The Scourge of Child Poverty: A Plague on Both Developing and Developed Countries

The Scourge of Child Poverty: A Plague on Both Developing and Developed Countries

Chester Alexis C. Buama

SOCIETY Publishing

www.societypublishing.com

The Scourge of Child Poverty: A Plague on Both Developing and Developed Countries

Chester Alexis C. Buama

Society Publishing
224 Shoreacres Road
Burlington, ON L7L 2H2
Canada
www.societypublishing.com
Email: orders@arclereducation.com

ISBN: 978-1-77469-056-7 (Hardcover)

ABOUT THE AUTHOR

Hon. Chester Alexis C. Buama, PhD, is a College Professor at Laguna State Polytechnic University under the Faculty of College of Arts and Sciences and currently serving as Regent of the LSPU Board of Regents the highest policy-making body of the university. He previously served as the College Research Coordinator and Coordinator of Curriculum, Instruction Quality Assurance, A Consultant of the Department of Education Central Office for Learning Assessment and National Trainer of the Commission on Higher Education for General Education Courses. He is also a member of local and international organizations: he is a Fellow and Senior Member of the Royal Institute of Management and the Royal Institute of Educators, Singapore, Reading Association of the Philippines, and International English Learners Training Institute. He was a Philippine Youth Ambassador to ASEAN countries and Japan which was sponsored by the Cabinet Office of Japan and Office of the President of the Philippines in 2010. He has a Master's degree in Management major in Public Administration and a Bachelor's degree in Journalism. He was conferred a Doctorate Degree in Philosophy major in Public Administration in 2016 and graduated with a Doctorate Degree in Philosophy major in Business Management in 2018. At present he is teaching Human Behavior in Organization, Social Philosophy, Principles of Management and Organization, Good Governance and Social Responsibility, Business Communication, Macro and, Micro Economics and Philippine History and Constitution both in the undergraduate and graduate levels. Moreover, he has actively participated in the Civic Activities of the Global Cooperation Society International, Philippine National Chapter and is often invited as resource speaker in various management and research writing seminars. Recently, he was awarded the Ambassador Seal of Excellence for Education as Research Practitioner and as 2018 Outstanding Premier College Professor and Humanitarian Service Excellence Award by the Asia Pacific Excellence Council, Inc.

TABLE OF CONTENTS

LIST OF FIGURES

LIST OF ABBREVIATIONS

ASU	Arab Socialist Union
AU	African Union
BEIP	Bucharest Early Intervention Project
CDI	Child Development Index
CFI	ChildFund International
COE	Council of Europe
DLM	Dual Labor Market
EFA	Education For All
ESRI	Economic and Social Research Institute
HAI	Housing Affordability Index
ID	Intellectually Disabled
IGOs	Intergovernmental Organizations
ILO	International Labor Organization
IMF	International Monetary Fund
INGOs	International Nongovernmental Organizations
INTERPOL	International Police Organization
LCPS	Low-Cost Private Schools
MIT	Massachusetts Institute of Technology
NEPAD	New Partnership for Africa's Development
NGOs	Non-Government Organizations
OAU	Organization of African Unity
OECD	Organization for Economic Co-operation and Development
OJJDP	Office of Juvenile Justice and Delinquency Prevention
OSCE	Organization for Security and Co-operation in Europe
PFC	Physiological Functional Capacity
PSID	Panel Study of Income Dynamics
RECs	Regional Economic Communities
SAPs	Structural Adjustment Programs

SDGs	Sustainable Development Goals
SOAS	School of Oriental and African Studies
UN	United Nations
UNAIDS	United Nations Program on HIV and AIDS
UNDP	United Nations Development Program
UNICEF	United Nations Children's Fund
WHO	World Health Organization

PREFACE

The tragedy of child poverty is the fact that it tends to affect some of the most vulnerable sections of the community. By their vulnerability, these communities are unable to launch effective responses to the poverty within which they exist. Moreover, the fact that they are vulnerable also makes it difficult for them to build the necessary resilience so that they can overcome extreme poverty in the range of its guises. Perhaps one of the most surprising things about child poverty is that it can exist in both developing and developed nations. Just because a country can report high gross domestic product (GDP) figures does not automatically mean that it can provide an equitable welfare system for its citizenry. Indeed, there have been instances where income inequality has increased even as the country develops and prospers. There are systemic societal issues that determine who are the winners and losers of economic development. If these issues are not addressed through a clear policy formulation process and a review of outcomes; the most vulnerable will likely continue getting a raw deal in the child poverty stakes.

This book has been written from that context to tie together many of the issues that have created and fostered child poverty. The book is primarily aimed at those who study undergraduate courses addressing poverty as one of the key contemporary issues in society today. The implication is that this book is in some way relevant to virtually all courses at university, given the fact that poverty has repeatedly manifested itself to be a primary and underlying cause of human suffering across the globe. The book attempts to distinguish child poverty from other forms of poverty such as adult poverty or the poverty that afflicts those who have a disability. Not only does this distinction help to focus the book; it also highlights the unique issues that children living in poverty face. Moreover, this book examines some of the causal aspects of child poverty and its overreaching consequences that can impact other segments of society. Above all, the book is meant to stimulate debate and action concerning child poverty. Both the Millennium Development Goals (MDGs) and Sustainable Development Goals (SDGs) have identified the elimination of child poverty as an important societal goal that requires international coordination.

This book will explore case studies of child poverty in a range of countries, including those that are highly industrialized; those that are considered to be middle-income countries; and the least developed countries. Throughout, the book will highlight the similarities of experience, which call for an international and coordinated response. At the same time, the book will also highlight the localized experiences of child poverty which may vary greatly. The implication is that international efforts have to be complemented with more localized approaches that are contextualized. Additionally, the book will critically examine some of the policy formulations that are designed to deal with the problem of child poverty. However, this critique will be done in such a way as to highlight the possibilities, limitations, and suggestions for improvement concerning policies that are designed to alleviate or eliminate child poverty. In doing so, this book adopts a progressive and perhaps the interventionist approach to child poverty. Hopefully, that means that children in need are not left to their own devices, but are instead supported better.

Chapter 1

Conceptualizing Child Poverty

CONTENTS

This initial chapter in the book will attempt to conceptualize the notion of child poverty. We will consider the technical, academic, and practical definitions of child poverty as they are used in contemporary developmental economics. The chapter will identify the children that are currently living in poverty as well as explaining briefly the factors that have placed them in such a situation. The chapter explores the conceptualizations of "poor families" and the challenges that they represent for the communities within which they exist. This then leads to an example of a specific vulnerable population of orphans who experience child poverty in a, particularly challenging way. The chapter closes with an overview of the lives that communities lead when dealing with poverty in all its forms. By the end of this chapter, the reader should have a grasp of what child poverty means and how it differs from other forms of poverty or social problems.

1.1. WHAT IS CHILD POVERTY?

Child poverty refers to the state of children living in poverty and applies to children from poor families or orphans being raised with limited or, in some cases absent, state resources (Ansell, 2016; Ashiabi, 2000; Ashworth, Hill, and Walker, 1994; Bäckman, and Nilsson, 2007; Bhargava et al., 2004; Bloom and Canning, 2001; Bourdillon and Boyden, 2011; Boyden and James, 2014). Children that fail to meet the minimum acceptable standard of the nation where that child lives are said to be poor (Bruch and Touraine, 1940; Chamberlain et al., 2016; Chiputwa, Spielman, and Qaim, 2015; Corcoran and Chaudry, 1997). In developing countries, these standards are low and, when combined with the increased number of orphans, the effects are more extreme (Deaton, 2006; Dreyer, 2013; Duncan and Magnuson, 2013; Lichter, Shanahan, and Gardner, 2002; Lipina, 2016; Lipina et al., 2013; Lopez and Velasco, 2011). The definition of children in most countries is 'people under the age of 18' (Lyytikäinen et al., 2006; Magnuson and Votruba-Drzal, 2008; Duncan and Rodgers, 1988; Evans, 2004, 2016; Farah et al., 2006). However, biologically the transition from childhood to adulthood is said to occur with the onset of puberty (Duncan, Kalil, and Ziol-Guest, 2008, 2013; Fierman et al., 2016; Evans and Cassells, 2014). Culturally defining the end of childhood is more complex, and takes into account factors such as the commencement of work, end of schooling and marriage as well as class, gender, and race (Fujiura and Yamaki, 2000; Garrett, Ng'andu, and Ferron, 1994; Duncan et al., 2012; Evans and Fuller-Rowell, 2013; Guest and Biasini, 2001; Duncan et al., 1998). According to the United Nations

Children's Fund (UNICEF), "children living in poverty are those who experience deprivation of the material, spiritual, and emotional resources needed to stay alive, develop, and thrive, leaving them unable to enjoy their rights, achieve their full potential, and participate as full and equal members of society." As Figure 1.1 shows, child poverty is not the exclusive reserve of developing nations; but can also exist in some of the most developed countries in the world (Ansell, 2016; Ashiabi, 2000; Ashworth, Hill, and Walker, 1994; Bäckman, and Nilsson, 2007).

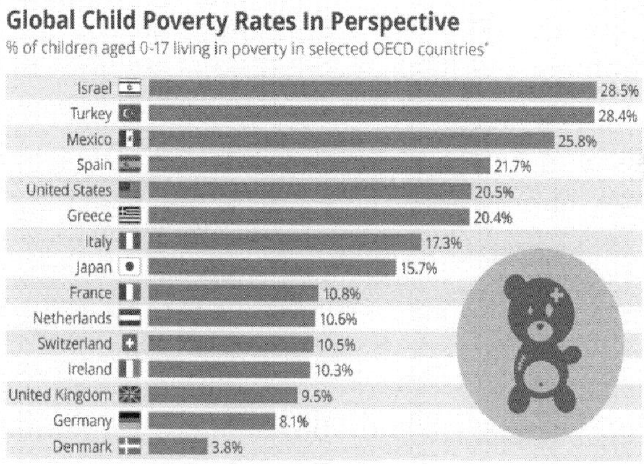

Figure 1.1. Global child poverty rates in perspective.

Source: Forbes and Statista.

The ChildFund International (CFI) definition is based on deprivation or the lack of materialistic conditions and services (Bhargava et al., 2004; Bloom and Canning, 2001; Bourdillon and Boyden, 2011; Boyden and James, 2014). Another definition is based on exclusion or the denial of rights and safety (Bruch and Touraine, 1940; Chamberlain et al., 2016). The third definitional element relates to vulnerability, particularly when society cannot deal with threats to children (Chiputwa, Spielman, and Qaim, 2015; Corcoran and Chaudry, 1997; Lipina et al., 2013). Other charitable organizations also use this multi-dimensional approach to child poverty (Deaton, 2006; Dreyer, 2013; Duncan and Magnuson, 2013; Lichter, Shanahan, and Gardner, 2002; Lipina, 2016; Lopez and Velasco, 2011). This is achieved by defining it as a combination of economic, social, cultural, physical, environmental, and emotional factors (Lyytikäinen et al., 2006; Magnuson and Votruba-Drzal, 2008; Duncan and Rodgers, 1988). These definitions suggest that child poverty is multidimensional, relative to their current and changing living conditions and complex interactions of the body, mind, and emotions are involved (Evans, 2004, 2016; Farah et al., 2006). The easiest way to quantify child poverty is by setting an absolute or relative monetary threshold (Duncan, Kalil, and Ziol-Guest, 2008; Fierman et al., 2016). If a family does not earn above that threshold, the children of that family will be considered to live below the poverty line (Duncan, Kalil, and Ziol-Guest, 2013; Evans and Cassells, 2014; Guest and Biasini, 2001; Duncan et al., 1998). Absolute poverty thresholds are fixed and generally updated only for price changes, but relative poverty thresholds are developed concerning the actual income of the population and reflect changes in consumption (Fujiura and Yamaki, 2000; Garrett, Ng'andu, and Ferron, 1994; Duncan et al., 2012; Evans and Fuller-Rowell, 2013).

The absolute poverty threshold is the money needed to purchase a defined quantity of goods and services (Evans and Kim, 2007, 2013; Hannum, Liu, and Alvarado-Urbina, 2017; Hart, 2008). Moreover, every threshold generally reflects the minimum income required to acquire necessities of life (Hatcher et al., 2019; Evans and Kutcher, 2011; Hill and Sandfort, 1995). However, a caveat is that a family that earns above a set threshold may still choose to not spend on the need of their children (Hobcraft, 1998; Hobcraft and Kiernan, 2001; Evans and Schamberg, 2009; Holzer et al., 2008). Certain organizations, such as the World Bank and the International Monetary Fund (IMF), use the absolute poverty threshold of US$1 a day to measure poverty in developing countries (Hong, 2015; Jain and Vaachani, 2006; Jarjoura, Triplett, and Brinker, 2002; Kaplinsky, 2005; Kapoor, 1993; Jones, Vargas, and Villar, 2008). Since the 1960s, the US has used an absolute poverty threshold adjusted for family size and composition to determine those living in poverty (Javanbakht et al., 2015; Jones, Vargas, and Villar, 2007; Kalil, Duncan, and Ziol-Guest, 2016). Europe and many other developed countries use a relative poverty threshold, typically 50% of the countries' median income (Kendig, Mattingly, and Bianchi, 2014; Kim et al., 2013). Relative poverty does not necessarily mean the child is lacking anything but is more a reflection of inequality in society (Kim et al., 2015; Krason, 2015; Lesner, 2018). Child poverty, when measured using relative thresholds, will improve only if low-income families benefit more from economic advances than well-off families (Mazza et al., 2017; Kim et al., 2016). Measures of child poverty using income thresholds will vary depending on whether relative or absolute poverty is measured and what threshold limits are applied (Mbabazi and Pyeong, 2014; McLaughlin and Rank, 2018; McLoyd, Aikens, and Burton, 2007).

Using a relative measure, poverty is much higher in the US than in Europe (Mickelson, 2002; Miller and Chen, 2013; Miller et al., 2011). However, if an absolute measure is used, then poverty in some European countries is higher (Ministry of Finance, 2014; Morrow, 2013; Muñoz, Álvarez-Verdejo, and García-Fernández, 2016). It is argued that using income as the only threshold ignores the multidimensional aspect of child poverty (Nikulina and Widom, 2014; Nikulina, Widom, and Czaja, 2011; Okiror, 2015; Penn, 2004; Ratcliffe and McKernan, 2010). This aspect includes consumption requirements, access to resources, and the ability to interact in society safely and without discrimination (Ridge, 2002, 2006; Rowntree, 1901; Ryan, Fauth, and Brooks-Gunn, 2006; Sánchez, 2008). A 2003 study conducted by researchers out of Bristol attempted to provide a scientific basis for measuring severe deprivation based on levels of adequate nutrition, safe drinking water, decent sanitation facilities, health, shelter, education, and information (Schickedanz, Dreyer, and Halfon, 2015; Schmitz, Wagner, and Menke, 2001; Segretin et al., 2016). Measurable values were attributed to each indicator and these were used to establish how many children were living in poverty (Serbin et al., 2011; Zembe-Mkabile et al., 2015). The values included: heights and weights more than three deviations below the international median, children with access only to rivers and other surface water, no access to toilets, no immunizations, no access to medical advice, living in dwellings with more than five people per room, no school attendance and no access to newspapers or other media (Sinervo and Hill, 2011; Song and Lu, 2002; Sripada et al., 2014). Out of a population of 1.8 billion children from developing nations, 56% were below at least one of these measurements (State House Uganda, 2017; Stewart, 2005; Torres and Wong, 2013; Townsend, 1979; Twikirize et al., 2014). In Sub-Saharan Africa and Southern Asia, this number increased to over 80%, with the rural children from these areas the worst affected (Vallas, Fremstad, and Ekman, 2015; Van den Waeyenberg, and Hens, 2008; Waddington, 2004; Wells et al., 2010).

The Young Lives Project is investigating the changing nature of child poverty by following nearly 12,000 children for 15 years in four countries, including Ethiopia, Peru, Vietnam, and India (Ziol-Guest, Duncan, and Kalil, 2009; Ziol-Guest et al., 2012). These countries were chosen to reflect a wide range of cultural, political, geographical, and social contexts. Every 3 to 4 years, researchers will collect data on the children and their family's health, malnutrition, literacy, access to services, and other indicators of poverty. Reports are available for these four countries that comparing the initial data obtained in 2002 with data from 2006. Peru, Vietnam, and India have shown economic growth and a reduction in poverty over this time, but large inequalities still exist between rural and urban areas, and among ethnic groups (Ansell, 2016; Ashiabi, 2000; Ashworth, Hill, and Walker, 1994; Bäckman, and Nilsson, 2007; Bhargava et al., 2004). This is particularly obvious in India, a country with the second-largest population of billionaires but also home to 25% of the world's poor (Bloom and Canning, 2001; Bourdillon and Boyden, 2011; Boyden and James, 2014; Bruch and Touraine, 1940). Ethiopia, one of the poorest countries in the world, has also shown slight economic growth and reduction in poverty.

Inequalities still exist, with boys more likely to be malnourished than girls and more absolute poverty in rural areas, although relative poverty is higher in urban areas (Chamberlain et al., 2016; Chiputwa, Spielman, and Qaim, 2015).

This data was collected before the 2008 drought and the recent increase in food prices, which have had a severe impact on the ability of Ethiopia to feed its population (Corcoran and Chaudry, 1997; Deaton, 2006; Dreyer, 2013; Duncan and Magnuson, 2013).

Studies such as these provide a comparative analysis of poverty in a range of contexts (Mbabazi and Pyeong, 2014; McLaughlin and Rank, 2018; McLoyd, Aikens, and Burton, 2007).

That can help policy formulators when they are trying to understand the multi-level and multi-faceted ways in which poverty presents itself (Mickelson, 2002; Miller and Chen, 2013; Miller et al., 2011).

Moreover, the studies help us understand better how different parts of the world are developing appropriate responses to child poverty (Ministry of Finance, 2014; Morrow, 2013; Muñoz, Álvarez-Verdejo, and García-Fernández, 2016).

Ultimately, all these definitions of child poverty rely on benchmarks that reflect the minimum acceptable living standards in a given community (Lichter, Shanahan, and Gardner, 2002; Lipina, 2016; Lipina et al., 2013). However, some argue that absolute poverty is a more appropriate measure since it raises the prospect of allowing the least developed countries to catch up with their more industrialized counterparts (Lopez and Velasco, 2011; Lyytikäinen et al., 2006; Magnuson and Votruba-Drzal, 2008). It is also important to note that poverty is culturally defined and may differ according to contexts (Duncan and Rodgers, 1988; Evans, 2004; Farah et al., 2006). The things that children need or want in developed nations may differ significantly from those that are reflected in developing nations (Jones, Vargas, and Villar, 2007; Kalil, Duncan, and Ziol-Guest, 2016; Kaplinsky, 2005; Kapoor, 1993). For example, children are living in the world today who are not addicted to consumerism or portable electronics; yet they are markedly happier than those who rely on these materialistic elements (Kim et al., 2015; Krason, 2015; Lesner, 2018; Mazza et al., 2017). That is why it is important to understand the localized context and how it impacts our understanding of child poverty (Mazza et al., 2017; Kim et al., 2016). In the next section, we generally consider the kind of children that are presently living in poverty.

1.2. WHICH CHILDREN ARE LIVING IN POVERTY?

The majority of poverty-stricken children are born to poor parents (Nikulina and Widom, 2014; Nikulina, Widom, and Czaja, 2011; Okiror, 2015; Penn, 2004; Ratcliffe and McKernan, 2010). Therefore, the causes such as adult poverty, government policies, lack of education, unemployment, social services, disabilities, and discrimination significantly affect the presence of child poverty (Ridge, 2002, 2006; Rowntree, 1901; Ryan, Fauth, and Brooks-Gunn, 2006; Sánchez, 2008). Lack of parental economic resources such as disposable income restricts children's opportunities (Schickedanz, Dreyer, and Halfon, 2015; Schmitz, Wagner, and Menke, 2001; Segretin et al., 2016). Economic and demographic factors such as deindustrialization, globalization, residential segregation, labor market segmentation, and migration of middle-class residents from inner cities, constrain economic opportunities and choices across generations, isolating inner-city poor children (Serbin et al., 2011; Zembe-Mkabile et al., 2015). The decline of the nuclear family, illegitimacy, teen pregnancy, and increased numbers of single mothers, is also cited as a major cause of poverty and welfare dependency for women and their children (Sinervo and Hill, 2011; Song and Lu, 2002; Sripada et al., 2014). In the case of Africa, as is everywhere, child poverty remains a multidimensional concept (see Figure 1.2).

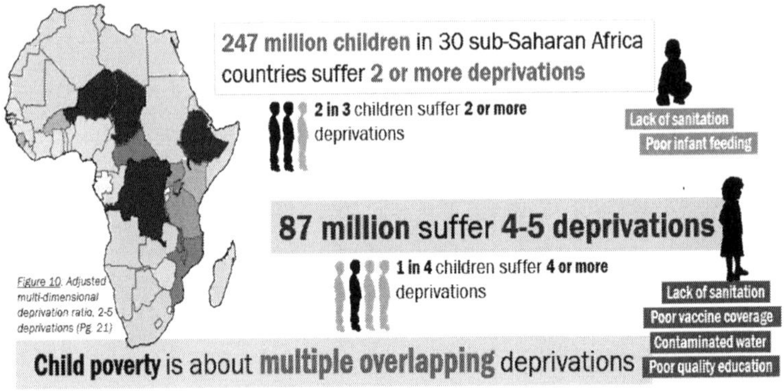

Figure 1.2. Multidimensional childhood poverty in Sub-Saharan Africa. *Source: UNICEF.*

Children resulting from unintended pregnancies are more likely to live in poverty (State House Uganda, 2017; Stewart, 2005; Torres and Wong, 2013; Townsend, 1979; Twikirize et al., 2014). This is because raising a child requires significant resources. Hence, each additional child increases demands on parental resources (Vallas, Fremstad, and Ekman, 2015; Van den Waeyenberg, and Hens, 2008; Waddington, 2004; Wells et al., 2010). Families raised by a single parent are generally poorer than those raised by couples (Ziol-Guest, Duncan, and Kalil, 2009; Ziol-Guest et al., 2012). In the United States, 6 of 10 long-term poor children have spent time in single-parent families (Ansell, 2016; Ashiabi, 2000; Ashworth, Hill, and Walker, 1994; Bäckman, and Nilsson, 2007; Bhargava et al., 2004). By 2007, children living in households headed by single mothers were five times as likely as children living in households headed by married parents to be living in poverty (Bloom and Canning, 2001; Bourdillon and Boyden, 2011; Boyden and James, 2014; Bruch and Touraine, 1940). Many of the apparent negative associations between growing up poor and children's attainments reflect unmeasured parental advantages that positively affect both parents' incomes and children's attainments, such as parental depression (Duncan and Rodgers, 1988; Evans, 2004; Farah et al., 2006). Developed countries also have a serious problem with child poverty (Chamberlain et al., 2016; Chiputwa, Spielman, and Qaim, 2015). If all the 16.7 million poor children in America were gathered in one place, they would form a city bigger than New York (Corcoran and Chaudry, 1997; Deaton, 2006; Dreyer, 2013; Duncan and Magnuson, 2013). Many published studies have demonstrated strong associations between childhood poverty and the child's adult outcomes in education, health, and socialization, fertility, labor market, and income (Lichter, Shanahan, and Gardner, 2002; Lipina, 2016; Lipina et al., 2013). Strong evidence suggests that children of low-income parents have an increased risk of intellectual and behavioral development problems (Lopez and Velasco, 2011; Lyytikäinen et al., 2006; Magnuson and Votruba-Drzal, 2008).

Large negative associations between poverty during early childhood and academic outcomes have been consistently found in many studies (Jones, Vargas, and Villar, 2008; Kendig, Mattingly, and Bianchi, 2014; Kim et al., 2013). Furthermore, children in poverty have a greater risk of displaying behavior and emotional problems, such as impulsiveness and difficulty getting along with peers, and family poverty is associated with a higher risk for teen childbearing, less positive peer relations, and lower self-esteem (Duncan et al., 1998; Evans and Kim, 2007; Hannum, Liu, and Alvarado-Urbina, 2017). These behaviors increase the chances of children who grew up in poverty to stay in poverty (Evans and Kim, 2013; Hart, 2008; Hatcher et al., 2019). In terms of economic disadvantages, adults who experienced persistent childhood poverty are more likely to fall below the poverty line at least once later in life (Evans and Kutcher, 2011; Hill and Sandfort, 1995; Hobcraft, 1998; Hobcraft and Kiernan, 2001). Poorboys work fewer hours per year, earn lower hourly wages, receive lower annual earnings, and spend more weeks idle in their mid-20s (Evans and Schamberg, 2009; Holzer et al., 2008; Hong, 2015).

Paternal income is also strongly associated with adult economic status (Jain and Vaachani, 2006; Jarjoura, Triplett, and Brinker, 2002; Javanbakht et al., 2015). The National Academy of Sciences found that "childhood poverty and chronic stress may lead to problems regulating emotions as an adult" (Duncan, Kalil, and Ziol-Guest, 2008; Evans, 2016; Fierman et al., 2016). Not only can growing up in poverty affect physical health, but it can also affect your future as well. Growing up in poverty has been statistically proven to increase an individual's probability of going to prison, becoming an addict, mental illness, or not completing high school (Jones, Vargas, and Villar, 2007; Kalil, Duncan, and Ziol-Guest, 2016; Kaplinsky, 2005; Kapoor, 1993). Because of these things, children who grow up in poverty often end up staying in poverty and repeating the cycle (Kim et al., 2015; Krason, 2015; Lesner, 2018; Mazza et al., 2017). Additionally, childhood poverty in the first 3 years of life is related to substandard nutritional status and poor motor skills. In contrast, poverty is also associated with child obesity (McLoyd, Aikens, and Burton, 2007; Mickelson, 2002; Miller and Chen, 2013; Miller et al., 2011). As they get older, poor children are more likely to have chronic health problems, such as asthma and anemia (Ministry of Finance, 2014;

Morrow, 2013; Muñoz, Álvarez-Verdejo, and García-Fernández, 2016; Nikulina and Widom, 2014). These impacts probably reflect issues related to poverty including a substandard diet, inferior housing conditions, poor neighborhood environment, reduced access to goods and activities, and the psychological stress stemming from these factors (Nikulina, Widom, and Czaja, 2011; Okiror, 2015; Penn, 2004; Ratcliffe and McKernan, 2010).

The relationship between childhood poverty and later negative adult outcomes is relatively small in other research (Ridge, 2002; Rowntree, 1901; Ryan, Fauth, and Brooks-Gunn, 2006; Sánchez, 2008). In one systematic analysis, family income only "modestly" affected the likelihood of teen pregnancy and male unemployment (Ridge, 2006; Schickedanz, Dreyer, and Halfon, 2015; Schmitz, Wagner, and Menke, 2001). Using a relative measure of child poverty, an impoverished child growing up in a developing country suffers more hardship than most children living in poverty in a developed country (Segretin et al., 2016; Serbin et al., 2011). Poverty in these countries is a condition usually characterized by severe deprivation of basic human needs (Sinervo and Hill, 2011; Song and Lu, 2002; Sripada et al., 2014; State House Uganda, 2017). It is estimated that one-third of all children in developing countries (about 700 million) are living in poverty, the highest rates being in the rural areas of Sub-Saharan Africa and South Asia (Stewart, 2005; Torres and Wong, 2013; Townsend, 1979; Twikirize et al., 2014; Vallas, Fremstad, and Ekman, 2015). War, disease, corruption, lack of resources, and harsh environmental conditions afflict many of these countries, contributing to their poverty (Van den Waeyenberg, and Hens, 2008; Waddington, 2004; Wells et al., 2010). These factors are a major cause of death, which in turn leads to a higher number of single parents and orphaned children (Zembe-Mkabile et al., 2015; Ziol-Guest, Duncan, and Kalil, 2009; Ziol-Guest et al., 2012).

All UN member states have ratified the 1989 Convention on the Rights of the Child, except for the United States and South Sudan, which aims at reducing violations to many rights relevant to reducing child poverty in different countries (Ansell, 2016; Dreyer, 2013; Evans, 2016; Evans and Kim, 2013; Jones, Vargas, and Villar, 2007; Mbabazi and Pyeong, 2014; Schickedanz, Dreyer, and Halfon, 2015). A review published by UNICEF in 2009, found declines in under-five mortalities, less child malnourishment, increases in breastfeeding, improved water systems, and better education access (Ashiabi, 2000; Duncan and Magnuson, 2013; Fierman et al., 2016). It also states that despite these improvements 24 000 children still die each day from mostly preventable diseases, 150 million 5- to 14-year-olds are involved in child labor and 100 million primary aged children go without schooling (Hart, 2008; Kalil, Duncan, and Ziol-Guest, 2016; Kaplinsky, 2005; McLaughlin and Rank, 2018; Schmitz, Wagner, and Menke, 2001). These violations have consequences for the economy as well as the children that are affected (Ashworth, Hill, and Walker, 1994; Lichter, Shanahan, and Gardner, 2002; Duncan, Kalil, and Ziol-Guest, 2013).

There are still great inequalities within populations (Hatcher et al., 2019; Kapoor, 1993; McLoyd, Aikens, and Burton, 2007). For example, girls, and children from rural areas more likely to suffer poor health, education, and survival than boys and urban populations (Bäckman, and Nilsson, 2007; Bhargava et al., 2004; Lipina, 2016; Evans and Cassells, 2014). Notable state attempts to tackle child poverty in the developing world, include Brazil's Bolsa Familia initiative which reaches 12 million households, and South Africa's Child Grant which reaches 7 million households (Evans and Kutcher, 2011; Mickelson, 2002; Segretin et al., 2016; Jones, Vargas, and Villar, 2008). Elsewhere, child-specific social protection policies and programs are few, and the institutions to implement them are often lacking (Bloom and Canning, 2001; Lipina et al., 2013). The cycle of poverty is when a family remains in poverty over many successive generations (Fujiura and Yamaki, 2000; Hill and Sandfort, 1995; Kendig, Mattingly, and Bianchi, 2014). For this reason, reducing child poverty has been a focus of almost all governments as a way to break this cycle (Miller and Chen, 2013; Miller et al., 2011). Improving the quality of education provided to the poor is seen by most as the best way to break this cycle (Bourdillon and Boyden, 2011; Lopez and Velasco, 2011; Garrett, Ng'andu, and Ferron, 1994). Improving the environment, ensuring access to health, and providing financial incentives (either through benefit schemes or reducing taxes) have all been suggested as ways to break the cycle (Hobcraft, 1998; Kim et al., 2013).

Boys and girls have equal rates of poverty through their childhoods (Muñoz, Álvarez-Verdejo, and García-Fernández, 2016; Sripada et al., 2014). However, as women enter their teens and childbearing years, the rates of poverty between the genders widen (Boyden and James, 2014; Lyytikäinen et al., 2006; Duncan et al., 2012). Globally, women are far more impoverished than men and poor children are more likely to live in female-headed households (Hobcraft and Kiernan, 2001; Kim et al., 2015; Nikulina and Widom, 2014). Attempts to combat the cycle of poverty, therefore, have often targeted mothers as a way to interrupt the negative patterns of poverty that affect the education, nutrition or health, and psychological or social outcomes for poor children (Bruch and Touraine, 1940; Magnuson and Votruba-Drzal, 2008; Evans and Fuller-Rowell, 2013). According to the Overseas Development Institute, greater visibility for children's rights issues is needed in donor policies and attempts should be made to emulate the success achieved using gender markers to develop gender-sensitive development policy (Guest and Biasini, 2001; Evans and Schamberg, 2009; Krason, 2015; Lesner, 2018). They believe major influential players in the children's rights community (such as UNICEF, UNFPA, and NGOs, such as Save the Children, Plan International and World Vision) should do more to highlight the impact of mainstream macro-policies issues on children (Nikulina, Widom, and Czaja, 2011; State House Uganda, 2017; Stewart, 2005; Torres and Wong, 2013). The Overseas Development Institute further suggests that an international commission be established to address the impact of the 3-F crisis (food, financial, and fuel) on children as a platform for dialog and new initiatives (Chamberlain et al., 2016).

Nevertheless, determining the appropriate policies for dealing with long-term childhood poverty and intergenerational economic inequality is hotly debated (Duncan et al., 1998; Mazza et al., 2017). This is because most proposed policy solutions, and depend on the effects that most impact the region (Chiputwa, Spielman, and Qaim, 2015; Evans and Kim, 2007; Okiror, 2015; Townsend, 1979). To combat the lack of resources available in developed nations, policies must be developed that deliver resources to poor families and raise skill levels of poor children by building on successful welfare-to-work initiatives and maintaining financial work supports, such as Earned Income Tax Credit, refundable child care tax credits and housing vouchers (Corcoran and Chaudry, 1997; Deaton, 2006; Kim et al., 2016; Twikirize et al., 2014). Combating poverty in developed countries also means improving the schools that exist there (Duncan and Rodgers, 1988; Holzer et al., 2008). To help children in poverty, schools need to invest more money in school meals, libraries, and healthcare (Evans, 2004; Jain and Vaachani, 2006; Ministry of Finance, 2014; Vallas, Fremstad, and Ekman, 2015). To effectively address economic, demographic, and cultural changes, economic, and social service strategies to reverse the factors that generated the urban underclass, such as providing jobs and social services policies that deal with the effects of isolation, should be implemented (Farah et al., 2006).

To reduce the cycle of poverty for children and families, policies should be aimed at expanding economic opportunities, especially for disadvantaged girls (Duncan, Kalil, and Ziol-Guest, 2008; Morrow, 2013; Song and Lu, 2002; Ziol-Guest et al., 2012). In the next section, we will concentrate on the notion and characteristics of poor families.

1.3. THE NOTION OF POOR FAMILIES

The poor family is often the starting point for childhood poverty (Hannum, Liu, and Alvarado-Urbina, 2017; Penn, 2004; Ratcliffe; Van den Waeyenberg, and Hens, 2008; Sinervo and Hill, 2011). In this case, the definitions of poverty have to be nuanced to incorporate as forms of social, political, economic, environmental, and legal deprivations (Hong, 2015; Jarjoura, Triplett, and Brinker, 2002; Ridge, 2002; Waddington, 2004; Ziol-Guest, Duncan, and Kalil, 2009). Poverty is not having enough material possessions or income for a person's needs. This is because poverty may include social, economic, and political elements (Javanbakht et al., 2015; Wells et al., 2010). Absolute poverty is the complete lack of the means necessary to meet basic personal needs, such as food, clothing, and shelter (Rowntree, 1901; Ryan, Fauth, and Brooks-Gunn, 2006; Sánchez, 2008; Ridge, 2006). The threshold at which absolute poverty is defined is always about the same, independent of the person's permanent location or era (Serbin et al., 2011; Zembe-Mkabile et al., 2015). By way of contrast, relative poverty occurs when a person cannot meet a minimum level of living standards, compared to others in the same time and place (Duncan et al., 2012; Evans and Fuller-Rowell, 2013; Guest and Biasini, 2001). Therefore, the threshold at which relative poverty is defined varies from one country to another, or from one society to another (Kim et al., 2016; Mbabazi and Pyeong, 2014; McLaughlin and Rank, 2018). In Figure 1.3, we see that the juvenilization of poverty is creeping up to the levels that it was in the late 1950s.

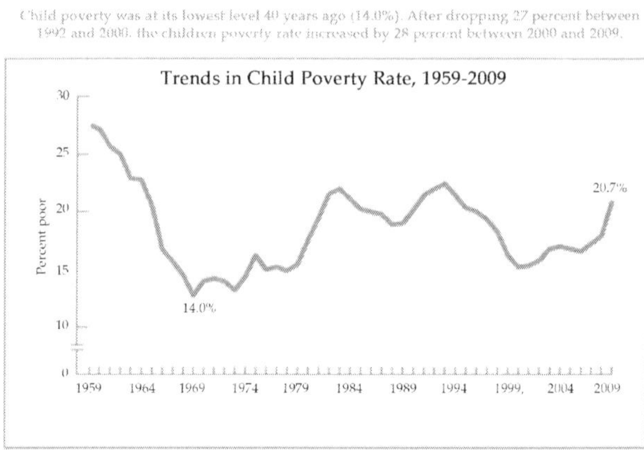

Figure 1.3. The juvenilization of poverty 1959 to 2009.

Source: Department of Commerce and the Bureau of the Census.

Governments and non-governmental organizations try to reduce poverty because they consider it to be a social problem that requires intervention (Duncan, Kalil, and Ziol-Guest, 2013; Evans and Cassells, 2014; Fujiura and Yamaki, 2000; Garrett, Ng'andu, and Ferron, 1994). Providing basic needs to people who are unable to earn a sufficient income can be hampered by constraints on the government's ability to deliver services, such as corruption, tax avoidance, debt, and loan conditionalities, and by the brain drain of health care and educational professionals (Ansell, 2016; Ashiabi, 2000; Ashworth, Hill, and Walker, 1994; Bäckman, and Nilsson, 2007). Strategies of increasing income to make basic needs more affordable typically include welfare, economic freedoms, and providing financial services (Bhargava et al., 2004; Bloom and Canning, 2001; Bourdillon and Boyden, 2011; Boyden and James, 2014). There are several definitions of poverty depending on the context of the situation it is placed in, and the views of the person giving the definition (Bruch and Touraine, 1940; Chamberlain et al., 2016).

According to the United Nations (UN), poverty is fundamentally the inability of having choices and opportunities (Chiputwa, Spielman, and Qaim, 2015; Corcoran and Chaudry, 1997; Lipina et al., 2013). This constitutes a violation of human dignity. It means a lack of basic capacity to participate effectively in society (Deaton, 2006; Dreyer, 2013; Duncan and Magnuson, 2013; Lichter, Shanahan, and Gardner, 2002; Lipina, 2016; Lopez and Velasco, 2011). Poverty means not having enough to feed and clothe a family, not having a school or clinic to go to, not having the land on which to grow one's food or a job to earn one's living, not having access to credit (Lyytikäinen et al., 2006; Magnuson and Votruba-Drzal, 2008; Duncan and Rodgers, 1988). For some communities, poverty means insecurity, powerlessness, and exclusion of individuals, households, and communities (Evans, 2004; Farah et al., 2006). It also means susceptibility to violence, and it often implies living in marginal or fragile environments, without access to clean water or sanitation (Duncan, Kalil, and Ziol-Guest, 2008; Evans, 2016; Fierman et al., 2016). The World Bank suggests that poverty is a pronounced deprivation in well-being, and comprises many dimensions (Duncan, Kalil, and Ziol-Guest, 2013; Evans and Cassells, 2014; Guest and Biasini, 2001; Duncan et al., 1998). It includes low incomes and the inability to acquire the basic goods and services necessary for survival with dignity (Fujiura and Yamaki, 2000; Garrett, Ng'andu, and Ferron, 1994; Duncan et al., 2012; Evans and Fuller-Rowell, 2013). Poverty also encompasses low levels of health and education, poor access to clean water and sanitation, inadequate physical security, lack of voice, and insufficient capacity and opportunity to better one's life (Evans and Kim, 2007, 2013; Hannum, Liu, and Alvarado-Urbina, 2017; Hart, 2008).

Absolute poverty refers to a set standard that is consistent over time and between countries (Hatcher et al., 2019; Evans and Kutcher, 2011; Hill and Sandfort, 1995). First introduced in 1990, the dollar-a-day poverty line measured absolute poverty by the standards of the world's poorest countries (Hobcraft, 1998; Hobcraft and Kiernan, 2001; Evans and Schamberg, 2009; Holzer et al., 2008). The World Bank defined the new international poverty line as $1.25 a day in 2008 for 2005 (equivalent to $1.00 a day in 1996 US prices). In October 2015, they reset it to $1.90 a day (Hong, 2015; Jain and Vaachani, 2006; Jarjoura, Triplett, and Brinker, 2002; Kaplinsky, 2005; Kapoor, 1993; Jones, Vargas, and Villar, 2008). Absolute poverty, extreme poverty, or abject poverty is characterized by severe deprivation of basic human needs, including food, safe drinking water, sanitation facilities, health, shelter, education, and information (Javanbakht et al., 2015; Jones, Vargas, and Villar, 2007; Kalil, Duncan, and Ziol-Guest, 2016). It depends not only on income but also on access to services (Kendig, Mattingly, and Bianchi, 2014; Kim et al., 2013). The term 'absolute poverty,' when used in this fashion, is usually synonymous with 'extreme poverty (Kim et al., 2015; Krason, 2015; Lesner, 2018). Robert McNamara, the former president of the World Bank, described absolute or extreme poverty as, "a condition so limited by malnutrition, illiteracy, disease, squalid surroundings, high infant mortality, and low life expectancy as to be beneath any reasonable definition of human decency."

For a few years starting in 1990, the World Bank anchored the absolute poverty line as $1 per day (Mazza et al., 2017; Kim et al., 2016). This was revised in 1993, and through 2005, absolute poverty was $1.08 a day for all countries on a purchasing power parity basis, after adjusting for inflation to the 1993 US dollar (Mbabazi and Pyeong, 2014; McLaughlin and Rank, 2018; McLoyd, Aikens, and Burton, 2007). In 2005, after extensive studies of the cost of living across the world, The World Bank raised the measure for the global poverty line to reflect the observed higher cost of living (Mickelson, 2002; Miller and Chen, 2013; Miller et al., 2011). In 2015, the World Bank defines extreme poverty as living on less than US$1.90 (PPP) per day, and moderate poverty as less than $2 or $5 a day (Ministry of Finance, 2014; Morrow, 2013; Muñoz, Álvarez-Verdejo, and García-Fernández, 2016). However, it is notable that a person or family with access to subsistence resources (e.g., subsistence farmers), may have a low cash income without a correspondingly low standard of living (Nikulina and Widom, 2014; Nikulina, Widom, and Czaja, 2011; Okiror, 2015; Penn, 2004; Ratcliffe and McKernan, 2010). These categories of people are not living "on" their cash income but using it as a top-up. It estimated that "in 2001, 1.1 billion people had consumption levels below $1 a day and 2.7 billion lived on less than $2 a day" (Ridge, 2002, 2006; Rowntree, 1901; Ryan, Fauth, and Brooks-Gunn, 2006; Sánchez, 2008). A 'dollar a day,' in nations that do not use the US dollar as currency, does not translate to living a day on the equivalent amount of local currency as determined by the exchange rate (Schickedanz, Dreyer, and Halfon, 2015; Schmitz, Wagner, and Menke, 2001; Segretin et al., 2016). Rather, it is determined by the purchasing power parity rate, which would look at how much local currency is needed to buy the same things that a dollar could buy in the United States (Serbin et al., 2011; Zembe-Mkabile et al., 2015). Usually, this would translate to less local currency than the exchange rate in poorer countries as the United States is a relatively more expensive country (Sinervo and Hill, 2011; Song and Lu, 2002; Sripada et al., 2014).

The poverty line threshold of $1.90 per day, as set by the World Bank, is controversial (State House Uganda, 2017; Stewart, 2005; Torres and Wong, 2013; Townsend, 1979; Twikirize et al., 2014). Each nation has its threshold for absolute poverty line (Vallas, Fremstad, and Ekman, 2015; Van den Waeyenberg, and Hens, 2008; Waddington, 2004; Wells et al., 2010). In the United States, for example, the absolute poverty line was US$15.15

per day in 2010 (US$22,000 per year for a family of four), while in India it was US$1.0 per day (Ziol-Guest, Duncan, and Kalil, 2009; Ziol-Guest et al., 2012). In China, the absolute poverty line was US$0.55 per day, each on a PPP basis in 2010 (Ansell, 2016; Ashiabi, 2000; Ashworth, Hill, and Walker, 1994; Bäckman, and Nilsson, 2007; Bhargava et al., 2004). These different poverty lines make data comparison between each nation's official reports qualitatively difficult (Bloom and Canning, 2001; Bourdillon and Boyden, 2011; Boyden and James, 2014; Bruch and Touraine, 1940). Some scholars argue that the World Bank method sets the bar too high, others argue it is too low (Duncan and Rodgers, 1988; Evans, 2004; Farah et al., 2006). Still, others suggest that the poverty line misleads as it measures everyone below the poverty line the same when in reality someone living on $1.20 per day is in a different state of poverty than someone living on $0.20 per day (Chamberlain et al., 2016; Chiputwa, Spielman, and Qaim, 2015). In other words, the depth and intensity of poverty vary across the world and in any regional population, and $1.25 per day poverty line and headcounts are inadequate measures (Corcoran and Chaudry, 1997; Deaton, 2006; Dreyer, 2013; Duncan and Magnuson, 2013).

Relative poverty views poverty as socially defined and dependent on social context, hence relative poverty is a measure of income inequality (Lichter, Shanahan, and Gardner, 2002; Lipina, 2016; Lipina et al., 2013). Usually, relative poverty is measured as the percentage of the population with income less than some fixed proportion of median income (Lopez and Velasco, 2011; Lyytikäinen et al., 2006; Magnuson and Votruba-Drzal, 2008). There are several other different income inequality metrics, for example, the Gini coefficient or the Theil Index (Jones, Vargas, and Villar, 2008; Kendig, Mattingly, and Bianchi, 2014; Kim et al., 2013). Relative poverty is the most useful measure for ascertaining poverty rates in wealthy developed nations (Duncan et al., 1998; Evans and Kim, 2007; Hannum, Liu, and Alvarado-Urbina, 2017). The relative poverty measure is used by the United Nations Development Program (UNDP), the UNICEF, the Organization for Economic Co-operation and Development (OECD), and Canadian poverty researchers (Evans and Kim, 2013; Hart, 2008; Hatcher et al., 2019). In the European Union, the relative poverty measure is the most prominent and most-quoted of the EU social inclusion indicators (Evans and Kutcher, 2011; Hill and Sandfort, 1995; Hobcraft, 1998; Hobcraft and Kiernan, 2001). Relative poverty reflects better the cost of social inclusion and equality of opportunity in a specific time and space (Evans and Schamberg, 2009; Holzer et al., 2008; Hong, 2015). Once economic development has progressed beyond a certain minimum level, the essence of the poverty problem (from the point of view of both the poor individual and of the societies in which they live) is not so much the effects of poverty in any absolute form but the effects of the contrast, which is perceived regularly, between the lives of the poor and the lives of those around them (Jain and Vaachani, 2006; Jarjoura, Triplett, and Brinker, 2002; Javanbakht et al., 2015). For practical purposes, the problem of poverty in the industrialized nations today is a problem of relative poverty (Duncan, Kalil, and Ziol-Guest, 2008; Evans, 2016; Fierman et al., 2016).

Various scholars have defined relative poverty and its usefulness to economic planning (Jones, Vargas, and Villar, 2007; Kalil, Duncan, and Ziol-Guest, 2016; Kaplinsky, 2005; Kapoor, 1993). For example, Adam Smith in the Wealth of Nations (1776) argued that poverty is the inability to afford not only the commodities which are indispensably necessary for the support of life; but also whatever the custom of the country renders it indecent for creditable people, even of the lowest order, to be without. In 1958 Galbraith argued that people are poverty-stricken when their income, even if adequate for survival, falls markedly behind that of their community. In 1964 in a joint committee economic President's report in the United States, Republicans endorsed the concept of relative poverty. They argued that no objective definition of poverty exists (Kim et al., 2015; Krason, 2015; Lesner, 2018; Mazza et al., 2017). Hence, the definition varies from place to place and time to time (McLoyd, Aikens, and Burton, 2007; Mickelson, 2002; Miller and Chen, 2013; Miller et al., 2011). As our standard of living rises, so does our idea of what is substandard (Ministry of Finance, 2014; Morrow, 2013; Muñoz, Álvarez-Verdejo, and García-Fernández, 2016; Nikulina and Widom, 2014). In 1965 Rose Friedman argued for the use of relative poverty, claiming that the definition of poverty changes with general living standards (Nikulina, Widom, and Czaja, 2011; Okiror, 2015; Penn, 2004; Ratcliffe and McKernan, 2010). Those labeled as poor in 1995 would have had a higher standard of living than many labeled not poor" in 1965 for example (Ridge, 2002; Rowntree, 1901; Ryan, Fauth, and Brooks-Gunn, 2006; Sánchez, 2008). In 1979, British sociologist, Peter Townsend published his famous definition where "*individuals. can be said to be in poverty when they lack the resources to obtain the types of diet, participate in the activities, and have the living conditions and amenities which are customary or are at least widely encouraged or approved, in the societies to which they belong*" (p.31). Brian Nolan and Christopher T. Whelan of the Economic and Social Research Institute (ESRI) in Ireland explained that poverty has to be seen in terms of the standard of living of the society in question (Ridge, 2006; Schickedanz, Dreyer, and Halfon, 2015; Schmitz, Wagner, and Menke, 2001). Relative poverty measures are used as official poverty rates by the European Union, UNICEF, and the OECD (Segretin et al., 2016; Serbin et al., 2011). The main poverty line used in the OECD and the European Union is based on "economic distance," a level of income set at 60% of the median household income (Sinervo and Hill, 2011; Song and Lu, 2002; Sripada et al., 2014; State House Uganda, 2017). Many wealthy nations have seen an increase in relative poverty rates ever since the Great Recession (Stewart, 2005; Torres and Wong, 2013; Townsend, 1979; Twikirize et al., 2014; Vallas, Fremstad, and Ekman, 2015). This poverty is experienced particularly among children from impoverished families who often reside in substandard housing and find educational opportunities out of reach (Van den Waeyenberg, and Hens, 2008; Waddington, 2004; Wells et al., 2010). The poverty rate is a calculation of the percentage of people whose family household income falls below the Poverty Line (Zembe-Mkabile et al., 2015; Ziol-Guest, Duncan, and Kalil, 2009; Ziol-Guest et al., 2012). The United States federal government typically regulates this line, and typically the cost of the line is set to three times the cost of an adequate meal (Ansell, 2016; Dreyer, 2013; Evans, 2016; Evans and Kim, 2013; Jones, Vargas, and Villar, 2007; Mbabazi and Pyeong, 2014; Schickedanz, Dreyer, and Halfon, 2015). This line is subject to change based on the level of price changes and the size of the family (Ashiabi, 2000; Duncan and Magnuson, 2013; Fierman et al., 2016). According to the census, the poverty rate helped determine that around 14.8% of the US population had household incomes that were below the poverty line for their family size in 2014 (Hart, 2008; Kalil, Duncan, and Ziol-Guest, 2016; Kaplinsky, 2005; McLaughlin and Rank, 2018; Schmitz, Wagner, and Menke, 2001). In the next section, we consider a specific population in terms of orphans who experience childhood poverty in a, particularly pernicious way.

1.4. ORPHANS LIVING IN POVERTY

An orphan is a child whose parents have died, are unknown, or have permanently abandoned them. In common usage, only a child who has lost both parents due to death is called an orphan (Ashworth, Hill, and Walker, 1994; Lichter, Shanahan, and Gardner, 2002; Duncan, Kalil, and Ziol-Guest, 2013). Various groups use different definitions to identify orphans (Hatcher et al., 2019; Kapoor, 1993; McLoyd, Aikens, and Burton, 2007). One legal definition used in the United States is a minor bereft through "death or disappearance of, abandonment or desertion by, or separation or loss from, both parents" (Bäckman, and Nilsson, 2007; Bhargava et al., 2004; Lipina, 2016; Evans and Cassells, 2014). In common use, an orphan does not have any surviving parent to care for them (Evans and Kutcher, 2011; Mickelson, 2002; Segretin et al., 2016; Jones, Vargas, and Villar, 2008). However, the UNICEF, Joint United Nations Program on HIV and AIDS (UNAIDS), and other groups label any child who has lost one parent as an orphan (Bloom and Canning, 2001; Lipina et al., 2013). In this approach, a maternal orphan is a child whose mother has died, while a paternal orphan is a child whose father has died (Fujiura and Yamaki, 2000; Hill and Sandfort, 1995; Kendig, Mattingly, and Bianchi, 2014). A double orphan is a child or tenor infant who has lost both parents (Miller and Chen, 2013; Miller et al., 2011). This contrasts with the older use of half-orphans to describe children who had lost only one parent (Bourdillon and Boyden, 2011; Lopez and Velasco, 2011; Garrett, Ng'andu, and Ferron, 1994). As Figure 1.4 demonstrates, even the wealthiest countries on the globe sometimes struggle to look after young people.

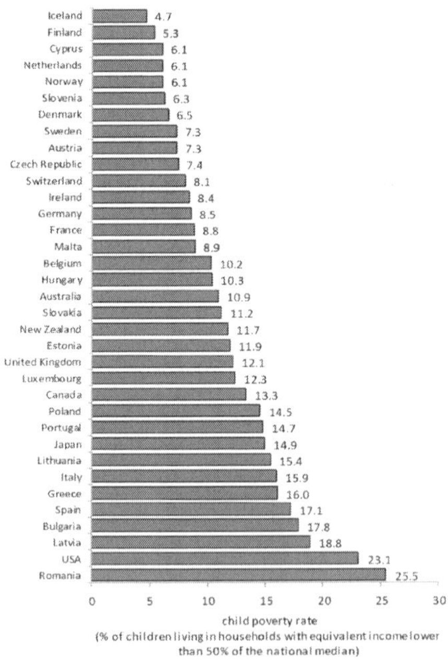

Figure 1.4. Child poverty among high-income countries.

Source: ResearchGate.

The 2001 figures from the 2002 UNICEF/UNAIDS report attempt to provide some insight into the numbers of orphans that are spread across the globe (Hobcraft, 1998; Kim et al., 2013). In China, a survey conducted by the Ministry of Civil Affairs in 2005 showed that China has about 573,000 orphans below 18 years old (Muñoz, Álvarez-Verdejo, and García-Fernández, 2016; Sripada et al., 2014). According to Russian reports from 2002 cited in the New York Times, 650,000 children are housed in orphanages (Boyden and James, 2014; Lyytikäinen et al., 2006; Duncan et al., 2012). They are released at age 16, and 40% become homeless, while 30% become criminals or commit suicide (Hobcraft and Kiernan, 2001; Kim et al., 2015; Nikulina and Widom, 2014). Street children have a major presence in Latin America (Bruch and Touraine, 1940; Magnuson and Votruba-Drzal, 2008; Evans and Fuller-Rowell, 2013). For example, some estimate that there are as many as 40 million street children in Latin America (Guest and Biasini, 2001; Evans and Schamberg, 2009; Krason, 2015; Lesner, 2018). Although not all street children are orphans, all street children work and many do not have significant family support (Nikulina, Widom, and Czaja, 2011; State House Uganda, 2017; Stewart, 2005; Torres and Wong, 2013).

Wars and great epidemics such as AIDS have created many orphans (Chamberlain et al., 2016). The Second World War, with its massive numbers of deaths and population movements, created large numbers of orphans in many countries (Duncan et al., 1998; Mazza et al., 2017). There was wide variability in reporting with estimates for Europe ranging from 1,000,000 to 13,000,000. Judt (2006) estimates there were 9,000 orphaned children in Czechoslovakia, 60,000 in the Netherlands 300,000 in Poland, and 200,000 in Yugoslavia, plus many more in the Soviet Union, Germany, Italy, and elsewhere (Chiputwa, Spielman, and Qaim, 2015; Evans and Kim, 2007; Okiror, 2015; Townsend, 1979). The notion of an orphan is not new to cultural understanding (Corcoran and Chaudry, 1997; Deaton, 2006; Kim et al., 2016; Twikirize et al., 2014). For example, orphans were frequently quoted in Victorian literature and they were invariably associated with extreme neediness and poverty, as well as abuse by those that were supposed to look after them (Evans, 2004; Jain and Vaachani, 2006; Ministry of Finance, 2014; Vallas, Fremstad, and Ekman, 2015). Orphaned characters are extremely common as literary protagonists, especially in children's and fantasy literature (Duncan and Rodgers, 1988; Holzer et al., 2008). The lack of parents leaves the characters to pursue more interesting and adventurous lives, by freeing them from familial obligations and controls and depriving them of more prosaic lives (Farah et al., 2006). It creates characters that are self-contained and introspective and who strive for affection (Duncan, Kalil, and Ziol-Guest, 2008; Morrow, 2013; Song and Lu, 2002; Ziol-Guest et al., 2012). Orphans can metaphorically search for self-understanding through attempting to know their roots (Hannum, Liu, and Alvarado-Urbina, 2017; Penn, 2004; Ratcliffe; Van den Waeyenberg, and Hens, 2008; Sinervo and Hill, 2011). Parents can also be allies and sources of aid for children, and removing the parents makes the character's difficulties more severe (Hong, 2015; Jarjoura, Triplett, and Brinker, 2002; Ridge, 2002; Waddington, 2004; Ziol-Guest, Duncan, and Kalil, 2009). Parents, furthermore, can be irrelevant to the theme a writer is trying to develop, and orphaning the character frees the writer from the necessity to depict such an irrelevant relationship; if one parent-child relationship is important, removing the other parent prevents complicating the necessary relationship (Javanbakht et al., 2015; Wells et al., 2010). All these characteristics make orphans attractive characters for authors (Rowntree, 1901; Ryan, Fauth, and Brooks-Gunn, 2006; Sánchez, 2008; Ridge, 2006).

The use of government-run orphanages has been phased out in the United States, Canada, the United Kingdom, and in the European Union member-states during the latter half of the 20th century but continue to operate in many other regions internationally (Serbin et al., 2011; Zembe-Mkabile et al., 2015). While the term "orphanage" is no longer typically used in the United States, nearly every US state continues to operate residential group homes for children in need of a safe place to live and in which to be supported in their educational and life-skills pursuits (Duncan et al., 2012; Evans and Fuller-Rowell, 2013; Guest and Biasini, 2001). Homes like the Milton Hershey School in Pennsylvania, Mooseheart in Illinois, and the Crossnore School and Children's Home in North Carolina continue to provide care and support for children in need (Kim et al., 2016; Mbabazi and Pyeong, 2014; McLaughlin and Rank, 2018). While a place like the Milton Hershey School houses nearly 2,000 children, each child lives in a small group-home environment with "house parents" who often live many years in that home (Duncan, Kalil, and Ziol-Guest, 2013; Evans and Cassells, 2014; Fujiura and Yamaki, 2000; Garrett, Ng'andu, and Ferron, 1994). Children who grow up in these residential homes have higher rates of high school and college graduation than those who spend equivalent numbers of years in the US Foster Care system, wherein only 44% to 66% of children graduate from high school (Ansell, 2016; Ashiabi, 2000; Ashworth, Hill, and Walker, 1994; Bäckman, and Nilsson, 2007).

Research from the Bucharest Early Intervention Project (BEIP) is often cited as demonstrating that residential institutions negatively impact the wellbeing of children (Bhargava et al., 2004; Bloom and Canning, 2001; Bourdillon and Boyden, 2011; Boyden and James, 2014). The BEIP selected orphanages in Bucharest, Romania that raised abandoned children in socially and emotionally deprived environments to study the changes in the development of infants and children after they had been placed with specially trained foster families in the local community (Bruch and Touraine, 1940; Chamberlain et al., 2016). This powerful study demonstrated how the lack of loving attention typically provided to children by their parents or caregivers is pivotal for optimal human development, specifically of the brain; adequate nutrition is not enough (Chiputwa, Spielman, and Qaim, 2015; Corcoran and Chaudry, 1997; Lipina et al., 2013). Further research of children who were adopted from institutions in Eastern European countries to the US demonstrated that for every 3.5 months that an infant spent in the institution, they lagged behind their peers in growth by 1 month (Deaton, 2006; Dreyer, 2013; Duncan and Magnuson, 2013; Lichter, Shanahan, and Gardner, 2002; Lipina, 2016; Lopez and Velasco, 2011). Further, a meta-analysis of research on the IQs of children in orphanages found lower IQs among the children in many institutions, but this result was not found in the low-income country setting (Lyytikäinen et al., 2006; Magnuson and Votruba-Drzal, 2008; Duncan and Rodgers, 1988).

Worldwide, residential institutions like orphanages can often be detrimental to the psychological development of affected children (Evans, 2004; Farah et al., 2006). In countries where orphanages are no longer in use, the long-term care of unawarded children by the state has been transitioned to a domestic environment, with an emphasis on replicating a family home (Duncan, Kalil, and Ziol-Guest, 2008; Evans, 2016; Fierman et al., 2016). Many of these countries, such as the United States, utilize a system of monetary stipends paid to foster parents to incentivize and subsidize the care of state wards in private homes (Duncan, Kalil, and Ziol-Guest, 2013; Evans and Cassells, 2014; Guest and Biasini, 2001; Duncan et al., 1998). A distinction must be made between foster care and adoption (Fujiura and Yamaki, 2000; Garrett, Ng'andu, and Ferron, 1994; Duncan et al., 2012; Evans and Fuller-Rowell, 2013). An adoption would remove the child from the care of the state and transfer the legal responsibility for that child's care to the adoptive parent completely and irrevocably (Evans and Kim, 2007, 2013; Hannum, Liu, and Alvarado-Urbina, 2017; Hart, 2008). In the case of foster care, the child would remain a ward of the state with the foster parent acting only as a caregiver (Hatcher et al., 2019; Evans and Kutcher, 2011; Hill and Sandfort, 1995). Most children who live in orphanages are not orphans (Hobcraft, 1998; Hobcraft and Kiernan, 2001; Evans and Schamberg, 2009; Holzer et al., 2008). For example, four out of five children in orphanages have at least one living parent, and most having some extended family (Hong, 2015; Jain and Vaachani, 2006; Jarjoura, Triplett, and Brinker, 2002; Kaplinsky, 2005; Kapoor, 1993; Jones, Vargas, and Villar, 2008). Developing countries and their governments rely on kinship care to aid in the orphan crisis because it is cheaper to financially help extended families in taking in an orphaned child than it is to institutionalize them (Javanbakht et al., 2015; Jones, Vargas, and Villar, 2007; Kalil, Duncan, and Ziol-Guest, 2016). Additionally, developing nations are lacking in child welfare and their well-being because of a lack of resources (Kendig, Mattingly, and Bianchi, 2014; Kim et al., 2013).

Research that is being collected in the developing world shows that these countries focus purely on survival indicators instead of a combination of their survival and other positive indicators like a developed nation would do (Kim et al., 2015; Krason, 2015; Lesner, 2018). This speaks to the way that many developed countries treat an orphan crisis, as the only focus is to obtain a way to ensure their survival (Mazza et al., 2017; Kim et al., 2016). In the developed nations, orphans can expect to find not only a home but also these countries will try and ensure a secure future as well (Mbabazi and Pyeong, 2014; McLaughlin and Rank, 2018; McLoyd, Aikens, and Burton, 2007). Furthermore, orphans in developing nations are seen as a problem that needs to be solved, this also makes them vulnerable to exploitation or neglect (Mickelson, 2002; Miller and Chen, 2013; Miller et al., 2011). In Pakistan, alternative care for orphans often falls on to extended families and Pakistan society as the government feels puts the burden of caring for orphans on them (Ministry of Finance, 2014; Morrow, 2013; Muñoz, Álvarez-Verdejo, and García-Fernández, 2016). Although it is very common for Pakistan citizens to take in orphans because of their culture and religion, only orphans whose parents have died are taken in (Nikulina and Widom, 2014; Nikulina, Widom, and Czaja, 2011; Okiror, 2015; Penn, 2004; Ratcliffe and McKernan, 2010). This neglects a population of children who need alternative care, either due to abuse, or parents who are unable to care for their child because of poverty, mental, or physical issues (Ridge, 2002, 2006; Rowntree, 1901; Ryan, Fauth, and Brooks-Gunn, 2006; Sánchez, 2008).

A few large international charities continue to fund orphanages, but most are still commonly founded by smaller charities and religious groups (Schickedanz, Dreyer, and Halfon, 2015; Schmitz, Wagner, and Menke, 2001; Segretin et al., 2016). Especially in developing countries, orphanages may prey on vulnerable families at risk of breakdown and actively recruit children to ensure continued funding (Serbin et al., 2011; Zembe-Mkabile et al., 2015). Orphanages in developing countries are rarely run by the state (Sinervo and Hill, 2011; Song and Lu, 2002; Sripada et al., 2014). However, not all orphanages that are state-run are less corrupted (State House Uganda, 2017; Stewart, 2005; Torres and Wong, 2013; Townsend, 1979; Twikirize et al., 2014). For example, the Romanian orphanages, like those in Bucharest, were founded due to the soaring population numbers catalyzed by dictator Nicolae Ceau□escu, who banned abortion and birth control and incentivized procreation to increase the Romanian workforce (Vallas, Fremstad, and Ekman, 2015; Van den Waeyenberg, and Hens, 2008; Waddington, 2004; Wells et al., 2010). Today's residential institutions for children, also described as congregate care, include group homes, residential child care communities, children's homes, refuges, rehabilitation centers, night shelters, and youth treatment centers (Ziol-Guest, Duncan, and Kalil, 2009; Ziol-Guest et al., 2012) (Ansell, 2016; Ashiabi, 2000; Ashworth, Hill, and Walker, 1994; Bäckman, and Nilsson, 2007; Bhargava et al., 2004).

Evidence from a variety of studies supports the vital importance of attachment security and later development of children (Bloom and Canning, 2001; Bourdillon and Boyden, 2011; Boyden and James, 2014; Bruch and Touraine, 1940). Deinstitutionalization of orphanages and children's homes program in the United States began in the 1950s, after a series of scandals involving the coercion of birth parents and abuse of orphans (Duncan and Rodgers, 1988; Evans, 2004; Farah et al., 2006). A notorious case was identified at the Georgia Tann's Tennessee Children's Home Society. In Romania, a decree was established that aggressively promoted population growth, banning contraception and abortions for women with fewer than four children (Chamberlain et al., 2016; Chiputwa, Spielman, and Qaim, 2015). This decree was implemented despite the wretched poverty of most families. After Ceausescu was overthrown, he left a society unable and unwilling to take care of its children (Corcoran and Chaudry, 1997; Deaton, 2006; Dreyer, 2013; Duncan and Magnuson, 2013). Researchers conducted a study to see what the implications of this early childhood neglect were on development (Lichter, Shanahan, and Gardner, 2002; Lipina, 2016; Lipina et al., 2013). Typically reared Romanian children showed high rates of secure attachment (Lopez and Velasco, 2011; Lyytikäinen et al., 2006; Magnuson and Votruba-Drzal, 2008). Whereas the institutionally raised children showed huge rates of disorganized attachment (Jones, Vargas, and Villar, 2008; Kendig, Mattingly, and Bianchi, 2014; Kim et al., 2013). Many countries accepted the need to de-institutionalize the care of vulnerable children (Duncan et al., 1998; Evans and Kim, 2007; Hannum, Liu, and Alvarado-Urbina, 2017). In effect, this meant closing down orphanages in favor of foster care and accelerated adoption (Evans and Kim, 2013; Hart, 2008; Hatcher et al., 2019).

Foster care operates by taking in children from their homes due to the lack of care or abuse of their parents, where orphanages take in children with no parents or children whose parents have dropped them off for a better life, typically due to income (Evans and Kutcher, 2011; Hill and Sandfort, 1995; Hobcraft, 1998; Hobcraft and Kiernan, 2001). Major charities are increasingly focusing their efforts on the re-integration of orphans to keep them with their parents or extended family and communities (Evans and Schamberg, 2009; Holzer et al., 2008; Hong, 2015). Orphanages are no longer common in the European Community. Romania, in particular, has struggled greatly to reduce the visibility of its children's institutions to meet conditions of its entry into the European Union (Jain and Vaachani, 2006; Jarjoura, Triplett, and Brinker, 2002; Javanbakht et al., 2015). Some have stated it is important to understand the reasons for child abandonment, then set up targeted alternative services to support vulnerable families at risk of separation such as mother and baby units and daycare centers (Duncan, Kalil, and Ziol-Guest, 2008; Evans, 2016; Fierman et al., 2016). This chapter will close with a review of the lives of communities that are existing amidst poverty.

1.5. COMMUNITIES LIVING IN POVERTY

Many communities are living in poverty, even though they may even have a relatively good income. An example of that is secondary poverty (Kim et al., 2015; Krason, 2015; Lesner, 2018; Mazza et al., 2017). Secondary poverty refers to those that earn enough income to not be impoverished, but who spend their income on unnecessary pleasures, such as alcoholic beverages, thus placing them below it in practice (McLoyd, Aikens, and Burton, 2007; Mickelson, 2002; Miller and Chen, 2013; Miller et al., 2011). In 18th- and 19th-century Great Britain, the practice of temperance among Methodists, as well as their rejection of gambling, allowed them to eliminate secondary poverty and accumulate capital (Ministry of Finance, 2014; Morrow, 2013; Muñoz, Álvarez-Verdejo, and García-Fernández, 2016; Nikulina and Widom, 2014). Economic aspects of poverty focus on material needs, typically including the necessities of daily living, such as food, clothing, shelter, or safe drinking water (Nikulina, Widom, and Czaja, 2011; Okiror, 2015; Penn, 2004; Ratcliffe and McKernan, 2010). Poverty in this sense may be understood as a condition in which a person or community is lacking in the basic needs for a minimum standard of well-being and life, particularly as a result of a persistent lack of income (Ridge, 2002; Rowntree, 1901; Ryan, Fauth, and Brooks-Gunn, 2006; Sánchez, 2008). The increase in poverty runs parallel sides with unemployment, hunger, and a higher crime rate (Ridge, 2006; Schickedanz, Dreyer, and Halfon, 2015; Schmitz, Wagner, and Menke, 2001). Figure 1.5 is a snapshot of comparative rates of population versus child poverty in selected countries.

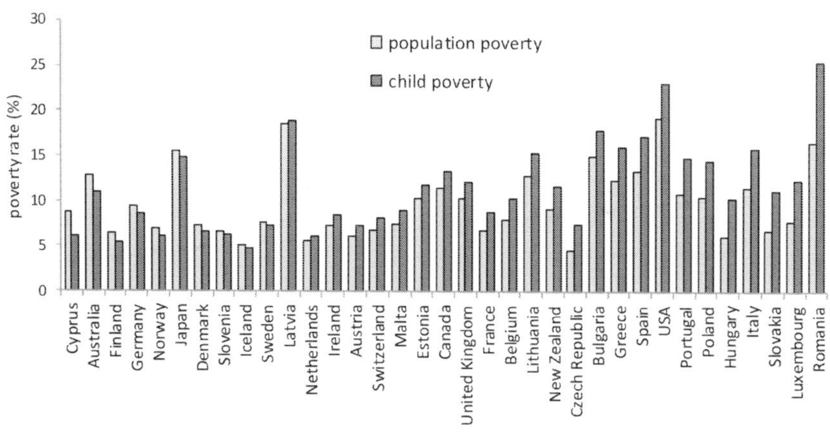

Figure 1.5. Comparison of overall and childhood poverty.

Source: ResearchGate.

Analysis of social aspects of poverty links conditions of scarcity to aspects of the distribution of resources and power in a society and recognizes that poverty may be a function of the diminished "capability" of people to live the kinds of lives they value (Segretin et al., 2016; Serbin et al., 2011). The social aspects of poverty may include lack of access to information, education, health care, social capital, or political power (Sinervo and Hill, 2011; Song and Lu, 2002; Sripada et al., 2014; State House Uganda, 2017). Poverty levels are snapshot pictures in time that omits the transitional dynamics between levels (Stewart, 2005; Torres and Wong, 2013; Townsend, 1979; Twikirize et al., 2014; Vallas, Fremstad, and Ekman, 2015). Mobility statistics supply additional information about the fraction who leave the poverty level (Van den Waeyenberg, and Hens, 2008; Waddington, 2004; Wells et al., 2010). For example, one study finds that in 16 years (1975 to 1991 in the US) only 5% of those in the lower 5th of the income level were still at that level, while 95% transitioned to a higher income category (Zembe-Mkabile et al., 2015; Ziol-Guest, Duncan, and Kalil, 2009; Ziol-Guest et al., 2012). Poverty levels can remain the same while those who rise out of poverty are replaced by others (Ansell, 2016; Dreyer, 2013; Evans, 2016; Evans and Kim, 2013; Jones, Vargas, and Villar, 2007; Mbabazi and Pyeong, 2014; Schickedanz, Dreyer, and Halfon, 2015). The transient poor and chronic poor differ in each society (Ashiabi, 2000; Duncan and Magnuson, 2013; Fierman et al., 2016). In 9 years ending in 2005 for the US, 50% of the poorest quintile transitioned to a higher quintile (Hart, 2008; Kalil, Duncan, and Ziol-Guest, 2016; Kaplinsky, 2005; McLaughlin and Rank, 2018; Schmitz, Wagner, and Menke, 2001).

Poverty may also be understood as an aspect of unequal social status and inequitable social relationships, experienced as social exclusion, dependency, and diminished capacity to participate, or to develop meaningful connections with other people in society (Ashworth, Hill, and Walker, 1994; Lichter, Shanahan, and Gardner, 2002; Duncan, Kalil, and Ziol-Guest, 2013). Such social exclusion can be minimized through strengthened connections with the mainstream, such as through the provision of relational care to those who are experiencing poverty (Hatcher et al., 2019; Kapoor, 1993; McLoyd, Aikens, and Burton, 2007). The World Bank's "Voices of the Poor," based on research with over 20,000 poor people in 23 countries, identifies a range of factors that poor people identify as part of poverty (Bäckman, and Nilsson, 2007; Bhargava et al., 2004; Lipina, 2016; Evans and Cassells, 2014). These include abuse by those in power, dis-empowering institutions, excluded locations, gender relationships, lack of security, limited capabilities, physical limitations, precarious livelihoods, problems in social relationships, weak community organizations, and discrimination (Evans and Kutcher, 2011; Mickelson, 2002; Segretin et al., 2016; Jones, Vargas, and Villar, 2008). David Moore, in his book "*The World Bank*," argues that some analysis of poverty reflects certain pejorative, sometimes racial, stereotypes of impoverished people as powerless victims and passive recipients of aid programs (Bloom and Canning, 2001; Lipina et al., 2013).

Ultra-poverty is a term coined by Michael Lipton. It connotes being amongst the poorest of the poor in low-income countries (Fujiura and Yamaki, 2000; Hill and Sandfort, 1995; Kendig, Mattingly, and Bianchi, 2014). Lipton defined ultra-poverty as receiving less than 80% of minimum caloric intake whilst spending more than 80% of income on food (Miller and Chen, 2013; Miller et al., 2011). Alternatively, a 2007 report issued by International Food Policy Research Institute defined ultra-poverty as living on less than 54 cents per day (Bourdillon and Boyden, 2011; Lopez and Velasco, 2011; Garrett, Ng'andu, and Ferron, 1994). Asset poverty is an economic and social condition that is more persistent and prevalent than income poverty (Hobcraft, 1998; Kim et al., 2013). It can be defined as a household's inability to access wealth resources that are enough to provide for basic needs for three months (Muñoz, Álvarez-Verdejo, and García-Fernández, 2016; Sripada et al., 2014).

Basic needs refer to the minimum standards for consumption and acceptable needs (Boyden and James, 2014; Lyytikäinen et al., 2006; Duncan et al., 2012). Wealth resources consist of homeownership, another real estate (second home, rented properties, etc.), the net value of farm and business assets, stocks, checking, and savings accounts, and other savings (including money in savings bonds, life insurance policy cash values, and the like (Hobcraft and Kiernan, 2001; Kim et al., 2015; Nikulina and Widom, 2014). Wealth is measured in three forms: net worth, net worth minus home equity, and liquid assets (Bruch and Touraine, 1940; Magnuson and Votruba-Drzal, 2008; Evans and Fuller-Rowell, 2013). Net worth consists of all the aspects mentioned above (Guest and Biasini, 2001; Evans and Schamberg, 2009; Krason, 2015; Lesner, 2018). Net worth minus home equity is the same except it does not include home ownership in asset calculations (Nikulina, Widom, and Czaja, 2011; State House Uganda, 2017; Stewart, 2005; Torres and Wong, 2013). Liquid assets are resources that are readily available such as cash, checking, and savings accounts, stocks, and other sources of savings (Chamberlain et al., 2016). There are two types of assets: tangible and intangible (Duncan et al., 1998; Mazza et al., 2017). Tangible assets most closely resemble liquid assets in that they include stocks, bonds, property, natural resources, and hard assets not in the form of real estate (Chiputwa, Spielman, and Qaim, 2015; Evans and Kim, 2007; Okiror, 2015; Townsend, 1979). Intangible assets are simply the access to credit, social capital, cultural capital, political capital, and human capital (Corcoran and Chaudry, 1997; Deaton, 2006; Kim et al., 2016; Twikirize et al., 2014).

The absolute poverty measure trends are supported by human development indicators, which have also been improving (Evans, 2004; Jain and Vaachani, 2006; Ministry of Finance, 2014; Vallas, Fremstad, and Ekman, 2015). Life expectancy has greatly increased in the developing world since World War II and is starting to close the gap to the developed world (Duncan and Rodgers, 1988; Holzer et al., 2008). Child mortality has decreased in every developing region of the world (Farah et al., 2006). The proportion of the world's population living in countries where per-capita food supplies are less than 2,200 calories (9,200 kilojoules) per day decreased from 56% in the mid-1960s to below 10% by the 1990s (Duncan, Kalil, and Ziol-Guest, 2008; Morrow, 2013; Song and Lu, 2002; Ziol-Guest et al., 2012). Similar trends can be observed for literacy, access to clean water and electricity, and basic consumer items (Hannum, Liu, and Alvarado-Urbina, 2017; Penn, 2004; Ratcliffe; Van den Waeyenberg, and Hens, 2008; Sinervo and Hill, 2011). In the United Kingdom, the second David Cameron ministry came under attack for their redefinition of poverty; poverty is no longer classified by a family's income, but as to whether a family is in work or not. Considering that two-thirds of people who found work were accepting wages that are below the living wage according to the Joseph Rowntree Foundation. Hence, this has been criticized by anti-poverty campaigners as an unrealistic view of poverty in the United Kingdom (Hong, 2015; Jarjoura, Triplett, and Brinker, 2002; Ridge, 2002; Waddington, 2004; Ziol-Guest, Duncan, and Kalil, 2009).

The share of the world's population living in absolute poverty fell from 43% in 1981 to 14% in 2011 (Javanbakht et al., 2015; Wells et al., 2010). The absolute number of people in poverty fell from 1.95 billion in 1981 to 1.01 billion in 2011 (Rowntree, 1901; Ryan, Fauth, and Brooks-Gunn, 2006; Sánchez, 2008; Ridge, 2006). The economist Max Roser estimates that the number of people in poverty is therefore roughly the same as 200 years ago (Serbin et al., 2011; Zembe-Mkabile et al., 2015). This is the case since the world population was just a little more than 1 billion in 1820 and the majority (84% to 94%) of the world population was living in poverty (Duncan et al., 2012; Evans and Fuller-Rowell, 2013; Guest and Biasini, 2001). The proportion of the developing world's population living in extreme economic poverty fell from 28% in 1990 to 21% in 2001 (Kim et al., 2016; Mbabazi and Pyeong, 2014; McLaughlin and Rank, 2018). Most of this improvement has occurred in East and South Asia (Duncan, Kalil, and Ziol-Guest, 2013; Evans and Cassells, 2014; Fujiura and Yamaki, 2000; Garrett, Ng'andu, and Ferron, 1994). In East Asia, the World Bank reported that the poverty headcount rate at the \$2-a-day level is estimated to have fallen to about 27% down from 29.5% in 2006 and 69% in 1990 (Ansell, 2016; Ashiabi, 2000; Ashworth, Hill, and Walker, 1994; Bäckman, and Nilsson, 2007). In Sub-Saharan Africa, extreme poverty went up from 41% in 1981 to 46% in 2001 (Bhargava et al., 2004; Bloom and Canning, 2001; Bourdillon and Boyden, 2011; Boyden and James, 2014). This statistic, combined with the growing population increased the number of people living in extreme poverty from 231 million to 318 million (Bruch and Touraine, 1940; Chamberlain et al., 2016).

In the early 1990s, some of the transition economies of Central and Eastern Europe and Central Asia experienced a sharp drop in income (Chiputwa, Spielman, and Qaim, 2015; Corcoran and Chaudry, 1997; Lipina et al., 2013). The collapse of the Soviet Union resulted in large declines in GDP per capita, of about 30% to 35% between 1990 and the through the year 1998 when it was at its minimum (Deaton, 2006; Dreyer, 2013; Duncan and Magnuson, 2013; Lichter, Shanahan, and Gardner, 2002; Lipina, 2016; Lopez and Velasco, 2011). As a result, poverty rates tripled, excess mortality increased, and life expectancy declined. In subsequent years as per capita incomes recovered the poverty rate dropped from 31.4% of the population to 19.6% (Lyytikäinen et al., 2006; Magnuson and Votruba-Drzal, 2008; Duncan and Rodgers, 1988). The average post-communist country had returned to 1989 levels of per-capita GDP by 2005, although as of 2015, some are still far behind that (Evans, 2004; Farah et al., 2006). According to an article in Foreign Affairs, there were generally three paths to economic reform taken post-Soviet collapse (Duncan, Kalil, and Ziol-Guest, 2008; Evans, 2016; Fierman et al., 2016). Those nations that took a "radical" or "gradual" reform rate have GDP per capita similar to other nations in their stage of economic development at generally 150% of their transition year (1991) GDP (Duncan, Kalil, and Ziol-Guest, 2013; Evans and Cassells, 2014; Guest and Biasini, 2001; Duncan et al., 1998). Nations that took a "slow" approach (an approach that limited free-market reforms generally) had much slower, and lower economic growth, higher Gini coefficients, and poorer health outcomes (Fujiura and Yamaki, 2000; Garrett, Ng'andu, and Ferron, 1994; Duncan et al., 2012; Evans and Fuller-Rowell, 2013). Currently, those nations sit at 125% of their transition year GDP per capita (Evans and Kim, 2007, 2013; Hannum, Liu, and Alvarado-Urbina, 2017; Hart, 2008).

A 2009 study published in The Lancet suggested that radical economic changes and the resulting short-term unemployment led to temporary increases in the mortality rate of adult males (Hatcher et al., 2019; Evans and Kutcher, 2011; Hill and Sandfort, 1995). World Bank data shows that the percentage of the population living in households with consumption or income per person below the poverty line has decreased in each region of the world except the Middle East and North Africa since 1990 (Hobcraft, 1998; Hobcraft and Kiernan, 2001; Evans and Schamberg, 2009; Holzer et al., 2008). Despite the increasing prosperity and standards of living across the globe, there are still many people that are living in poverty (Hong, 2015; Jain and Vaachani, 2006; Jarjoura, Triplett, and Brinker, 2002; Kaplinsky, 2005; Kapoor, 1993; Jones, Vargas, and Villar, 2008). The increasing income inequality lends credence to the suggestion that economic development has not fostered social mobility for many swathes of the population (Javanbakht et al., 2015; Jones, Vargas, and Villar, 2007; Kalil, Duncan, and Ziol-Guest, 2016). The notion of distorted development has therefore been used to describe situations where the overall GDP is increasing, but the actual welfare of the majority of the population is not improving (Kendig, Mattingly, and Bianchi, 2014; Kim et al., 2013). This phenomenon has been particularly profound in those previously low-income countries that have been afflicted by the natural resource curse (Kim et al., 2015; Krason, 2015; Lesner, 2018). This refers to situations in which the discovery of a rich natural resource leads to increased mismanagement and corruption, which means that the resources never really get down to the people that need them (Mazza et al., 2017; Kim et al., 2016).

CHAPTER 1 SUMMARY

This initial chapter in the book has highlighted some of the challenges that are associated with the conceptualization of childhood poverty. For example, children can be living in poverty even though their community is on average wealthier than others. The chapter has shown how the institutionalization of vulnerable groups such as orphans has not been able to address their specific needs. Hence, childhood poverty continues to grow in these communities. Above all, the chapter has shown that poverty can manifest itself in some complex and multi-layered ways. The next chapter in this book considers the roles that are played by various stakeholders when dealing with childhood poverty.

Chapter 2

Stakeholders in Childhood Poverty

CONTENTS

There are many stakeholders in childhood poverty. However, these can be broadly divided into three categories. The first category is those people that are affected by childhood poverty. The second category comprises those who can intervene in the status quo to reduce or eliminate child poverty. The third category comprises those who cause, foster and maintain child poverty. The latter category might fall into that classification advertently or inadvertently. Hence, poverty can exist through action or inaction. This chapter highlights some of the stakeholders in child poverty and critically examines their role. By the end of this chapter, the reader should have an idea of the role that families, communities, local authorities, state agencies, and international agencies play in childhood poverty. There is an underlying assumption that any of these stakeholders can be victims, interventionists, or contributors to child poverty depending on their knowledge, attitudes, and behavior.

2.1. ROLE OF THE FAMILY IN CHILD POVERTY

In human society, a family is a group of people related (Mbabazi and Pyeong, 2014; McLaughlin and Rank, 2018; McLoyd, Aikens, and Burton, 2007). This can be by either consanguinity in which the relationship is recognized by birth; or by affinity where the relationship is recognized through marriage or other relationship (Mickelson, 2002; Miller and Chen, 2013; Miller et al., 2011). The purpose of families is to maintain the well-being of its members and society (Ministry of Finance, 2014; Morrow, 2013; Muñoz, Álvarez-Verdejo, and García-Fernández, 2016). Ideally, families would offer predictability, structure, and safety as members mature and participate in the community (Nikulina and Widom, 2014; Nikulina, Widom, and Czaja, 2011; Okiror, 2015; Penn, 2004; Ratcliffe and McKernan, 2010). In most societies, it is within families that children acquire socialization for life outside the family (Ridge, 2002, 2006; Rowntree, 1901; Ryan, Fauth, and Brooks-Gunn, 2006; Sánchez, 2008). Additionally, as the basic unit for meeting the basic needs of its members, it provides a sense of boundaries for performing tasks in a safe environment, ideally builds a person into a functional adult, transmits culture, and ensures continuity of humankind with precedents of knowledge (Schickedanz, Dreyer, and Halfon, 2015; Schmitz, Wagner, and Menke, 2001; Segretin et al., 2016).

Anthropologists generally classify most family organizations into five broad categories that may overlap (Serbin et al., 2011; Zembe-Mkabile et al., 2015). The first is the matrifocal families comprising a mother and her children (Sinervo and Hill, 2011; Song and Lu, 2002; Sripada et al., 2014). The second is the patrifocal families comprising a father and his children (State House Uganda, 2017; Stewart, 2005; Torres and Wong, 2013; Townsend, 1979; Twikirize et al., 2014). The third is a conjugal family comprising a wife, her husband, and children (Vallas, Fremstad, and Ekman, 2015; Van den Waeyenberg, and Hens, 2008; Waddington, 2004; Wells et al., 2010). This is also called the nuclear family (Ziol-Guest, Duncan, and Kalil, 2009; Ziol-Guest et al., 2012). The 4th category is that of the avuncular family which may include, for example, a grandparent, a brother, his sister, and her children (Ansell, 2016; Ashiabi, 2000; Ashworth, Hill, and Walker, 1994; Bäckman, and Nilsson, 2007; Bhargava et al., 2004). The 5th category is that of an extended family comprising parents and children co-reside with other members of one parent's family (Bloom and Canning, 2001; Bourdillon and Boyden, 2011; Boyden and James, 2014; Bruch and Touraine, 1940). To explain the persistent existence of child poverty among wealthy nations (see Figure 2.1), some have argued that the breakdown of the family is to blame.

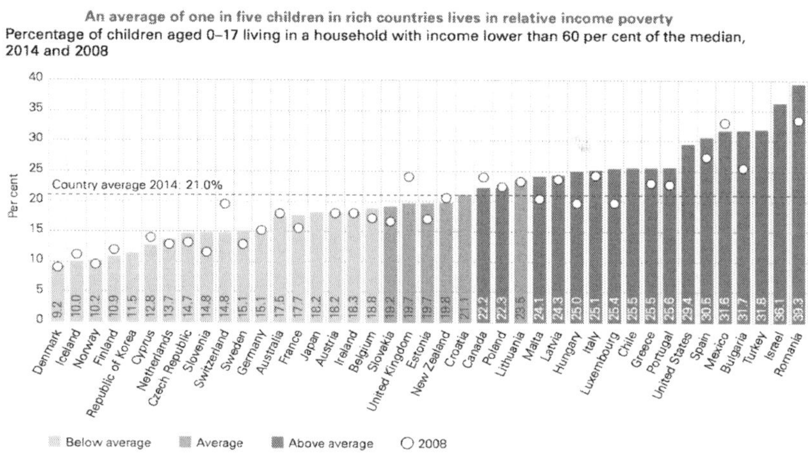

Figure 2.1. Child poverty among the richest nations on earth.

Source: World Economic Forum.

Members of the immediate family may include spouses, parents, grandparents, brothers, sisters, sons, and daughters (Duncan and Rodgers, 1988; Evans, 2004; Farah et al., 2006). Sometimes these are also considered members of the immediate family, depending on an individual's specific relationship with them, and the legal definition of "immediate family" varies (Chamberlain et al., 2016; Chiputwa, Spielman, and Qaim, 2015). Sexual relations with family members are regulated by rules concerning incest such as the incest taboo (Corcoran and Chaudry, 1997; Deaton, 2006; Dreyer, 2013; Duncan and Magnuson, 2013). Regardless of the makeup of the family, it can offer support, resilience, and social capital which ameliorates the effects of childhood poverty (Lichter, Shanahan, and Gardner, 2002; Lipina, 2016; Lipina et al., 2013). Dysfunctional families fail in this respect and can therefore increase child poverty (Lopez and Velasco, 2011; Lyytikäinen et al., 2006; Magnuson and Votruba-Drzal, 2008). It is not surprising that dysfunctional families have been traditionally associated with child poverty, although wealthy families can also be dysfunctional (Jones, Vargas, and Villar, 2008; Kendig, Mattingly, and Bianchi, 2014; Kim et al., 2013).

The field of genealogy aims to trace family lineages through history (Duncan et al., 1998; Evans and Kim, 2007; Hannum, Liu, and Alvarado-Urbina, 2017). The family is also an important economic unit studied in family economics (Evans and Kim, 2013; Hart, 2008; Hatcher et al., 2019). The word "families" can be used metaphorically to create more inclusive categories such as community, nationhood, and global village (Evans and Kutcher, 2011; Hill and Sandfort, 1995; Hobcraft, 1998; Hobcraft and Kiernan, 2001). One of the primary functions of the family involves providing a framework for the production and reproduction of persons biologically and socially (Evans and Schamberg, 2009; Holzer et al., 2008; Hong, 2015). This can occur through the sharing of material substances (such as food); the giving and receiving of care and nurture or nurture kinship (Jain and Vaachani, 2006; Jarjoura, Triplett, and Brinker, 2002; Javanbakht et al., 2015). Membership of a family elicits jural rights and obligations (Duncan, Kalil, and Ziol-Guest, 2008; Evans, 2016; Fierman et al., 2016). The family may also create moral and sentimental ties. Thus, one's experience of one's family shifts over time (Jones, Vargas, and Villar, 2007; Kalil, Duncan, and Ziol-Guest, 2016; Kaplinsky, 2005; Kapoor, 1993). From the perspective of children, the family is a "family of orientation" (Kim et al., 2015; Krason, 2015; Lesner, 2018; Mazza et al., 2017). In this case, the family serves to locate children socially and plays a major role in their enculturation and socialization (McLoyd, Aikens, and Burton, 2007; Mickelson, 2002; Miller and Chen, 2013; Miller et al., 2011). From the point of view of the parent or parents, the family is a "family of procreation," the goal of which is to produce, enculturate and socialize children (Ministry of Finance, 2014; Morrow, 2013; Muñoz, Álvarez-Verdejo, and García-Fernández, 2016; Nikulina and Widom, 2014). However, producing children is not the only function of the family (Nikulina, Widom, and Czaja, 2011; Okiror, 2015;

Penn, 2004; Ratcliffe and McKernan, 2010). For example, in societies with a sexual division of labor, marriage, and the resulting relationship between two people; it is necessary for the formation of an economically productive household (Ridge, 2002; Rowntree, 1901; Ryan, Fauth, and Brooks-Gunn, 2006; Sánchez, 2008).

Christopher Harris notes that the western conception of family is ambiguous and confused with the household, as revealed in the different contexts in which the word is used (Ridge, 2006; Schickedanz, Dreyer, and Halfon, 2015; Schmitz, Wagner, and Menke, 2001). Olivia Harris states this confusion is not accidental, but indicative of the familial ideology of capitalist, western countries that pass social legislation that insists members of a nuclear family should live together, and that those not so related should not live together (Segretin et al., 2016; Serbin et al., 2011). Despite the ideological and legal pressures, a large percentage of families do not conform to the ideal nuclear family type (Sinervo and Hill, 2011; Song and Lu, 2002; Sripada et al., 2014; State House Uganda, 2017).

Similarly, the reproductive roles of the family have been challenged in Western society where the birthrates are continuously falling (Stewart, 2005; Torres and Wong, 2013; Townsend, 1979; Twikirize et al., 2014; Vallas, Fremstad, and Ekman, 2015). The total fertility rate of women varies from country to country, from a high of 6.76 children born/woman in Niger to a low of 0.81 in Singapore as of 2015 (Van den Waeyenberg, and Hens, 2008; Waddington, 2004; Wells et al., 2010). Fertility is low in most Eastern European and Southern European countries, and high in most Sub-Saharan African countries (Zembe-Mkabile et al., 2015; Ziol-Guest, Duncan, and Kalil, 2009; Ziol-Guest et al., 2012). In some cultures, the mother's preference of family size influences that of the children through early adulthood (Ansell, 2016; Dreyer, 2013; Evans, 2016; Evans and Kim, 2013; Jones, Vargas, and Villar, 2007; Mbabazi and Pyeong, 2014; Schickedanz, Dreyer, and Halfon, 2015). A parent's number of children strongly correlates with the number of children that their children will eventually have (Ashiabi, 2000; Duncan and Magnuson, 2013; Fierman et al., 2016). High fertility rates may lead to large families and this can have a dampening effect in deprived regions (Hart, 2008; Kalil, Duncan, and Ziol-Guest, 2016; Kaplinsky, 2005; McLaughlin and Rank, 2018; Schmitz, Wagner, and Menke, 2001). Indeed, there are instances where child poverty is positively associated with large family size (Ashworth, Hill, and Walker, 1994; Lichter, Shanahan, and Gardner, 2002; Duncan, Kalil, and Ziol-Guest, 2013).

Early western cultural anthropologists and sociologists considered family and kinship to be universally associated with relations by "blood" (Hatcher et al., 2019; Kapoor, 1993; McLoyd, Aikens, and Burton, 2007). This was based on ideas common in their own cultures. However, later research has shown that many societies instead understand family through ideas of living together, the sharing of food (e.g., milk kinship), and sharing care and nurture (Bäckman, and Nilsson, 2007; Bhargava et al., 2004; Lipina, 2016; Evans and Cassells, 2014). Sociologists have a special interest in the function and status of family forms in stratified (especially capitalist) societies (Evans and Kutcher, 2011; Mickelson, 2002; Segretin et al., 2016; Jones, Vargas, and Villar, 2008).

According to the work of scholars Max Weber, Alan Macfarlane, Steven Ozment, Jack Goody, and Peter Laslett, the huge transformation that led to modern marriage in Western democracies was fueled by the religio-cultural value system provided by elements of Judaism, early Christianity, Roman Catholic canon law and the Protestant Reformation (Bloom and Canning, 2001; Lipina et al., 2013). The term "nuclear family" is commonly used, especially in the United States of America, to refer to conjugal families (Fujiura and Yamaki, 2000; Hill and Sandfort, 1995; Kendig, Mattingly, and Bianchi, 2014).

A "conjugal" family includes only the spouses and unmarried children who are not of age (Miller and Chen, 2013; Miller et al., 2011). Some sociologists distinguish between conjugal families which are relatively independent of the kindred of the parents and other families in general; and nuclear families which maintain relatively close ties with their kindred (Bourdillon and Boyden, 2011; Lopez and Velasco, 2011; Garrett, Ng'andu, and Ferron, 1994). Other family structures (e.g., blended parents, single parents, and domestic partnerships) have begun to challenge the normality of the nuclear family (Hobcraft, 1998; Kim et al., 2013).

A single-parent family consists of one parent together with their children, where the parent is either widowed, divorced (and not remarried), or never married (Muñoz, Álvarez-Verdejo, and García-Fernández, 2016; Sripada et al., 2014). The parent may have sole custody of the children, or separated parents may have a shared-parenting arrangement where the children divide their time (possibly equally) between two different single-parent families or between one single-parent family and one blended family (Boyden and James, 2014; Lyytikäinen et al., 2006; Duncan et al., 2012). As compared to sole custody, the physical, mental, and social well-being of children may be improved by shared-parenting arrangements and by children having greater access to both parents (Hobcraft and Kiernan, 2001; Kim et al., 2015; Nikulina and Widom, 2014). The number of single-parent families has been increasing over time (Bruch and Touraine, 1940; Magnuson and Votruba-Drzal, 2008; Evans and Fuller-Rowell, 2013). For example, about half of all children in the United States will live in a single-parent family at some point before they reach the age of 18 (Guest and Biasini, 2001; Evans and Schamberg, 2009; Krason, 2015; Lesner, 2018). Most single-parent families are headed by a mother, but the number of single-parent families headed by fathers is increasing (Nikulina, Widom, and Czaja, 2011; State House Uganda, 2017; Stewart, 2005; Torres and Wong, 2013).

A "matrifocal" family consists of a mother and her children (Chamberlain et al., 2016). Generally, these children are her biological offspring, although adoption of children is a practice in nearly every society (Duncan et al., 1998; Mazza et al., 2017). This kind of family occurs commonly where women have the resources to rear their children by themselves, or where men are more mobile than women (Chiputwa, Spielman, and Qaim, 2015; Evans and Kim, 2007; Okiror, 2015; Townsend, 1979). This is a family or domestic group which is centered on a woman and her children (Corcoran and Chaudry, 1997; Deaton, 2006; Kim et al., 2016; Twikirize et al., 2014). In this case, the father or fathers of these children are intermittently present in the life of the group and occupy a secondary place (Evans, 2004; Jain and Vaachani, 2006; Ministry of Finance, 2014; Vallas, Fremstad, and Ekman, 2015). The children's mother is not necessarily the wife of one of the children's fathers (Duncan and Rodgers, 1988; Holzer et al., 2008).

The term family of choice, also sometimes referred to as "chosen family" or "found family," is common within the LGBT community, veterans, individuals who have suffered abuse, and those who have no contact with biological "parents" (Farah et al., 2006). It refers to the group of people in an individual's life that satisfies the typical role of the family as a support system (Duncan, Kalil, and Ziol-Guest, 2008; Morrow, 2013; Song and Lu, 2002; Ziol-Guest et al., 2012).

The term differentiates between the "family of origin" (the biological family or that in which people are raised) and those that actively assume that ideal role (Hannum, Liu, and Alvarado-Urbina, 2017; Penn, 2004; Ratcliffe; Van den Waeyenberg, and Hens, 2008; Sinervo and Hill, 2011). The family of choice may or may not include some or all of the members of the family of origin. This terminology stems from the fact that many LGBT individuals, upon coming out, face rejection or shame from the families they were raised in (Hong, 2015; Jarjoura, Triplett, and Brinker, 2002; Ridge, 2002; Waddington, 2004; Ziol-Guest, Duncan, and Kalil, 2009). The term family of choice is also used by individuals in the 12 step communities, who create close-knit "family" ties through the recovery process (Javanbakht et al., 2015; Wells et al., 2010). As a family system, families of choice face unique issues (Rowntree, 1901; Ryan, Fauth, and Brooks-Gunn, 2006; Sánchez, 2008; Ridge, 2006). Without legal safeguards, families of choice may struggle when medical, educational, or governmental institutions fail to recognize their legitimacy (Serbin et al., 2011; Zembe-Mkabile et al., 2015). If members of the chosen family have been disowned by their family of origin, they may experience surrogate grief, displacing anger, loss, or anxious attachment onto their new family (Duncan et al., 2012; Evans and Fuller-Rowell, 2013; Guest and Biasini, 2001).

The term blended family or stepfamily describes families with mixed parents (Kim et al., 2016; Mbabazi and Pyeong, 2014; McLaughlin and Rank, 2018). In this case, one or both parents are remarried, bringing children of the former family into the new family (Duncan, Kalil, and Ziol-Guest, 2013; Evans and Cassells, 2014; Fujiura and Yamaki, 2000; Garrett, Ng'andu, and Ferron, 1994). Moreover, in sociology, particularly in the works of social psychologist Michael Lamb, traditional family refers to "a middle-class family with a bread-winning father and a stay-at-home mother, married to each other and raising their biological children," and nontraditional to exceptions to this rule (Ansell, 2016; Ashiabi, 2000; Ashworth, Hill, and Walker, 1994; Bäckman, and Nilsson, 2007). Most of the US households are now non-traditional under this definition (Bhargava et al., 2004; Bloom and Canning, 2001; Bourdillon and Boyden, 2011; Boyden and James, 2014). Critics of the term "traditional family" point out that in most cultures and at most times, the extended family model has been most common, not the nuclear family (Bruch and Touraine, 1940; Chamberlain et al., 2016). However, this tradition of the nuclear family has had a long tradition in England than in other parts of Europe and Asia which contributed large numbers of immigrants to the Americas (Chiputwa, Spielman, and Qaim, 2015; Corcoran and Chaudry, 1997; Lipina et al., 2013). The nuclear family became the most common form in the US in the 1960s and 1970s (Deaton, 2006; Dreyer, 2013; Duncan and Magnuson, 2013; Lichter, Shanahan, and Gardner, 2002; Lipina, 2016; Lopez and Velasco, 2011). In the next section, we consider the various roles that the community can play.

2.2. ROLE OF THE COMMUNITY AS A WHOLE IN FIGHTING POVERTY

A community is a social unit (a group of living things) with a commonality such as norms, religion, values, customs, or identity (Lyytikäinen et al., 2006; Magnuson and Votruba-Drzal, 2008; Duncan and Rodgers, 1988). Communities may share a sense of place situated in a given geographical area (Evans, 2004; Farah et al., 2006). This shared location may be a country, village, town, or neighborhood (Duncan, Kalil, and Ziol-Guest, 2008; Evans, 2016; Fierman et al., 2016). More recently, communities have been created and sustained in virtual space through communication platforms (Duncan, Kalil, and Ziol-Guest, 2013; Evans and Cassells, 2014; Guest and Biasini, 2001; Duncan et al., 1998). Even within relatively wealthy communities (see Figure 2.2), income inequality might mean that child poverty has implications for economic planning and delivery (Hong, 2015; Jain and Vaachani, 2006; Jarjoura, Triplett, and Brinker, 2002; Kaplinsky, 2005; Kapoor, 1993; Jones, Vargas, and Villar, 2008).

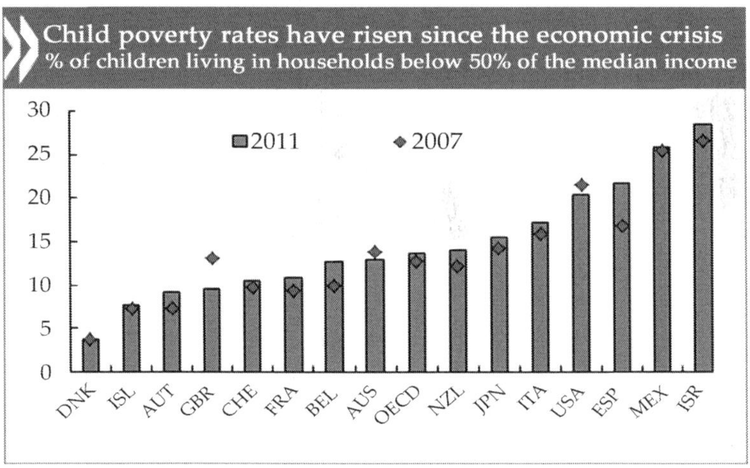

Figure 2.2. The price of income inequality among developed nations.

Source: OECD.

Durable relations that extend beyond immediate genealogical ties also define a sense of community (Fujiura and Yamaki, 2000; Garrett, Ng'andu, and Ferron, 1994; Duncan et al., 2012; Evans and Fuller-Rowell, 2013). These are important to their identity, practice, and roles in social institutions such as family, home, work, government, society, or humanity at large

(Evans and Kim, 2007, 2013; Hannum, Liu, and Alvarado-Urbina, 2017; Hart, 2008). Although communities are usually small relative to personal social ties, "community" may also refer to large group affiliations such as national communities, international communities, and virtual communities (Hatcher et al., 2019; Evans and Kutcher, 2011; Hill and Sandfort, 1995). Human communities may share intent, belief, resources, preferences, needs, and risks in common, affecting the identity of the participants and their degree of cohesiveness (Hobcraft, 1998; Hobcraft and Kiernan, 2001; Evans and Schamberg, 2009; Holzer et al., 2008).

Archaeological studies of social communities use the term "community" in two ways, paralleling usage in other areas (Javanbakht et al., 2015; Jones, Vargas, and Villar, 2007; Kalil, Duncan, and Ziol-Guest, 2016). The first is an informal definition of community as a place where people used to live (Kendig, Mattingly, and Bianchi, 2014; Kim et al., 2013). In this sense community is synonymous with the concept of an ancient settlement; regardless of whether or not it is a hamlet, village, town, or city (Kim et al., 2015; Krason, 2015; Lesner, 2018). The second meaning resembles the usage of the term in other social sciences: a community is a group of people living near one another who interact socially (Mazza et al., 2017; Kim et al., 2016). Social interaction on a small scale can be difficult to identify with archaeological data (Mbabazi and Pyeong, 2014; McLaughlin and Rank, 2018; McLoyd, Aikens, and Burton, 2007). Most reconstructions of social communities by archaeologists rely on the principle that social interaction in the past was conditioned by physical distance (Mickelson, 2002; Miller and Chen, 2013; Miller et al., 2011). Therefore, a small village settlement likely constituted a social community, and spatial subdivisions of cities and other large settlements may have formed communities (Ministry of Finance, 2014; Morrow, 2013; Muñoz, Álvarez-Verdejo, and García-Fernández, 2016). Archaeologists typically use similarities in material culture, which can range from house types to styles of pottery, to reconstruct communities in the past (Nikulina and Widom, 2014; Nikulina, Widom, and Czaja, 2011; Okiror, 2015; Penn, 2004; Ratcliffe and McKernan, 2010). This classification method relies on the assumption that people or households will share more similarities in the types and styles of their material goods with other members of a social community than they will with outsiders (Ridge, 2002, 2006; Rowntree, 1901; Ryan, Fauth, and Brooks-Gunn, 2006; Sánchez, 2008).

The process of learning to adopt the behavior patterns of the community is called socialization (Schickedanz, Dreyer, and Halfon, 2015; Schmitz,

Wagner, and Menke, 2001; Segretin et al., 2016). The most fertile time of socialization is usually the early stages of life, during which individuals develop the skills and knowledge and learn the roles necessary to function within their culture and social environment (Serbin et al., 2011; Zembe-Mkabile et al., 2015). For some psychologists, especially those in the psychodynamic tradition, the most important period of socialization is between the ages of one and ten (Sinervo and Hill, 2011; Song and Lu, 2002; Sripada et al., 2014). But socialization also includes adults moving into a significantly different environment where they must learn a new set of behaviors (State House Uganda, 2017; Stewart, 2005; Torres and Wong, 2013; Townsend, 1979; Twikirize et al., 2014). Socialization is influenced primarily by the family, through which children first learn community norms (Vallas, Fremstad, and Ekman, 2015; Van den Waeyenberg, and Hens, 2008; Waddington, 2004; Wells et al., 2010). Other important influences include schools, peer groups, people, mass media, the workplace, and government (Ziol-Guest, Duncan, and Kalil, 2009; Ziol-Guest et al., 2012). The degree to which the norms of a particular society or community are adopted determines one's willingness to engage with others (Ansell, 2016; Ashiabi, 2000; Ashworth, Hill, and Walker, 1994; Bäckman, and Nilsson, 2007; Bhargava et al., 2004). The norms of tolerance, reciprocity, and trust are important "habits of the heart," in an individual's involvement in the community (Bloom and Canning, 2001; Bourdillon and Boyden, 2011; Boyden and James, 2014; Bruch and Touraine, 1940).

The community can be the scene for interventions that not only develop the community generally but also specifically address the problem of child poverty (Duncan and Rodgers, 1988; Evans, 2004; Farah et al., 2006). Community development is often linked with community work or community planning and may involve stakeholders, foundations, governments, or contracted entities including non-government organizations (NGOs), universities, or government agencies to progress the social well-being of local, regional, and, sometimes, national communities (Chamberlain et al., 2016; Chiputwa, Spielman, and Qaim, 2015). More grassroots efforts, called community building or community organizing, seek to empower individuals and groups of people by providing them with the skills they need to effect change in their communities (Corcoran and Chaudry, 1997; Deaton, 2006; Dreyer, 2013; Duncan and Magnuson, 2013). These skills often assist in building political power through the formation of large social groups working for a common agenda (Lichter, Shanahan, and Gardner, 2002; Lipina, 2016; Lipina et al., 2013). Community development practitioners must understand both how to work with individuals and how to affect communities' positions within the context of larger social institutions (Lopez and Velasco, 2011; Lyytikäinen et al., 2006; Magnuson and Votruba-Drzal, 2008). Public administrators, in contrast, need to understand community development in the context of rural and urban development, housing, and economic development, and community, organizational, and business development (Jones, Vargas, and Villar, 2008; Kendig, Mattingly, and Bianchi, 2014; Kim et al., 2013).

The three basic types of community organizing are grassroots organizing, coalition building, and "institution-based community organizing" (Duncan et al., 1998; Evans and Kim, 2007; Hannum, Liu, and Alvarado-Urbina, 2017). This is also called "broad-based community organizing," an example of which is faith-based community organizing, or Congregation-based Community Organizing (Evans and Kim, 2013; Hart, 2008; Hatcher et al., 2019). Community building can use a wide variety of practices, ranging from simple events such as potlucks, small book clubs; to larger-scale efforts such as mass festivals, construction projects that involve local participants rather than outside contractors (Evans and Kutcher, 2011; Hill and Sandfort, 1995; Hobcraft, 1998; Hobcraft and Kiernan, 2001). Community building that is geared toward citizen action is usually termed "community organizing." In these cases, organized community groups seek accountability from elected officials and increased direct representation within decision-making bodies (Evans and Schamberg, 2009; Holzer et al., 2008; Hong, 2015). Where good-faith negotiations fail, these constituency-led organizations seek to pressure the decision-makers through a variety of means, including picketing, boycotting, sit-ins, petitioning, and electoral politics (Jain and Vaachani, 2006; Jarjoura, Triplett, and Brinker, 2002; Javanbakht et al., 2015).

Community organizing can focus on more than just resolving specific issues (Duncan, Kalil, and Ziol-Guest, 2008; Evans, 2016; Fierman et al., 2016). Organizing often means building a widely accessible power structure, often with the end goal of distributing power equally throughout the community (Jones, Vargas, and Villar, 2007; Kalil, Duncan, and Ziol-Guest, 2016; Kaplinsky, 2005; Kapoor, 1993). Community organizers generally seek to build groups that are open and democratic in governance (Kim et al., 2015; Krason, 2015; Lesner, 2018; Mazza et al., 2017). Such groups facilitate and encourage consensus decision-making with a focus on the general health of the community rather than a specific interest group (McLoyd, Aikens, and Burton, 2007; Mickelson, 2002; Miller and Chen, 2013; Miller et al., 2011). If communities are developed based on something they share in common, whether location or values, then one challenge for developing communities is how to incorporate individuality and differences (Ministry of Finance, 2014; Morrow, 2013; Muñoz, Álvarez-Verdejo, and García-Fernández, 2016; Nikulina and Widom, 2014). Rebekah Nathan suggests, in "*My Freshman Year*," that we are drawn to developing communities based on sameness, despite stated commitments to diversity, such as those found on university websites. Regardless of their formation or foundation, communities not only demonstrate the problems associated with childhood poverty; but can also be used as scenes of intervention (Nikulina, Widom, and Czaja, 2011; Okiror, 2015; Penn, 2004; Ratcliffe and McKernan, 2010). Indeed, where the community is broadly supportive of these interventions; they have a much higher chance of success (Ridge, 2002; Rowntree, 1901; Ryan, Fauth, and Brooks-Gunn, 2006; Sánchez, 2008). The next section examines the role of local authorities in causing and managing child poverty.

2.3. LOCAL AUTHORITIES AND CHILD POVERTY

A local government is a form of public administration which, in a majority of contexts, exists as the lowest tier of administration within a given state (Lichter, Shanahan, and Gardner, 2002; Lipina, 2016; Lipina et al., 2013). The term is used to contrast with offices at the state level, which are referred to as the central government, national government, or (where appropriate) federal government, and also to the supranational government which deals with governing institutions between states (Lopez and Velasco, 2011; Lyytikäinen et al., 2006; Magnuson and Votruba-Drzal, 2008). Local governments generally act within powers delegated to them by legislation or directives of the higher level of government (Jones, Vargas, and Villar, 2008; Kendig, Mattingly, and Bianchi, 2014; Kim et al., 2013). In federal states, the local government generally comprises the third (or sometimes 4th) tier of government, whereas, in unitary states, the local government usually occupies the second or third tier of government, often with greater powers than higher-level administrative divisions (Duncan et al., 1998; Evans and Kim, 2007; Hannum, Liu, and Alvarado-Urbina, 2017). Local authorities are often at the forefront of fighting child poverty since they are closer to communities than federal agencies (Evans and Kim, 2013; Hart, 2008; Hatcher et al., 2019). Local authorities might also pick up on the underlying patterns of poverty, such as the link between ethnicity and childhood deprivation (see Figure 2.3 for an example).

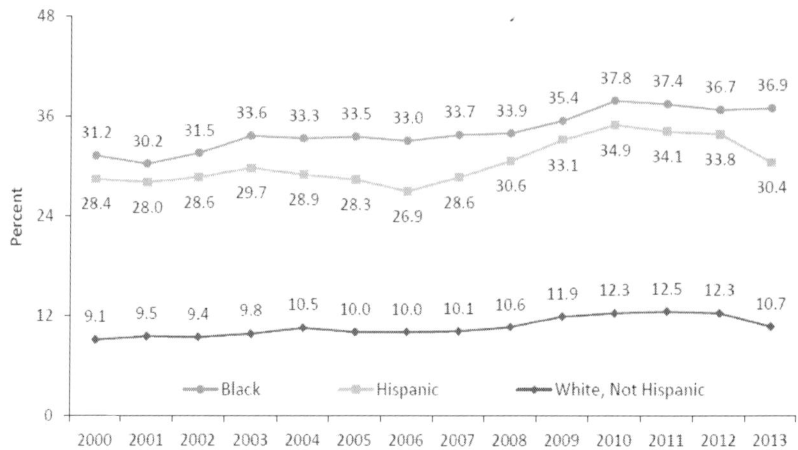

Figure 2.3. Linking child poverty and ethnicity.

Source: ASPE.

The question of municipal autonomy is a key question of public administration and governance (Evans and Kutcher, 2011; Hill and Sandfort, 1995; Hobcraft, 1998; Hobcraft and Kiernan, 2001). The institutions of local government vary greatly between countries, and even where similar arrangements exist, the terminology often varies (Evans and Schamberg, 2009; Holzer et al., 2008; Hong, 2015). Common designated names for local government entities include state, province, region, department, county, prefecture, district, city, township, town, borough, parish, municipality, shire, village, local service district, and local government area (Jain and Vaachani, 2006; Jarjoura, Triplett, and Brinker, 2002; Javanbakht et al., 2015). We can better understand the role of local authorities by considering some case studies (Duncan, Kalil, and Ziol-Guest, 2008; Evans, 2016; Fierman et al., 2016). Egypt is one such case study in which poverty remains an important consideration (Jones, Vargas, and Villar, 2007; Kalil, Duncan, and Ziol-Guest, 2016; Kaplinsky, 2005; Kapoor, 1993). Local government traditionally had limited power in Egypt's highly centralized state (Kim et al., 2015; Krason, 2015; Lesner, 2018; Mazza et al., 2017). Under the central government were 26 governorates. These were subdivided into districts and villages or towns. At each level, there was a governing structure that combined representative councils and government-appointed executive organs headed by governors, district officers, and mayors, respectively. Governors were appointed by the president, and they, in turn, appointed subordinate executive officers. The coercive backbone of the state apparatus ran downward from the Ministry of Interior through the governors' executive organs to the district police station and the village headman (McLoyd, Aikens, and Burton, 2007; Mickelson, 2002; Miller and Chen, 2013; Miller et al., 2011).

Before the revolution, state penetration of the rural areas was limited by the power of local notables (Ministry of Finance, 2014; Morrow, 2013; Muñoz, Álvarez-Verdejo, and García-Fernández, 2016; Nikulina and Widom, 2014). However, under Nasser, land reform reduced their socioeconomic dominance, and the incorporation of peasants into cooperatives transferred mass dependence from landlords to government (Nikulina, Widom, and Czaja, 2011; Okiror, 2015; Penn, 2004; Ratcliffe and McKernan, 2010). The extension of officials into the countryside permitted the regime to bring development and services to the village. The local branches of the ruling party, the Arab Socialist Union (ASU), fostered a certain peasant political activism and coopted the local notables (Ridge, 2002; Rowntree, 1901; Ryan, Fauth, and Brooks-Gunn, 2006; Sánchez, 2008). These included in particular the village headmen and checked their independence from the regime (Ridge, 2006; Schickedanz, Dreyer, and Halfon, 2015; Schmitz, Wagner, and Menke, 2001). State penetration did not retreat under Sadat and Mubarak. The earlier effort to mobilize peasants and deliver services disappeared as the local party and cooperative withered, but administrative controls over the peasants remained intact (Segretin et al., 2016; Serbin et al., 2011). The local power of the old families and the headmen revived but more at the expense of peasants than of the state (Sinervo and Hill, 2011; Song and Lu, 2002; Sripada et al., 2014; State House Uganda, 2017). The district police station balanced the notables, and the system of local government (the mayor and council) integrated them into the regime (Stewart, 2005; Torres and Wong, 2013; Townsend, 1979; Twikirize et al., 2014; Vallas, Fremstad, and Ekman, 2015).

Sadat took several measures to decentralize power to the provinces and towns (Van den Waeyenberg, and Hens, 2008; Waddington, 2004; Wells et al., 2010). Governors acquired more authority under Law Number 43 of 1979, which reduced the administrative and budgetary controls of the central government over the provinces (Zembe-Mkabile et al., 2015; Ziol-Guest, Duncan, and Kalil, 2009; Ziol-Guest et al., 2012). The elected councils acquired, at least formally, the right to approve or disapprove the local budget (Ansell, 2016; Dreyer, 2013; Evans, 2016; Evans and Kim, 2013; Jones, Vargas, and Villar, 2007; Mbabazi and Pyeong, 2014; Schickedanz, Dreyer, and Halfon, 2015). To reduce local demands on the central treasury, local government was given wider powers to raise local taxes (Ashiabi, 2000; Duncan and Magnuson, 2013; Fierman et al., 2016). But local representative councils became vehicles of pressure for government spending, and the soaring deficits of local government bodies had to be covered by the central government (Hart, 2008; Kalil, Duncan, and Ziol-Guest, 2016; Kaplinsky, 2005; McLaughlin and Rank, 2018; Schmitz, Wagner, and Menke, 2001). Local government was encouraged to enter into joint ventures with private investors, and these ventures stimulated an alliance between government officials and the local rich that paralleled the "*infitah alliance*" at the national level (Ashworth, Hill, and Walker, 1994; Lichter, Shanahan, and Gardner, 2002; Duncan, Kalil, and Ziol-Guest, 2013). Under Mubarak, decentralization and local autonomy became more of a reality, and local policies often reflected special local conditions (Hatcher et al., 2019; Kapoor, 1993; McLoyd, Aikens, and Burton, 2007). Thus, officials in Upper Egypt often bowed to the powerful Islamic movement there, while those in the port cities struck alliances with importers (Bäckman, and Nilsson, 2007; Bhargava et al., 2004; Lipina, 2016; Evans and Cassells, 2014).

Afghanistan is another example that was traditionally divided into provinces governed by centrally appointed governors with considerable autonomy in local affairs (Evans and Kutcher, 2011; Mickelson, 2002; Segretin et al., 2016; Jones, Vargas, and Villar, 2008). There are currently 34 provinces. During the Soviet occupation and the development of country-wide resistance, local areas came increasingly under the control of mujahidin groups that were largely independent of any higher authority (Bloom and Canning, 2001; Lipina et al., 2013). The local commanders, in some instances, asserted a measure of independence also from the mujahidin leadership in Pakistan (Fujiura and Yamaki, 2000; Hill and Sandfort, 1995; Kendig, Mattingly, and Bianchi, 2014). Hence, they often succeeded in establishing their systems of local government, collecting revenues, running educational and other facilities, and even engaging in local negotiations (Miller and Chen, 2013; Miller et al., 2011). Mujahidin groups retained links with the Peshawar parties to ensure access to weapons that were given out to the parties by the government of Pakistan for distribution to fighters inside Afghanistan (Bourdillon and Boyden, 2011; Lopez and Velasco, 2011; Garrett, Ng'andu, and Ferron, 1994). The Taliban set up a shura (assembly), made up of senior Taliban members and important tribal from the area (Hobcraft, 1998; Kim et al., 2013). Each shura made laws and collected taxes locally (Muñoz, Álvarez-Verdejo, and García-Fernández, 2016; Sripada et al., 2014). The Taliban set up a provisional government for the whole of

Afghanistan, but it did not exercise central control over the local shuras (Boyden and James, 2014; Lyytikäinen et al., 2006; Duncan et al., 2012). Regardless of the format that they take on, the primary role of these local authorities is to deploy the local resources to meet local problems, including child poverty (Hobcraft and Kiernan, 2001; Kim et al., 2015; Nikulina and Widom, 2014). However, the limited and uneven distribution of resources in various communities might mean that the central government has to step in and make appropriate supportive adjustments (Bruch and Touraine, 1940; Magnuson and Votruba-Drzal, 2008; Evans and Fuller-Rowell, 2013). In the next section, we specifically examine the role of state agencies in managing child poverty.

2.4. THE STATE AND CHILD POVERTY

A welfare state is a form of government in which the state protects and promotes the economic and social well-being of the citizens, based upon the principles of equal opportunity, equitable distribution of wealth, and public responsibility for citizens unable to avail themselves of the minimal provisions for a good life (Guest and Biasini, 2001; Evans and Schamberg, 2009; Krason, 2015; Lesner, 2018). Sociologist T. H. Marshall described the modern welfare state as a distinctive combination of democracy, welfare, and capitalism (Nikulina, Widom, and Czaja, 2011; State House Uganda, 2017; Stewart, 2005; Torres and Wong, 2013). As a type of mixed economy, the welfare state funds the governmental institutions for healthcare and education along with direct benefits given to individual citizens (Chamberlain et al., 2016). Early features of the welfare state, such as public pensions and social insurance, developed from the 1880s onwards in industrializing Western countries (Duncan et al., 1998; Mazza et al., 2017). The Great Depression, World War I, and World War II have been characterized as important events that ushered in expansions of the welfare state (Chiputwa, Spielman, and Qaim, 2015; Evans and Kim, 2007; Okiror, 2015; Townsend, 1979). The uneven distribution of child poverty across the globe (see Figure 2.4) means that often the neediest children are the ones that do not get adequate access to social welfare services (Corcoran and Chaudry, 1997; Deaton, 2006; Kim et al., 2016; Twikirize et al., 2014).

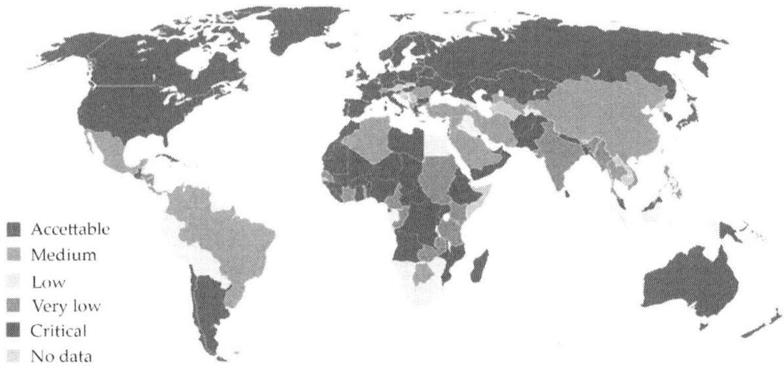

Figure 2.4. Global distribution of child poverty.

Source: Study.com.

The modern welfare state emerged in a reactive way to the Great Depression of the 1930s as a form of state interventionism to address unemployment, lost output, and collapse of the financial system (Evans, 2004; Jain and Vaachani, 2006; Ministry of Finance, 2014; Vallas, Fremstad, and Ekman, 2015). By the late 1970s, the contemporary capitalist welfare state began to decline, in part due to the economic crisis of post-World War II capitalism and Keynesianism and in part due to the lack of a well-articulated ideological foundation for the welfare state (Duncan and Rodgers, 1988; Holzer et al., 2008). The German term "social state" has been used since 1870 to describe state support programs devised by German "social politicians" and implemented as part of Bismarck's conservative reforms (Farah et al., 2006). In Germany, the term "welfare state," is used to describe Sweden's social insurance arrangements (Duncan, Kalil, and Ziol-Guest, 2008; Morrow, 2013; Song and Lu, 2002; Ziol-Guest et al., 2012). The literal English equivalent "social state" did not catch on in Anglophone countries (Hannum, Liu, and Alvarado-Urbina, 2017; Penn, 2004; Ratcliffe; Van den Waeyenberg, and Hens, 2008; Sinervo and Hill, 2011). However, during the Second World War, Anglican Archbishop William Temple, author of the book titled "*Christianity and the Social Order*" (1942), popularized the concept using the phrase "welfare state" (Hong, 2015; Jarjoura, Triplett, and Brinker, 2002; Ridge, 2002; Waddington, 2004; Ziol-Guest, Duncan, and Kalil, 2009). Bishop Temple's use of "welfare state" has been connected to Benjamin Disraeli's 1845 novel Sybil: or the Two Nations (in other words, the rich and the poor), where he writes "power has only one duty-to secure the social welfare of the people"(Javanbakht et al., 2015; Wells et al., 2010). At the time he wrote Sybil, Disraeli (later a prime minister) belonged to Young England, a conservative group of youthful Tories who disagreed with how the Whigs dealt with the conditions of the industrial poor (Rowntree, 1901; Ryan, Fauth, and Brooks-Gunn, 2006; Sánchez, 2008; Ridge, 2006). Members of Young England attempted to garner support among the privileged classes to assist the less fortunate and to recognize the dignity of labor that they imagined had characterized England during the Feudal Middle Ages (Serbin et al., 2011; Zembe-Mkabile et al., 2015).

The Swedish welfare state is called "the people's home") and goes back to the 1936 compromise, as well as to another important contract made in 1938 between Swedish trade unions and large corporations (Duncan et al., 2012; Evans and Fuller-Rowell, 2013; Guest and Biasini, 2001). Even though the country is often rated comparably economically free, Sweden's mixed economy remains heavily influenced by the legal framework and continual renegotiations of union contracts (Kim et al., 2016; Mbabazi and Pyeong, 2014; McLaughlin and Rank, 2018). This is a government-directed and municipality-administered system of social security, and a system of universal health care that is run by the more specialized and in theory more politically isolated county councils of Sweden (Duncan, Kalil, and Ziol-Guest, 2013; Evans and Cassells, 2014; Fujiura and Yamaki, 2000; Garrett, Ng'andu, and Ferron, 1994). Modern welfare programs are chiefly distinguished from earlier forms of poverty relief by their universal, comprehensive character (Ansell, 2016; Ashiabi, 2000; Ashworth, Hill, and Walker, 1994; Bäckman, and Nilsson, 2007). The institution of social insurance in Germany under Bismarck was an influential example (Bhargava et al., 2004; Bloom and Canning, 2001; Bourdillon and Boyden, 2011; Boyden and James, 2014). Some schemes were based largely on the development of the autonomous, mutualist provision of benefits. Others were founded on state provision (Bruch and Touraine, 1940; Chamberlain et al., 2016). In a highly influential essay, "*Citizenship and Social Class*" (1949), British sociologist T. H. Marshall identified modern welfare states as a distinctive combination of democracy, welfare, and capitalism. He argued that citizenship must encompass access to social, as well as to political and civil rights (Chiputwa, Spielman, and Qaim, 2015; Corcoran and Chaudry, 1997; Lipina et al., 2013). Examples of such states are Germany, all of the Nordic countries, the Netherlands, France, Uruguay, and New Zealand, and the United Kingdom in the 1930s (Deaton, 2006; Dreyer, 2013; Duncan and Magnuson, 2013; Lichter, Shanahan, and Gardner, 2002; Lipina, 2016; Lopez and Velasco, 2011). Since that time, the term welfare state applies only to states where social rights are accompanied by civil and political rights (Lyytikäinen et al., 2006; Magnuson and Votruba-Drzal, 2008; Duncan and Rodgers, 1988).

Changed attitudes in reaction to the worldwide Great Depression, which brought unemployment and misery to millions, were instrumental in the move to the welfare state in many countries (Evans, 2004; Farah et al., 2006). During the Great Depression, the welfare state was seen as a "middle way" between the extremes of communism on the left and unregulated laissez-faire capitalism on the right (Duncan, Kalil, and Ziol-Guest, 2008; Evans, 2016; Fierman et al., 2016). In the period following World War II, some countries in Western Europe moved from partial or selective provision of social services to relatively comprehensive "cradle-to-grave" coverage of the population (Duncan, Kalil, and Ziol-Guest, 2013; Evans and Cassells, 2014; Guest and Biasini, 2001; Duncan et al., 1998). Other Western European states did not, such as the United Kingdom, Ireland, Spain, and France (Fujiura and Yamaki, 2000; Garrett, Ng'andu, and Ferron, 1994; Duncan et al., 2012; Evans and Fuller-Rowell, 2013). Political scientist Eileen McDonagh has argued that a major determinant of where welfare states arose is whether or not a country had a historical monarchy with familial foundations, a trait that Max Weber called patrimonialism (Evans and Kim, 2007, 2013; Hannum, Liu, and Alvarado-Urbina, 2017; Hart, 2008). In places where the monarchic state was viewed as a parental steward of the populace, it was easier to shift into a mindset where the industrial state could also serve as a parental steward of the populace (Hatcher et al., 2019; Evans and Kutcher, 2011; Hill and Sandfort, 1995). The activities of present-day welfare states extend to the provision of both cash welfare benefits such as old-age pensions or unemployment benefits; and in-kind welfare services such as health or childcare services (Hobcraft, 1998; Hobcraft and Kiernan, 2001; Evans and Schamberg, 2009; Holzer et al., 2008). Through these provisions, welfare states can affect the distribution of well-being and personal autonomy among their citizens, as well as influence how their citizens consume and how they spend their time (Hong, 2015; Jain and Vaachani, 2006; Jarjoura, Triplett, and Brinker, 2002; Kaplinsky, 2005; Kapoor, 1993; Jones, Vargas, and Villar, 2008).

The Nordic welfare model refers to the welfare policies of the Nordic countries, which also tie into their labor market policies (Javanbakht et al., 2015; Jones, Vargas, and Villar, 2007; Kalil, Duncan, and Ziol-Guest, 2016).

The Nordic model of welfare is distinguished from other types of welfare states by its emphasis on maximizing labor force participation, promoting gender equality, egalitarian, and extensive benefit levels, the large magnitude of income redistribution, and liberal use of the expansionary fiscal policy (Kendig, Mattingly, and Bianchi, 2014; Kim et al., 2013). While there are differences among the Nordic countries, they all share a broad commitment to social cohesion, universal nature of welfare provision to safeguard individualism by providing protection for vulnerable individuals and groups in society and maximizing public participation in social decision-making (Kim et al., 2015; Krason, 2015; Lesner, 2018). It is characterized by flexibility and openness to innovation in the provision of welfare (Mazza et al., 2017; Kim et al., 2016). The Nordic welfare systems are mainly funded through taxation (Mbabazi and Pyeong, 2014; McLaughlin and Rank, 2018; McLoyd, Aikens, and Burton, 2007).

In contrast to the Nordic model, China traditionally relied on the extended family to provide welfare services (Mickelson, 2002; Miller and Chen, 2013; Miller et al., 2011). The one-child policy introduced in 1978 has made that unrealistic, and new models have emerged since the 1980s as China has rapidly become richer and more urban (Ministry of Finance, 2014; Morrow, 2013; Muñoz, Álvarez-Verdejo, and García-Fernández, 2016). Much discussion is underway regarding China's proposed path toward a welfare state (Nikulina and Widom, 2014; Nikulina, Widom, and Czaja, 2011; Okiror, 2015; Penn, 2004; Ratcliffe and McKernan, 2010). Chinese policies have been incremental and fragmented in terms of social insurance, privatization, and targeting (Ridge, 2002, 2006; Rowntree, 1901; Ryan, Fauth, and Brooks-Gunn, 2006; Sánchez, 2008). In the cities, where the rapid economic development has centered, lines of cleavage have developed between state-sector and non-state-sector employees, and between labor-market insiders and outsiders (Schickedanz, Dreyer, and Halfon, 2015; Schmitz, Wagner, and Menke, 2001; Segretin et al., 2016). Regardless of the actual format that it takes, the welfare state will intervene in issues of child poverty (Serbin et al., 2011; Zembe-Mkabile et al., 2015). This chapter will close with an overview of international agencies in eliminating the worst forms of child poverty.

2.5. INTERNATIONAL AGENCIES AND CHILD POVERTY

An international organization (an intergovernmental organization) is an organization established by a treaty or other instrument governed by international law and possessing its international legal personalities, such as the United Nations (UN), the World Health Organization (WHO), and NATO (Sinervo and Hill, 2011; Song and Lu, 2002; Sripada et al., 2014). International organizations are composed of primarily Member states, but may also include other entities, such as other international organizations (State House Uganda, 2017; Stewart, 2005; Torres and Wong, 2013; Townsend, 1979; Twikirize et al., 2014). Additionally, entities (including states) may hold observer status. Notable examples include the UN, Organization for Security and Co-operation in Europe (OSCE), Council of Europe (COE), International Labor Organization (ILO), and International Police Organization (INTERPOL). Because of their wide resource base and experience in dealing with development issues, international organizations are often involved in activities that directly or indirectly intervene in situations of child poverty or even general deprivation of children's rights (Vallas, Fremstad, and Ekman, 2015; Van den Waeyenberg, and Hens, 2008; Waddington, 2004; Wells et al., 2010). As seen in Figure 2.5, the challenge of managing child poverty rates is a long one that is full of ups and downs. Indeed, there are cases where the presence of international organizations has paradoxically worsened the situation (Ziol-Guest, Duncan, and Kalil, 2009; Ziol-Guest et al., 2012).

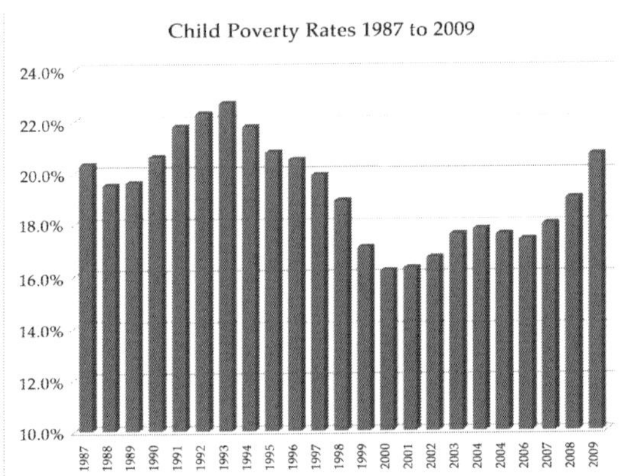

Figure 2.5. Fluctuating levels of child poverty 1987 to 2009.

Source: National Conference of State Legislatures.

The first and oldest intergovernmental organization (being established employing a treaty, and creating a permanent secretariat) is the International Telecommunication Union which was founded in 1865. The first general international organization was the League nations which were tasked with addressing a variety of issues. Although this later turned out to be a "toothless tiger," it set the precedent for countries working together to resolve problems rather than engaging in unilateral actions that could be damaging to the entire world in the long run (Ansell, 2016; Ashiabi, 2000; Ashworth, Hill, and Walker, 1994; Bäckman, and Nilsson, 2007; Bhargava et al., 2004). The UN followed this model after World War II. The role of international organizations is helping to set the international agenda, mediating political bargaining, providing a place for political initiatives, and acting as catalysts for the coalition formation (Bloom and Canning, 2001; Bourdillon and Boyden, 2011; Boyden and James, 2014; Bruch and Touraine, 1940). They facilitate cooperation and coordination among member nations (Duncan and Rodgers, 1988; Evans, 2004; Farah et al., 2006).

International organizations typically have member states from the whole world (Chamberlain et al., 2016; Chiputwa, Spielman, and Qaim, 2015). However, in some cases, organizations have geographic limitations, such as the European Union, African Union (AU), and NATO (Corcoran and Chaudry, 1997; Deaton, 2006; Dreyer, 2013; Duncan and Magnuson, 2013). The UN also has regional organizations, such as UNECE and UNECA (Lichter, Shanahan, and Gardner, 2002; Lipina, 2016; Lipina et al., 2013). The oldest regional organization is the Central Commission for Navigation on the Rhine, created in 1815 by the Congress of Vienna (Lopez and Velasco, 2011; Lyytikäinen et al., 2006; Magnuson and Votruba-Drzal, 2008). The UN organizes its work into agencies, such as UN Relief Works Agency, which are generally considered as international organizations in their own right (Jones, Vargas, and Villar, 2008; Kendig, Mattingly, and Bianchi, 2014; Kim et al., 2013). Additionally, the UN uses specialized agencies which are organizations within the UN System (Duncan et al., 1998; Evans and Kim, 2007; Hannum, Liu, and Alvarado-Urbina, 2017). From its establishment in 1963, the Organization of African Unity (OAU) identified the need for the economic integration of the continent as a prerequisite for economic development (Evans and Kim, 2013; Hart, 2008; Hatcher et al., 2019). The 1980 Lagos Plan of Action for the Development of Africa, followed by the 1991 treaty to establish the African Economic Community (also referred to as the Abuja Treaty), proposed the creation of regional economic communities (RECs) as the basis for African integration, with a timetable for regional and then continental integration to follow (Evans and Kutcher, 2011; Hill and Sandfort, 1995; Hobcraft, 1998; Hobcraft and Kiernan, 2001). The Treaty provides for the African Economic Community to be set up through a gradual process, in six stages over 34 years, i.e., by 2028 (Evans and Schamberg, 2009; Holzer et al., 2008; Hong, 2015).

International Organizations are sometimes referred to as Intergovernmental Organizations (IGOs), to clarify the distinction from International Nongovernmental Organizations (INGOs), which are non-governmental organizations (NGOs) that operate internationally (Jain and Vaachani, 2006; Jarjoura, Triplett, and Brinker, 2002; Javanbakht et al., 2015). These include international non-profit organizations such as the World Organization of the Scout Movement, the International Committee of the Red Cross, and Médecins Sans Frontières (Duncan, Kalil, and Ziol-Guest, 2008; Evans, 2016; Fierman et al., 2016). They may include lobby groups that represent the interest of multinational corporations, such as the World Economic Forum (Jones, Vargas, and Villar, 2007; Kalil, Duncan, and Ziol-Guest, 2016; Kaplinsky, 2005; Kapoor, 1993). The RECs in Africa group together individual countries in sub-regions to achieve greater economic integration (Kim et al., 2015; Krason, 2015; Lesner, 2018; Mazza et al., 2017). They are described as the "building blocks" of the AU and are also central to the strategy for implementing the New Partnership for Africa's Development (NEPAD). One of the criticisms of these international organizations is that they have disjointed agendas and are subject to the corrosive power of corruption in the localities where they operate (McLoyd, Aikens, and Burton, 2007; Mickelson, 2002; Miller and Chen, 2013; Miller et al., 2011). Others have accused these international organizations of disempowering local communities and hence rendering them reliant on tied foreign aid (Ministry of Finance, 2014; Morrow, 2013; Muñoz, Álvarez-Verdejo, and García-Fernández, 2016; Nikulina and Widom, 2014). The anti-colonialists argue that these international organizations are the now acceptable face of latent colonialism (Nikulina, Widom, and Czaja, 2011; Okiror, 2015; Penn, 2004; Ratcliffe and McKernan, 2010). For example, these organizations have been accused of driving a pro-Western agenda to the detriment of any other geopolitical force (Ridge, 2002; Rowntree, 1901; Ryan, Fauth, and Brooks-Gunn, 2006; Sánchez, 2008).

CHAPTER 2 SUMMARY

There are many stakeholders when dealing with child poverty. However, it is not clear whether these stakeholders engage with the issue positively and helpfully. For example, families may deny children the social and other resources that are due to them by right. Moreover, the community may fail to support those who are poor. Local authorities may not have the funding and expertise to deal with a significant problem such as child poverty. Similarly, these problems may be elevated at the national level. The help that comes from international organizations may not fully and effectively address the problem. That is why child poverty remains an enduring social problem despite all the interventions made over time. The next chapter seeks to clarify the benchmarks of childhood poverty.

Chapter 3

Benchmarks of Childhood Poverty

CONTENTS

Benchmarking child poverty is an onerous task, not least because of the diversity of communities that experience this social problem. This chapter explores some of the aspects that have traditionally been used to understand and measure poverty. Some of these benchmarks may include health, housing, education, income, and access to justice. By the end of this chapter, the reader should have an appreciation of the difficulties of measuring and comparing child poverty. At the same time, the reader should have an indicator of some of the measures that can be used as well as their limitations.

3.1. HEALTH STATUS AS AN INDICATOR OF CHILDHOOD POVERTY

Health is a state of physical, mental, and social well-being in which disease and infirmity are absent (Ridge, 2006; Schickedanz, Dreyer, and Halfon, 2015; Schmitz, Wagner, and Menke, 2001). The meaning of health has evolved. In keeping with the biomedical perspective, early definitions of health focused on the theme of the body's ability to function (Segretin et al., 2016; Serbin et al., 2011). Health was seen as a state of normal function that could be disrupted from time to time by disease (Sinervo and Hill, 2011; Song and Lu, 2002; Sripada et al., 2014; State House Uganda, 2017). An example of such a definition of health is the notion that health is "a state characterized by anatomic, physiologic, and psychological integrity; ability to perform personally valued family, work, and community roles; ability to deal with physical, biological, psychological, and social stress (Stewart, 2005; Torres and Wong, 2013; Townsend, 1979; Twikirize et al., 2014; Vallas, Fremstad, and Ekman, 2015). Then in 1948, in a radical departure from previous definitions, the WHO proposed a definition that aimed higher in terms of linking health to well-being (Van den Waeyenberg, and Hens, 2008; Waddington, 2004; Wells et al., 2010). Hence, health was defined in terms of "physical, mental, and social well-being, and not merely the absence of disease and infirmity" (Zembe-Mkabile et al., 2015; Ziol-Guest, Duncan, and Kalil, 2009; Ziol-Guest et al., 2012). Although this definition was welcomed by some as being innovative, it was also criticized as being vague, excessively broad, and was not construed as measurable (Ansell, 2016; Dreyer, 2013; Evans, 2016; Evans and Kim, 2013; Jones, Vargas, and Villar, 2007; Mbabazi and Pyeong, 2014; Schickedanz, Dreyer, and Halfon, 2015). For a long time, it was set aside as an impractical ideal, and most discussions of health returned to the practicality of the biomedical model (Ashiabi, 2000; Duncan and Magnuson, 2013; Fierman et al., 2016). Just as there was a shift from viewing disease as a state to thinking of it as a process, the same shift happened in definitions of health (Hart, 2008; Kalil, Duncan, and Ziol-Guest, 2016; Kaplinsky, 2005; McLaughlin and Rank, 2018; Schmitz, Wagner, and Menke, 2001). Again, the WHO played a leading role when it fostered the development of the health promotion movement in the 1980s (Ashworth, Hill, and Walker, 1994; Lichter, Shanahan, and Gardner, 2002; Duncan, Kalil, and Ziol-Guest, 2013). This brought in a new conception of health, not as a state, but in dynamic terms of resiliency. In other words, health is perceived as "a resource for living" (Hatcher et al., 2019; Kapoor, 1993; McLoyd, Aikens, and Burton, 2007). In 1984 WHO revised the definition of health defined it as "the extent to which an individual or group can realize aspirations and satisfy needs and to change or cope with the environment (Bäckman, and Nilsson, 2007; Bhargava et al., 2004; Lipina, 2016; Evans and Cassells, 2014). Health is a resource for everyday life, not the objective of living; it is a positive concept, emphasizing social and personal resources, as well as physical capacities" (Evans and Kutcher, 2011; Mickelson, 2002; Segretin et al., 2016; Jones, Vargas, and Villar, 2008). Thus, health referred to the ability to maintain homeostasis and recover from insults (Bloom and Canning, 2001; Lipina et al., 2013). Mental, intellectual, emotional, and social health referred to a person's ability to handle stress, to acquire skills, to maintain relationships, all of which form resources for resiliency and independent living (Fujiura and Yamaki, 2000; Hill and Sandfort, 1995; Kendig, Mattingly, and Bianchi, 2014). This opens up many possibilities for health to be taught, strengthened, and learned (Miller and Chen, 2013; Miller et al., 2011). As we can see in Figure 3.1, there may be other underlying social factors such as race which not only affect child poverty rates; but also indirectly reduce health levels (Bourdillon and Boyden, 2011; Lopez and Velasco, 2011; Garrett, Ng'andu, and Ferron, 1994).

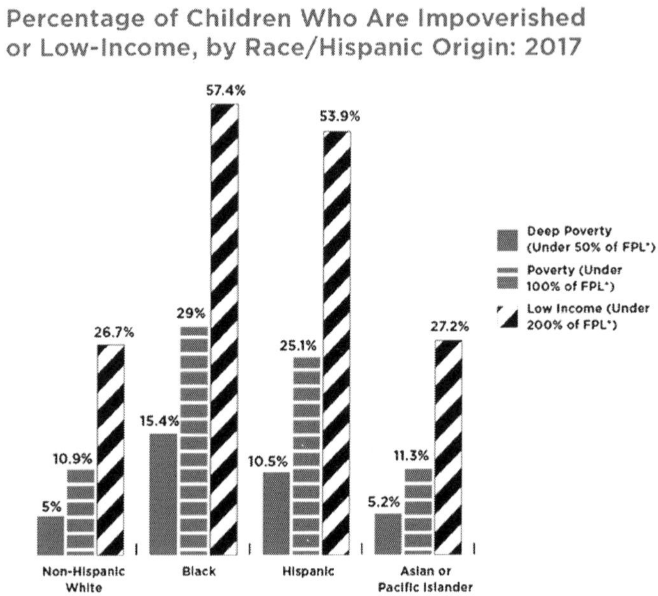

Figure 3.1. Relationship between child poverty and race in 2017.

Source: US Census Bureau via Child Trends.

Since the late 1970s, the federal Healthy People Initiative has been a visible component of the United States' approach to improving population health (Hobcraft, 1998; Kim et al., 2013). In each decade, a new version of Healthy People is issued, featuring updated goals and identifying topic areas and quantifiable objectives for health improvement during the succeeding 10 years, with assessment at that point of progress or lack thereof (Muñoz, Álvarez-Verdejo, and García-Fernández, 2016; Sripada et al., 2014). Progress has been limited to many objectives, leading to concerns about the effectiveness of Healthy People in shaping outcomes in the context of a decentralized and uncoordinated US health system (Boyden and James, 2014; Lyytikäinen et al., 2006; Duncan et al., 2012). Healthy People 2020 gives more prominence to health promotion and preventive approaches and adds a substantive focus on the importance of addressing social determinants of health (Hobcraft and Kiernan, 2001; Kim et al., 2015; Nikulina and Widom, 2014). A new expanded digital interface facilitates use and dissemination rather than bulky printed books as produced in the past (Bruch and Touraine, 1940; Magnuson and Votruba-Drzal, 2008; Evans and Fuller-Rowell, 2013). The impact of these changes on Healthy People will be determined in the coming years (Guest and Biasini, 2001;

Evans and Schamberg, 2009; Krason, 2015; Lesner, 2018). Systematic activities to prevent or cure health problems and promote good health in humans are undertaken by health care providers (Nikulina, Widom, and Czaja, 2011; State House Uganda, 2017; Stewart, 2005; Torres and Wong, 2013). Applications concerning animal health are covered by the veterinary sciences (Chamberlain et al., 2016). The term "healthy" is also widely used in the context of many types of non-living organizations and their impacts for the benefit of humans, such as in the sense of healthy communities, healthy cities, or healthy environments (Duncan et al., 1998; Mazza et al., 2017). In addition to health care interventions and a person's surroundings, some other factors are known to influence the health status of individuals, including their background, lifestyle, and economic, social conditions, and spirituality (Chiputwa, Spielman, and Qaim, 2015; Evans and Kim, 2007; Okiror, 2015; Townsend, 1979). These are collectively referred to as the determinants of health. Studies have shown that high levels of stress can affect human health, for example (Corcoran and Chaudry, 1997; Deaton, 2006; Kim et al., 2016; Twikirize et al., 2014). Hence, interventions may target stress, rather than just focusing on organic diseases (Evans, 2004; Jain and Vaachani, 2006; Ministry of Finance, 2014; Vallas, Fremstad, and Ekman, 2015).

In the first decade of the 21st century, the conceptualization of health as an ability opened the door for self-assessments to become the main indicators to judge the performance of efforts aimed at improving human health (Duncan and Rodgers, 1988; Holzer et al., 2008). It also created the opportunity for every person to feel healthy, even in the presence of multiple chronic diseases, or a terminal condition, and for the re-examination of determinants of health, away from the traditional approach that focuses on the reduction of the prevalence of diseases (Farah et al., 2006). Generally, the context in which an individual's life is of great importance for both his health status and quality of their life (Duncan, Kalil, and Ziol-Guest, 2008; Morrow, 2013; Song and Lu, 2002; Ziol-Guest et al., 2012). It is increasingly recognized that health is maintained and improved not only through the advancement and application of health science, but also through the efforts and intelligent lifestyle choices of the individual and society (Hannum, Liu, and Alvarado-Urbina, 2017; Penn, 2004; Ratcliffe; Van den Waeyenberg, and Hens, 2008; Sinervo and Hill, 2011). According to the World Health Organization (WHO), the main determinants of health include the social and economic environment, the physical environment, and the person's characteristics and behaviors (Hong, 2015; Jarjoura, Triplett, and

Brinker, 2002; Ridge, 2002; Waddington, 2004; Ziol-Guest, Duncan, and Kalil, 2009).

More specifically, key factors that have been found to influence whether people are healthy or unhealthy include the following: income and social status, social support networks, education, and literacy, employment or working conditions, social environments, and physical environments (Javanbakht et al., 2015; Wells et al., 2010). Other factors that may be considered include personal health practices and coping skills, healthy child development, biology, and genetics, health care services, gender, and culture (Rowntree, 1901; Ryan, Fauth, and Brooks-Gunn, 2006; Sánchez, 2008; Ridge, 2006). An increasing number of studies and reports from different organizations and contexts examine the linkages between health and different factors (Serbin et al., 2011; Zembe-Mkabile et al., 2015). Such factors may include lifestyles, environments, health care organization, and health policy, one specific health policy brought into many countries in recent years was the introduction of the sugar tax (Duncan et al., 2012; Evans and Fuller-Rowell, 2013; Guest and Biasini, 2001). Beverage taxes came into light with increasing concerns about obesity, particularly among youth. Sugar-sweetened beverages have become a target of anti-obesity initiatives with increasing evidence of their link to obesity (Kim et al., 2016; Mbabazi and Pyeong, 2014; McLaughlin and Rank, 2018). Some of the specific studies that are referenced in health policy include the 1974 Lalonde report from Canada; the Alameda County Study in California; and the series of World Health Reports of the WHO (Duncan, Kalil, and Ziol-Guest, 2013; Evans and Cassells, 2014; Fujiura and Yamaki, 2000; Garrett, Ng'andu, and Ferron, 1994). These reports focus on global health issues, including access to health care and improving public health outcomes, especially in developing countries (Ansell, 2016; Ashiabi, 2000; Ashworth, Hill, and Walker, 1994; Bäckman, and Nilsson, 2007). The next section focuses on good quality housing as a determinant and indicator of health.

3.2. HOUSING AS AN INDICATOR OF CHILDHOOD POVERTY

Housing, or more general living spaces, refers to the construction and assigned usage of houses or buildings collectively, to shelter people (Bhargava et al., 2004; Bloom and Canning, 2001; Bourdillon and Boyden, 2011; Boyden and James, 2014). It may also refer to the housing planning or provision delivered by an authority as well as being associated with related meanings (Bruch and Touraine, 1940; Chamberlain et al., 2016). The social issue is of ensuring that members of society have a home in which to live, whether this is a house, or some other kind of dwelling, lodging, or shelter (Chiputwa, Spielman, and Qaim, 2015; Corcoran and Chaudry, 1997; Lipina et al., 2013). Many governments have one or more housing authorities, sometimes also called a housing ministry, or housing department (Deaton, 2006; Dreyer, 2013; Duncan and Magnuson, 2013; Lichter, Shanahan, and Gardner, 2002; Lipina, 2016; Lopez and Velasco, 2011). One of the basic unmet needs that children in poverty face is the lack of safe, sustainable, and durable housing. Indeed, housing has been mentioned in both the Millennium Development Goals and sustainable development goals (SDGs) as a key objective of these developmental frameworks (Lyytikäinen et al., 2006; Magnuson and Votruba-Drzal, 2008; Duncan and Rodgers, 1988). As Figure 3.2 demonstrates; there is a link between living standards, poverty, and inequality (Evans, 2004; Farah et al., 2006).

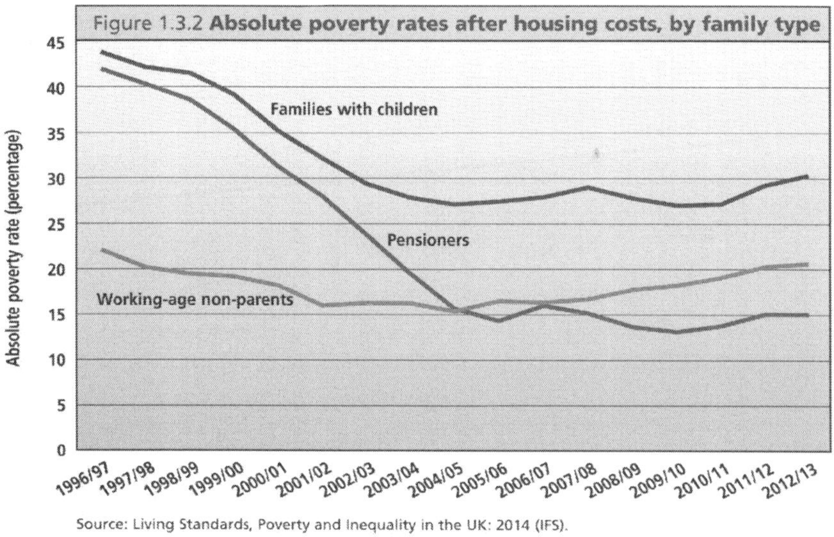

Figure 3.2. Living standards, poverty, and inequality in the UK 2015.

Source: IFS via Two Worlds.

Previous research shows that housing price is affected by the macroeconomic conditions in a given context (Duncan, Kalil, and Ziol-Guest, 2008; Evans, 2016; Fierman et al., 2016). Recent research showed that a 1% increase in the Consumer Price Index leads to a $3,559,715 increase in housing prices and raises the property price per square feet by $119 (Duncan, Kalil, and Ziol-Guest, 2013; Evans and Cassells, 2014; Guest and Biasini, 2001; Duncan et al., 1998). Money Supply has a positive relationship with housing prices (Fujiura and Yamaki, 2000; Garrett, Ng'andu, and Ferron, 1994; Duncan et al., 2012; Evans and Fuller-Rowell, 2013). As Money Supply increases by one unit, housing prices will rise by 0.06 in a study conducted in Hong Kong (Evans and Kim, 2007, 2013; Hannum, Liu, and Alvarado-Urbina, 2017; Hart, 2008). When there is a 1% increase in the best lending rate, housing prices drop by between $18,237 and $28,681 in the established models (Hatcher et al., 2019; Evans and Kutcher, 2011; Hill and Sandfort, 1995). Mortgage repayments lead to a rise in the discount window base rate (Hobcraft, 1998; Hobcraft and Kiernan, 2001; Evans and Schamberg, 2009; Holzer et al., 2008). A 1% rise in the rate leads to a $14,314 drop in housing prices, and an average selling price drop of $585,335 (Hong, 2015; Jain and Vaachani, 2006; Jarjoura, Triplett, and Brinker, 2002; Kaplinsky, 2005; Kapoor, 1993; Jones, Vargas, and Villar, 2008). As the US real interest rate increases, the interest rates in Hong Kong must follow, increasing the mortgage repayments (Javanbakht et al., 2015; Jones, Vargas, and Villar, 2007; Kalil, Duncan, and Ziol-Guest, 2016). When there is a 1% increase in the US real interest rate, the property prices decreased from $9302 to $4957, and the saleable area drops by $4.96 and $14 (Kendig, Mattingly, and Bianchi, 2014; Kim et al., 2013). When there is a 1% rise in overnight Hong Kong Interbank Offered Rate, the housing prices drop to about 3455, and the price per square foot will drop by $187 (Kim et al., 2015; Krason, 2015; Lesner, 2018).

Affordability is an important consideration when developing and allocating housing stock (Mazza et al., 2017; Kim et al., 2016). The median multiple indicators, recommended by the World Bank and the UN, rates affordability of housing by dividing the median house price by gross (before tax) annual median household income (Mbabazi and Pyeong, 2014; McLaughlin and Rank, 2018; McLoyd, Aikens, and Burton, 2007). A common measure of community-wide affordability is the number of homes that a household with a certain percentage of median income can afford (Mickelson, 2002; Miller and Chen, 2013; Miller et al., 2011). For example, in a perfectly balanced housing market, the median household (the wealthier half of households) could officially afford the median housing option, while those poorer than the median income could not afford the median home (Ministry of Finance, 2014; Morrow, 2013; Muñoz, Álvarez-Verdejo, and García-Fernández, 2016). Hence, 50% affordability for the median home indicates a balanced market (Nikulina and Widom, 2014; Nikulina, Widom, and Czaja, 2011; Okiror, 2015; Penn, 2004; Ratcliffe and McKernan, 2010). Determining housing affordability is complex and the commonly used housing-expenditure-to-income-ratio tool has been challenged (Ridge, 2002, 2006; Rowntree, 1901; Ryan, Fauth, and Brooks-Gunn, 2006; Sánchez, 2008). In the United States and Canada, a commonly accepted guideline for housing affordability is a housing cost that does not exceed 30% of a household's gross income (Schickedanz, Dreyer, and Halfon, 2015; Schmitz, Wagner, and Menke, 2001; Segretin et al., 2016). Canada, for example, switched to a 25% rule from a 20% rule in the 1950s (Serbin et al., 2011; Zembe-Mkabile et al., 2015). In the 1980s this was replaced by a 30% rule. India uses a 40% rule (Sinervo and Hill, 2011; Song and Lu, 2002; Sripada et al., 2014).

The housing affordability index (HAI) is one of the affordability measures that are widely used (State House Uganda, 2017; Stewart, 2005; Torres and Wong, 2013; Townsend, 1979; Twikirize et al., 2014). One of the greatest strengths of the HAI developed by the Massachusetts Institute of Technology (MIT) is its ability to capture the total cost of ownership of individuals' housing choices (Vallas, Fremstad, and Ekman, 2015; Van den Waeyenberg, and Hens, 2008; Waddington, 2004; Wells et al., 2010). In computing the index, the obvious cost of rents and mortgage payments are modified by the hidden costs of those choices. Income is the primary factor, not just referring to price and availability, when determining housing affordability (Ziol-Guest, Duncan, and Kalil, 2009; Ziol-Guest et al., 2012). In a market economy, the distribution of income is the key determinant of the quantity and quality of housing obtained (Ansell, 2016; Ashiabi, 2000; Ashworth, Hill, and Walker, 1994; Bäckman, and Nilsson, 2007; Bhargava et al., 2004). Therefore, understanding affordable housing challenges requires understanding trends and disparities in income and wealth (Bloom and Canning, 2001; Bourdillon and Boyden, 2011; Boyden and James, 2014; Bruch and Touraine, 1940). Housing is often the single biggest expenditure of low- and middle-income families (Duncan and Rodgers, 1988; Evans, 2004; Farah et al., 2006). For low- and middle-income families, their house is also the greatest source of wealth (Chamberlain et al., 2016; Chiputwa, Spielman, and Qaim, 2015). The most common approach to measure the affordability of housing has been to consider the percentage of income that a household spends on housing expenditures (Corcoran and Chaudry, 1997; Deaton, 2006; Dreyer, 2013; Duncan and Magnuson, 2013). Another method of studying affordability looks at the regular hourly wage of full-time workers who are paid only the minimum wage; as set by their local, regional, or national government (Lichter, Shanahan, and Gardner, 2002; Lipina, 2016; Lipina et al., 2013). The expectation is that full-time workers will be able to afford at least a small apartment in the area where they work (Lopez and Velasco, 2011; Lyytikäinen et al., 2006; Magnuson and Votruba-Drzal, 2008). Some countries look at those living in relative poverty, which is usually defined as making less than 60% of the median household income (Jones, Vargas, and Villar, 2008; Kendig, Mattingly, and Bianchi, 2014; Kim et al., 2013). In their policy reports, they consider the presence or absence of housing for people making 60% of the median income (Duncan et al., 1998; Evans and Kim, 2007; Hannum, Liu, and Alvarado-Urbina, 2017).

Housing affordability can be measured by the changing relationships between house prices and rents and between house prices and incomes (Evans and Kim, 2013; Hart, 2008; Hatcher et al., 2019). There has been an increase among policymakers in affordable housing as the price of housing has increased dramatically, creating a crisis in affordable housing (Evans and Kutcher, 2011; Hill and Sandfort, 1995; Hobcraft, 1998; Hobcraft and Kiernan, 2001). Since 2000 the world experienced an unprecedented house price boom in terms of magnitude and duration, but also of synchronization across countries (Evans and Schamberg, 2009; Holzer et al., 2008; Hong, 2015). This is why house prices have risen so fast, for so long, in so many countries (Jain and Vaachani, 2006; Jarjoura, Triplett, and Brinker, 2002; Javanbakht et al., 2015). Prices doubled in many countries and nearly tripled in Ireland (Duncan, Kalil, and Ziol-Guest, 2008; Evans, 2016; Fierman et al., 2016). The bursting of the biggest financial bubble in history in 2008 wreaked havoc globally on the housing market (Jones, Vargas, and Villar, 2007; Kalil, Duncan, and Ziol-Guest, 2016; Kaplinsky, 2005; Kapoor, 1993). By 2011 home prices in Ireland had plunged by 45% from their peak in 2007 (Kim et al., 2015; Krason, 2015; Lesner, 2018; Mazza et al., 2017). In the United States, prices fell by 34% while foreclosures increased exponentially (McLoyd, Aikens, and Burton, 2007; Mickelson, 2002; Miller and Chen, 2013; Miller et al., 2011). In Spain and Denmark home prices dropped by 15% (Ministry of Finance, 2014; Morrow, 2013; Muñoz, Álvarez-Verdejo, and García-Fernández, 2016; Nikulina and Widom, 2014). However, despite the bust, home prices continue to be overvalued by about 25% or more in Australia, Belgium, Canada, France, New Zealand, Britain, the Netherlands, Spain, and Sweden (Nikulina, Widom, and Czaja, 2011; Okiror, 2015; Penn, 2004; Ratcliffe and McKernan, 2010).

Some researchers argue that a shortage of affordable housing, at least in the USA, is caused in part by income inequality (Ridge, 2002; Rowntree, 1901; Ryan, Fauth, and Brooks-Gunn, 2006; Sánchez, 2008). David Rodda noted that from 1984 and 1991, the number of quality rental units decreased as the demand for higher-quality housing increased (Ridge, 2006; Schickedanz, Dreyer, and Halfon, 2015; Schmitz, Wagner, and Menke, 2001). Through gentrification of older neighborhoods, for example, in East New York, rental prices increased rapidly as landlords found new residents willing to pay higher market rates for housing (Segretin et al., 2016; Serbin et al., 2011). This left lower-income families without rental units (Sinervo and Hill, 2011; Song and Lu, 2002; Sripada et al., 2014; State House Uganda, 2017). The ad valorem property tax policy combined with rising prices made it difficult or impossible for low-income residents to keep pace (Stewart, 2005; Torres and Wong, 2013; Townsend, 1979; Twikirize et al., 2014; Vallas, Fremstad, and Ekman, 2015). In measuring the affordability of housing, there are various expenditures beyond the price of the actual housing stock itself, that are considered depending on the index being used (Van den Waeyenberg, and Hens, 2008; Waddington, 2004; Wells et al., 2010). Some organizations and agencies consider the cost of purchasing a single-family home (Zembe-Mkabile et al., 2015; Ziol-Guest, Duncan, and Kalil, 2009; Ziol-Guest et al., 2012). Others look exclusively at the cost of renting an apartment (Ansell, 2016; Dreyer, 2013; Evans, 2016; Evans and Kim, 2013; Jones, Vargas, and Villar, 2007; Mbabazi and Pyeong, 2014; Schickedanz, Dreyer, and Halfon, 2015). Many US studies, for example, focus primarily on the median cost of renting a two-bedroom apartment in a large apartment complex for a new tenant (Ashiabi, 2000; Duncan and Magnuson, 2013; Fierman et al., 2016). These studies often lump together luxury apartments and slums, as well as desirable and undesirable neighborhoods (Hart, 2008; Kalil, Duncan, and Ziol-Guest, 2016; Kaplinsky, 2005; McLaughlin and Rank, 2018; Schmitz, Wagner, and Menke, 2001). While this practice is known to distort the true costs, it is difficult to provide accurate information for the wide variety of situations without the report being unwieldy (Ashworth, Hill, and Walker, 1994; Lichter, Shanahan, and Gardner, 2002; Duncan, Kalil, and Ziol-Guest, 2013).

Normally, only legal, permitted, separate housing is considered when calculating the cost of housing (Hatcher et al., 2019; Kapoor, 1993; McLoyd, Aikens, and Burton, 2007). The low rent costs for a room in a single-family home, or an illegal garage conversion, or a college dormitory are generally excluded from the calculation (Bäckman, and Nilsson, 2007; Bhargava et al., 2004; Lipina, 2016; Evans and Cassells, 2014). This is regardless of how many people in an area live in such situations (Evans and Kutcher, 2011; Mickelson, 2002; Segretin et al., 2016; Jones, Vargas, and Villar, 2008). Because of this study methodology, median housing costs tend to be slightly inflated (Bloom and Canning, 2001; Lipina et al., 2013). Costs are generally considered on a cash (not accrual) basis (Fujiura and Yamaki, 2000; Hill and Sandfort, 1995; Kendig, Mattingly, and Bianchi, 2014). Thus a person making the last payment on a large home mortgage might live in officially unaffordable housing one month, and very affordable housing the following month, when the mortgage is paid off (Miller and Chen, 2013; Miller et al., 2011). The resultant distortion can be significant in areas where real estate costs are high, even if incomes are similarly high (Bourdillon and Boyden, 2011; Lopez and Velasco, 2011; Garrett, Ng'andu, and Ferron, 1994). This is because a high income allows a higher proportion of the income to be dedicated to buying an expensive home without endangering the household's ability to buy food or other necessities (Hobcraft, 1998; Kim et al., 2013).

Growing density convergence and regional urbanization has sometimes been associated with poor housing provision and even child poverty (Muñoz, Álvarez-Verdejo, and García-Fernández, 2016; Sripada et al., 2014). The majority of the more than 7 billion people on earth now live in cities, according to statistics released by the UN (Boyden and James, 2014; Lyytikäinen et al., 2006; Duncan et al., 2012). There are more than 500 city regions with more than 1 million inhabitants in the world (Hobcraft and Kiernan, 2001; Kim et al., 2015; Nikulina and Widom, 2014). Cities become megacities become megalopolitan city regions and even "galaxies" of more than 60 million inhabitants (Bruch and Touraine, 1940; Magnuson and Votruba-Drzal, 2008; Evans and Fuller-Rowell, 2013). The Yangtze Delta-Greater Shanghai region now surpasses 80 million (Guest and Biasini, 2001; Evans and Schamberg, 2009; Krason, 2015; Lesner, 2018). Tokyo-Yokohama adjacent to Osaka-Kobe-Kyoto has a combined population of 100 million (Nikulina, Widom, and Czaja, 2011; State House Uganda, 2017; Stewart, 2005; Torres and Wong, 2013). Rapid population growth leads to an increased need for affordable housing in most cities (Chamberlain et al., 2016). The availability of affordable housing in the proximity of mass transit and linked to job distribution has become severely imbalanced in this period of rapid regional urbanization and growing density convergence (Duncan et al., 1998; Mazza et al., 2017). In addition to the distress it causes families who cannot find a place to live, lack of affordable housing is considered by many urban planners to have negative effects on a community's overall health (Chiputwa, Spielman, and Qaim, 2015; Evans and Kim, 2007; Okiror, 2015; Townsend, 1979).

Affordable housing challenges in inner cities range from the homeless who are forced to live on the street to the relative deprivation of vital workers like police officers, firefighters, teachers, and nurses unable to find affordable accommodation near their place of work (Corcoran and Chaudry, 1997; Deaton, 2006; Kim et al., 2016; Twikirize et al., 2014). These workers are forced to live in suburbia, commuting up to two hours each way to work (Evans, 2004; Jain and Vaachani, 2006; Ministry of Finance, 2014; Vallas, Fremstad, and Ekman, 2015). Lack of affordable housing can make low-cost labor scarcer since workers travel longer distances. Lack of affordable housing places a particular burden on local economies (Duncan and Rodgers, 1988; Holzer et al., 2008). As well, individual consumers are faced with mortgage arrears and excessive debt and therefore cut back on consumption (Farah et al., 2006). A combination of high housing costs and high debt levels contributes to a reduction in savings (Duncan, Kalil, and Ziol-Guest, 2008; Morrow, 2013; Song and Lu, 2002; Ziol-Guest et al., 2012). These factors can lead to decreased investment in sectors that are essential to the long-term growth of the economy (Hannum, Liu, and Alvarado-Urbina, 2017; Penn, 2004; Ratcliffe; Van den Waeyenberg, and Hens, 2008; Sinervo and Hill, 2011). In some countries, the market has been unable to meet the growing demand to supply housing stock at affordable prices (Hong, 2015; Jarjoura, Triplett, and Brinker, 2002; Ridge, 2002; Waddington, 2004; Ziol-Guest, Duncan, and Kalil, 2009). Although demand for affordable housing, particularly rental housing that is affordable for low- and middle-income earners, has increased, the supply has not (Javanbakht et al., 2015; Wells et al., 2010). Potential homebuyers are forced to turn to the rental market, which is also under pressure (Rowntree, 1901; Ryan, Fauth, and Brooks-Gunn, 2006; Sánchez, 2008; Ridge, 2006). An inadequate supply of housing stock increases demand on the private and social rented sector, and in worse case scenarios, homelessness (Serbin et al., 2011; Zembe-Mkabile et al., 2015). The next section explores education as a benchmark of child poverty.

3.3. EDUCATION AS AN INDICATOR OF CHILDHOOD POVERTY

There is an implied assumption in development economics that the less educated one is, the poorer they are likely to be (Duncan et al., 2012;

Evans and Fuller-Rowell, 2013; Guest and Biasini, 2001). Education is the process of facilitating learning, or the acquisition of knowledge, skills, values, beliefs, and habits (Kim et al., 2016; Mbabazi and Pyeong, 2014; McLaughlin and Rank, 2018). Educational methods include teaching, training, storytelling, discussion, and directed research (Duncan, Kalil, and Ziol-Guest, 2013; Evans and Cassells, 2014; Fujiura and Yamaki, 2000; Garrett, Ng'andu, and Ferron, 1994). Education frequently takes place under the guidance of educators, however, learners can also educate themselves (Ansell, 2016; Ashiabi, 2000; Ashworth, Hill, and Walker, 1994; Bäckman, and Nilsson, 2007). Education can take place in formal or informal settings and any experience that has a formative effect on the way one thinks, feels, or acts may be considered educational (Bhargava et al., 2004; Bloom and Canning, 2001; Bourdillon and Boyden, 2011; Boyden and James, 2014). The methodology of teaching is called pedagogy (Bruch and Touraine, 1940; Chamberlain et al., 2016). Formal education is commonly divided formally into such stages as preschool or kindergarten, primary school, secondary school, and then college, university, or apprenticeship (Chiputwa, Spielman, and Qaim, 2015; Corcoran and Chaudry, 1997; Lipina et al., 2013). A right to education has been recognized by some governments and the UN (Deaton, 2006; Dreyer, 2013; Duncan and Magnuson, 2013; Lichter, Shanahan, and Gardner, 2002; Lipina, 2016; Lopez and Velasco, 2011). In most regions, education is compulsory up to a certain age (Lyytikäinen et al., 2006; Magnuson and Votruba-Drzal, 2008; Duncan and Rodgers, 1988). There is a movement for education reform, and in particular for evidence-based education (Evans, 2004; Farah et al., 2006). Because Africa remains an epicenter of poverty, these issues are often played out on that continent (Figure 3.3) (Lichter, Shanahan, and Gardner, 2002; Lipina, 2016; Lipina et al., 2013).

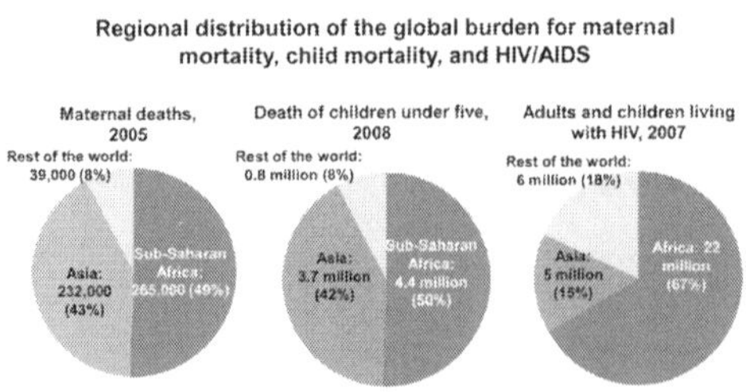

Figure 3.3. Africa as an epicenter of child poverty.

Source: PLoS.

There are development goals that are associated with education, hence making it an instrumentality of policy achievement as well as a policy in itself (Duncan, Kalil, and Ziol-Guest, 2008; Evans, 2016; Fierman et al., 2016). Joseph Chimombo pointed out education's role as a policy instrument, capable of instilling social change and economic advancement in developing countries by allowing communities to take control of their destinies (Duncan, Kalil, and Ziol-Guest, 2013; Evans and Cassells, 2014; Guest and Biasini, 2001; Duncan et al., 1998). The 2030 Agenda for Sustainable Development, adopted by the UN General Assembly in September 2015, calls for a new vision to address the environmental, social, and economic concerns facing the world today (Fujiura and Yamaki, 2000; Garrett, Ng'andu, and Ferron, 1994; Duncan et al., 2012; Evans and Fuller-Rowell, 2013). The Agenda includes 17 SDGs, including SDG 4 on education (Evans and Kim, 2007, 2013; Hannum, Liu, and Alvarado-Urbina, 2017; Hart, 2008). Since 1909, the percentage of children in the developing world attending school has increased. Before then, a small minority of boys attended school (Hatcher et al., 2019; Evans and Kutcher, 2011; Hill and Sandfort, 1995). By the start of the 21st century, the majority of children in most regions of the world attended school (Hobcraft, 1998; Hobcraft and Kiernan, 2001; Evans and Schamberg, 2009; Holzer et al., 2008).

Universal Primary Education is one of the 8 international Millennium Development Goals, towards which progress has been made in the past decade, though barriers remain (Hong, 2015; Jain and Vaachani, 2006; Jarjoura, Triplett, and Brinker, 2002; Kaplinsky, 2005; Kapoor, 1993; Jones, Vargas, and Villar, 2008). Securing charitable funding from prospective donors is one particularly persistent problem (Javanbakht et al., 2015; Jones, Vargas, and Villar, 2007; Kalil, Duncan, and Ziol-Guest, 2016). Researchers at the Overseas Development Institute have indicated that the main obstacles to funding for education include conflicting donor priorities, an immature aid architecture, and a lack of evidence and advocacy for the issue (Kendig, Mattingly, and Bianchi, 2014; Kim et al., 2013). Additionally, Transparency International has identified corruption in the education sector as a major stumbling block to achieving Universal Primary Education in Africa (Kim et al., 2015; Krason, 2015; Lesner, 2018). Furthermore, demand in the developing world for improved educational access is not as high as foreigners have expected (Mazza et al., 2017; Kim et al., 2016). Indigenous governments are reluctant to take on the ongoing costs involved (Mbabazi and Pyeong, 2014; McLaughlin and Rank, 2018; McLoyd, Aikens, and Burton, 2007). There is also economic pressure from some parents, who prefer their children to earn money in the short term rather than work towards the long-term benefits of education (Mickelson, 2002; Miller and Chen, 2013; Miller et al., 2011).

A study conducted by the UNESCO International Institute for Educational Planning indicates that stronger capacities in educational planning and management may have an important spill-over effect on the system as a whole (Ministry of Finance, 2014; Morrow, 2013; Muñoz, Álvarez-Verdejo, and García-Fernández, 2016). Sustainable capacity development requires complex interventions at the institutional, organizational, and individual levels that could be based on some foundational principles (Nikulina and Widom, 2014; Nikulina, Widom, and Czaja, 2011; Okiror, 2015; Penn, 2004; Ratcliffe and McKernan, 2010). First, there ought to be national leadership and ownership that is the touchstone of any intervention (Ridge, 2002, 2006; Rowntree, 1901; Ryan, Fauth, and Brooks-Gunn, 2006; Sánchez, 2008). Second, are strategies that must be context relevant and context specific (Schickedanz, Dreyer, and Halfon, 2015; Schmitz, Wagner, and Menke, 2001; Segretin et al., 2016). Third, there should be plans that employ an integrated set of complementary interventions, though implementation may need to proceed in steps (Serbin et al., 2011; Zembe-Mkabile et al., 2015). Fourth, partners should commit to a long-term investment in capacity development while working towards some short-term achievements (Sinervo and Hill, 2011; Song and Lu, 2002; Sripada et al., 2014). Fifth, outside intervention should be conditional on an impact assessment of national capacities at various levels (State House Uganda, 2017; Stewart, 2005; Torres and Wong, 2013; Townsend, 1979; Twikirize et al., 2014). Lastly, a certain percentage of students should be removed for improvisation of academics (Vallas, Fremstad, and Ekman, 2015; Van den Waeyenberg, and Hens, 2008; Waddington, 2004; Wells et al., 2010). This is usually practiced in schools, after 10th grade (Ziol-Guest, Duncan, and Kalil, 2009; Ziol-Guest et al., 2012). Nearly every country now has universal primary education (Ansell, 2016; Ashiabi, 2000; Ashworth, Hill, and Walker, 1994; Bäckman, and Nilsson, 2007; Bhargava et al., 2004). Similarities in systems or even in ideas that schools share internationally have led to an increase in international student exchanges (Bloom and Canning, 2001; Bourdillon and Boyden, 2011; Boyden and James, 2014; Bruch and Touraine, 1940). The European Socrates-Erasmus Program facilitates exchanges across European universities. The Soros Foundation provides many opportunities for students from central Asia and eastern Europe (Duncan and Rodgers, 1988; Evans, 2004; Farah et al., 2006). Programs such as the International Baccalaureate have contributed to the internationalization of education (Chamberlain et al., 2016; Chiputwa, Spielman, and Qaim, 2015). The global campus online, led by American universities, allows free access to class materials and lecture files recorded during the actual classes (Corcoran and Chaudry, 1997; Deaton, 2006; Dreyer, 2013; Duncan and Magnuson, 2013).

The Program for International Student Assessment and the International Association for the Evaluation of Educational Achievement objectively monitor and compare the proficiency of students from a wide range of different nations (Lopez and Velasco, 2011; Lyytikäinen et al., 2006; Magnuson and Votruba-Drzal, 2008). The internationalization of education is sometimes equated by critics with the westernization of education (Jones, Vargas, and Villar, 2008; Kendig, Mattingly, and Bianchi, 2014; Kim et al., 2013). These critics say that the internationalization of education leads to the erosion of local education systems and indigenous values and norms, which are replaced with Western systems and cultural and ideological values and orientation (Duncan et al., 1998; Evans and Kim, 2007; Hannum, Liu, and Alvarado-Urbina, 2017). Technology plays an increasingly significant role in improving access to education for people living in impoverished areas and developing countries (Evans and Kim, 2013; Hart, 2008; Hatcher et al., 2019). However, lack of technological advancement is still causing barriers with regards to quality and access to education in developing countries (Evans and Kutcher, 2011; Hill and Sandfort, 1995; Hobcraft, 1998; Hobcraft and Kiernan, 2001). Charities like One Laptop per Child are dedicated to providing infrastructures through which the disadvantaged may access educational materials (Evans and Schamberg, 2009; Holzer et al., 2008; Hong, 2015). The OLPC foundation, a group out of MIT Media Lab and supported by several major corporations, has a stated mission to develop a $100 laptop for delivering educational software (Jain and Vaachani, 2006; Jarjoura, Triplett, and Brinker, 2002; Javanbakht et al., 2015). The laptops were widely available as of 2008. They are sold at cost or given away based on donations (Duncan, Kalil, and Ziol-Guest, 2008; Evans, 2016; Fierman et al., 2016).

In Africa, the New Partnership for Africa's Development (NEPAD) has launched an "e-school program" to provide all 600,000 primary and high schools with computer equipment, learning materials, and internet access within 10 years (Jones, Vargas, and Villar, 2007; Kalil, Duncan, and Ziol-Guest, 2016; Kaplinsky, 2005; Kapoor, 1993). An International Development Agency project called nabuur.com started with the support of former American President Bill Clinton, uses the Internet to allow cooperation by individuals on issues of social development (Kim et al., 2015; Krason, 2015; Lesner, 2018; Mazza et al., 2017). India is developing technologies that will bypass land-based telephone and Internet infrastructure to deliver distance learning directly to its students (McLoyd, Aikens, and Burton, 2007; Mickelson, 2002; Miller and Chen, 2013; Miller et al., 2011). In 2004, the Indian Space Research Organization launched EDUSAT, a communications satellite providing access to educational materials that can reach more of the country's population at a greatly reduced cost (Ministry of Finance, 2014; Morrow, 2013; Muñoz, Álvarez-Verdejo, and García-Fernández, 2016; Nikulina and Widom, 2014). A survey of the literature of the research into low-cost private schools (LCPS) found that over 5 years to July 2013, the debate around LCPSs to achieving education for all (EFA) objectives was polarized and finding growing coverage in international policy (Nikulina, Widom, and Czaja, 2011; Okiror, 2015; Penn, 2004; Ratcliffe and McKernan, 2010). The polarization was due to disputes around whether the schools are affordable for the poor, reach disadvantaged groups, provide quality education, support or undermine equality, and are financially sustainable (Ridge, 2002; Rowntree, 1901; Ryan, Fauth, and Brooks-Gunn, 2006; Sánchez, 2008). The report examined the main challenges encountered by development organizations that support LCPS (Ridge, 2006; Schickedanz, Dreyer, and Halfon, 2015; Schmitz, Wagner, and Menke, 2001). Surveys suggest these types of schools are expanding across Africa and Asia. This success is attributed to excess demand (Segretin et al., 2016; Serbin et al., 2011).

These surveys found cause for concern with regards to LCPS in some spheres. The first issue is that of equity of access (Sinervo and Hill, 2011; Song and Lu, 2002; Sripada et al., 2014; State House Uganda, 2017). This concern is widely found in the literature, suggesting the growth in low-cost private schooling may be exacerbating or perpetuating already existing inequalities in developing countries, between urban and rural populations, lower-, and higher-income families, and between girls and boys (Stewart, 2005; Torres and Wong, 2013; Townsend, 1979; Twikirize et al., 2014; Vallas, Fremstad, and Ekman, 2015). The report findings suggest that girls may be underrepresented and that LCPS are reaching low-income families in smaller numbers than higher-income families (Van den Waeyenberg, and Hens, 2008; Waddington, 2004; Wells et al., 2010). Secondly, are concerns about the quality and educational outcomes. It is difficult to generalize about the quality of private schools (Zembe-Mkabile et al., 2015; Ziol-Guest, Duncan, and Kalil, 2009; Ziol-Guest et al., 2012). While most achieve better results than government counterparts, even after their social background is taken into account, some studies find the opposite (Ansell, 2016; Dreyer, 2013; Evans, 2016; Evans and Kim, 2013; Jones, Vargas, and Villar, 2007; Mbabazi and Pyeong, 2014; Schickedanz, Dreyer, and Halfon, 2015). Quality in terms of levels of teacher absence, teaching activity, and pupil-to-teacher ratios in some countries are better in LCPS than in government schools (Ashiabi, 2000; Duncan and Magnuson, 2013; Fierman et al., 2016).

Another concern about LCPS is the level of choice and affordability for the poor (Hart, 2008; Kalil, Duncan, and Ziol-Guest, 2016; Kaplinsky, 2005; McLaughlin and Rank, 2018; Schmitz, Wagner, and Menke, 2001). Parents can choose private schools because of perceptions of better-quality teaching and facilities, and an English language instruction preference (Ashworth, Hill, and Walker, 1994; Lichter, Shanahan, and Gardner, 2002; Duncan, Kalil, and Ziol-Guest, 2013).

Nevertheless, the concept of 'choice' does not apply in all contexts, or to all groups in society, partly because of limited affordability (which excludes most of the poorest) and other forms of exclusion, related to caste or social status (Hatcher et al., 2019; Kapoor, 1993; McLoyd, Aikens, and Burton, 2007). At the same time, three are concerns about the cost-effectiveness and financial sustainability of LCPS (Bäckman, and Nilsson, 2007; Bhargava et al., 2004; Lipina, 2016; Evans and Cassells, 2014).

There is evidence that private schools operate at low cost by keeping teacher salaries low, and their financial situation may be precarious where they are reliant on fees from low-income households (Evans and Kutcher, 2011; Mickelson, 2002; Segretin et al., 2016; Jones, Vargas, and Villar, 2008). The report showed some cases of successful vouchers where there was an oversupply of quality private places and an efficient administrative authority and of subsidy programs (Bloom and Canning, 2001; Lipina et al., 2013). Evaluations of the effectiveness of international support to the sector are rare (Fujiura and Yamaki, 2000; Hill and Sandfort, 1995; Kendig, Mattingly, and Bianchi, 2014). Addressing regulatory ineffectiveness is a key challenge. Emerging approaches stress the importance of understanding the political economy of the market for LCPS, specifically how relationships of power and accountability between users, government, and private providers can produce better education outcomes for the poor (Miller and Chen, 2013; Miller et al., 2011). The next section examines household incomes as a benchmark of child poverty.

3.4. HOUSEHOLD INCOMES AS AN INDICATOR OF CHILDHOOD POVERTY

Household income is a measure of the combined incomes of all people sharing a particular household or place of residence (Bourdillon and Boyden, 2011; Lopez and Velasco, 2011; Garrett, Ng'andu, and Ferron, 1994). It includes every form of income, e.g., salaries, and wages, retirement income, near cash government transfers like food stamps, and investment gains (Hobcraft, 1998; Kim et al., 2013). Average household incomes need not map directly to measures of an individual's earnings such as per capita income as numbers of people sharing households and numbers of income earners per household can vary significantly between regions and over time (Muñoz, Álvarez-Verdejo, and García-Fernández, 2016; Sripada et al., 2014). Average household income can be used as an indicator for the monetary well-being of a country's citizens (Boyden and James, 2014; Lyytikäinen et al., 2006; Duncan et al., 2012). Mean or median net household income, after taxes and mandatory contributions, is taken as indicators of standard of living (Bruch and Touraine, 1940; Magnuson and Votruba-Drzal, 2008; Evans and Fuller-Rowell, 2013). This is because they include only disposable income and acknowledge people sharing accommodation benefit from pooling at least some of their living costs (Hobcraft and Kiernan, 2001; Kim et al., 2015; Nikulina and Widom, 2014). Even in high-income countries such as the ones in Europe, household incomes can vary considerably (see Figure 3.4).

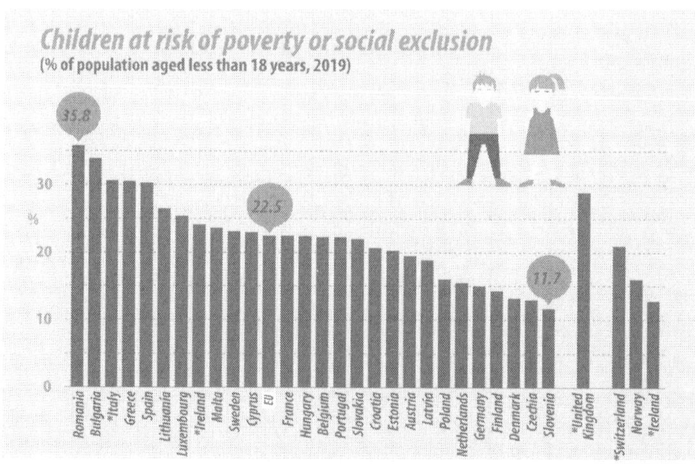

Figure 3.4. Children at risk of poverty or social exclusion.

Source: Statistics Explained via Europa. eu.

The median income is the amount that divides the income distribution into two equal groups, half having income above that amount, and half having income below that amount (Guest and Biasini, 2001; Evans and Schamberg, 2009; Krason, 2015; Lesner, 2018). Mean income (average) is the amount obtained by dividing the total aggregate income of a group by the number of units in that group (Nikulina, Widom, and Czaja, 2011; State House Uganda, 2017; Stewart, 2005; Torres and Wong, 2013). Caution should be made when comparing countries based on a strict ranking since not all datasets are capturing income equally (Chamberlain et al., 2016). For instance, income spent on private health insurance, which in 2004 was about $1300 per household in the US, is not subtracted (Duncan et al., 1998; Mazza et al., 2017). In terms of underreporting, the US dataset (US Census) captured only 80% of the gross income aggregate as of 2004 (Chiputwa, Spielman, and Qaim, 2015; Evans and Kim, 2007; Okiror, 2015; Townsend, 1979). By contrast, Finland, UK, and Norway registered much higher coverage with less underreporting (Corcoran and Chaudry, 1997; Deaton, 2006; Kim et al., 2016; Twikirize et al., 2014). Median equalized disposable household income (Evans, 2004; Jain and Vaachani, 2006; Ministry of Finance, 2014; Vallas, Fremstad, and Ekman, 2015).

Median household income divides households in a country or region into two equal segments with the first half of households earning less than the median household income and the other half earning more (Duncan and Rodgers, 1988; Holzer et al., 2008). It is considered by many statisticians to be a better indicator than the mean household income as it is not dramatically affected by unusually high or low values (Duncan, Kalil, and Ziol-Guest, 2008; Morrow, 2013; Song and Lu, 2002; Ziol-Guest et al., 2012). Typically, low household income means poverty (Farah et al., 2006). Therefore, some jurisdictions have attempted to lift children out of poverty by subsidizing or supplementing household income (Hannum, Liu, and Alvarado-Urbina, 2017; Penn, 2004; Ratcliffe; Van den Waeyenberg, and Hens, 2008; Sinervo and Hill, 2011). Such interventions will only work when there is a concerted effort by the parents or guardians to ensure that the additional income is spent on meeting the basic needs of the children (Hong, 2015; Jarjoura, Triplett, and Brinker, 2002; Ridge, 2002; Waddington, 2004; Ziol-Guest, Duncan, and Kalil, 2009). Otherwise, an increase in household income may not necessarily herald the disappearance of child poverty (Javanbakht et al., 2015; Wells et al., 2010). This chapter will close by considering how children from poor backgrounds engage with the criminal justice system.

3.5. CHILDHOOD POVERTY AND JUVENILE JUSTICE SYSTEM

There is a well-founded link between childhood poverty and engagement with the criminal justice system, particularly in terms of juvenile delinquency (Rowntree, 1901; Ryan, Fauth, and Brooks-Gunn, 2006; Sánchez, 2008; Ridge, 2006). Juvenile delinquency, also known as "juvenile offending," is the act of participating in unlawful behavior as a minor or individual younger than the statutory age of majority (Serbin et al., 2011; Zembe-Mkabile et al., 2015). For example, in the United States of America, a juvenile delinquent is a person who is typically below 18 (17 in the states of Georgia, New York, Michigan, Missouri, North Carolina, New Hampshire, Texas, and Wisconsin) years of age and commits an act that otherwise would have been charged as a crime if they were an adult (Duncan et al., 2012; Evans and Fuller-Rowell, 2013; Guest and Biasini, 2001).

Juvenile crimes can range from status offenses (such as underage smoking or drinking) to property crimes and violent crimes (Kim et al., 2016; Mbabazi and Pyeong, 2014; McLaughlin and Rank, 2018). Given the fact that some races experience child poverty at an elevated level (see Figure 3.5 for an example regarding Hispanic children); there is also a risk that they too will have negative experiences with the criminal justice system (Duncan, Kalil, and Ziol-Guest, 2013; Evans and Cassells, 2014; Fujiura and Yamaki, 2000; Garrett, Ng'andu, and Ferron, 1994). Therefore, the link between child poverty and juvenile delinquency can have far-reaching consequences on the individuals involved and the community as a whole (Ansell, 2016; Ashiabi, 2000; Ashworth, Hill, and Walker, 1994; Bäckman, and Nilsson, 2007).

Some scholars have found an increase in arrests for youth and have concluded that this may reflect more aggressive criminal justice and zero-tolerance policies rather than changes in youth behavior (Bhargava et al., 2004; Bloom and Canning, 2001; Bourdillon and Boyden, 2011; Boyden and James, 2014). Youth violence rates in the United States have dropped to approximately 12% of peak rates in 1993 according to official US government statistics, suggesting that most juvenile offending is non-violent (Bruch and Touraine, 1940; Chamberlain et al., 2016).

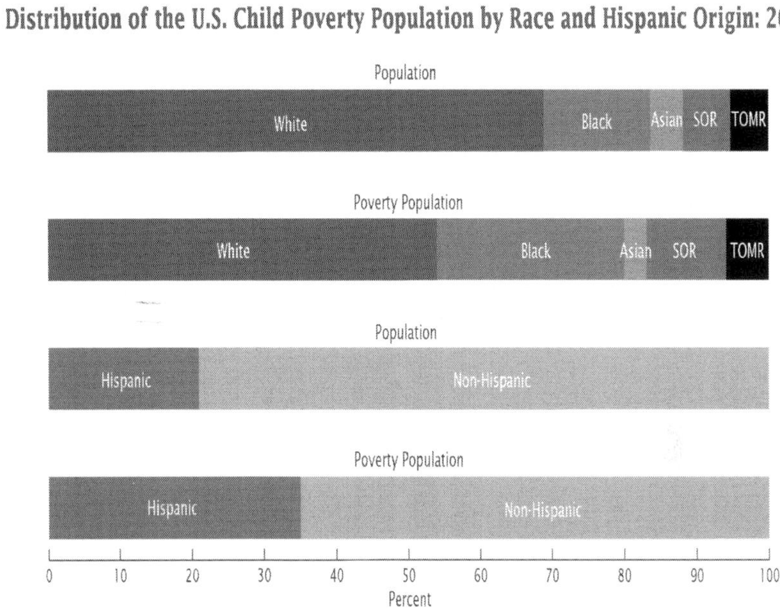

Figure 3.5. Hispanic experiences of child poverty in the USA.

Source: UC Davies Center for Poverty Research.

Many delinquent acts can be attributed to environmental factors such as family behavior or peer influence (Chiputwa, Spielman, and Qaim, 2015; Corcoran and Chaudry, 1997; Lipina et al., 2013). One contributing factor that has gained attention in recent years is the school-to-prison pipeline (Deaton, 2006; Dreyer, 2013; Duncan and Magnuson, 2013; Lichter, Shanahan, and Gardner, 2002; Lipina, 2016; Lopez and Velasco, 2011). The focus on punitive punishment has been seen to correlate with juvenile delinquency rates (Lyytikäinen et al., 2006; Magnuson and Votruba-Drzal, 2008; Duncan and Rodgers, 1988). Some have suggested shifting from zero-tolerance policies to restorative justice approaches (Evans, 2004; Farah et al., 2006). Juvenile detention centers, courts, and electronic monitoring are common structures of the juvenile legal system (Duncan, Kalil, and Ziol-Guest, 2008; Evans, 2016; Fierman et al., 2016). Juvenile courts are in place to address offenses for minors as civil rather than criminal cases in most instances (Duncan, Kalil, and Ziol-Guest, 2013; Evans and Cassells, 2014; Guest and Biasini, 2001; Duncan et al., 1998). The frequency of use and structure of these courts in the United States varies by state (Fujiura and Yamaki, 2000; Garrett, Ng'andu, and Ferron, 1994; Duncan et al., 2012; Evans and Fuller-Rowell, 2013). Depending on the type and severity of the offense committed, people under 18 can be charged and treated as adults (Evans and Kim, 2007, 2013; Hannum, Liu, and Alvarado-Urbina, 2017; Hart, 2008).

Juvenile delinquency, or offending, is often separated into three categories (Hatcher et al., 2019; Evans and Kutcher, 2011; Hill and Sandfort, 1995). The first category comprises delinquency, crimes committed by minors, which are dealt with by the juvenile courts and justice system (Hobcraft, 1998; Hobcraft and Kiernan, 2001; Evans and Schamberg, 2009; Holzer et al., 2008). The second category comprises criminal behavior and crimes dealt with by the criminal justice system (Hong, 2015; Jain and Vaachani, 2006; Jarjoura, Triplett, and Brinker, 2002; Kaplinsky, 2005; Kapoor, 1993; Jones, Vargas, and Villar, 2008). The third category comprises status offenses and offenses that are only classified as such because only a minor can commit them (Javanbakht et al., 2015; Jones, Vargas, and Villar, 2007; Kalil, Duncan, and Ziol-Guest, 2016). One example of this is the possession of alcohol by a minor. These offenses are also dealt with by the juvenile courts (Kendig, Mattingly, and Bianchi, 2014; Kim et al., 2013). Currently, there is not an agency whose jurisdiction is tracking worldwide juvenile delinquency, but UNICEF estimates that over 1 million children are in some type of detention globally (Kim et al., 2015; Krason, 2015; Lesner, 2018). Many countries do not keep records of the amount of delinquent or detained minors, but of the ones that do, the United States has the highest number of juvenile delinquency cases (Mazza et al., 2017; Kim et al., 2016). In the United States, the Office of Juvenile Justice and Delinquency Prevention (OJJDP) compiles data concerning trends in juvenile delinquency (Mbabazi and Pyeong, 2014; McLaughlin and Rank, 2018; McLoyd, Aikens, and Burton, 2007).

According to their most recent publication, 7 in 1000 juveniles in the US committed a serious crime (Fierman et al., 2016). A serious crime is defined by the US Department of Justice as one of the following 8 offenses: murder and non-negligent homicide; rape (legacy or revised); robbery; aggravated assault; burglary; motor vehicle theft; larceny-theft; and arson (Mickelson, 2002; Miller and Chen, 2013; Miller et al., 2011). According to research compiled by James Howell in 2009, the arrest rate for juveniles has been dropping consistently since its peak in 1994. Of the cases for juvenile delinquency that make it through the court system, probation is the most common consequence and males account for over 70% of the caseloads (Ministry of Finance, 2014; Morrow, 2013; Muñoz, Álvarez-Verdejo, and García-Fernández, 2016). According to developmental research, two different types of offenders emerge in adolescence (Nikulina and Widom, 2014; Nikulina, Widom, and Czaja, 2011; Okiror, 2015; Penn, 2004; Ratcliffe and McKernan, 2010). The first is an age-specific offender, referred to as the adolescence-limited offender (Vallas, Fremstad, and Ekman, 2015; Van den Waeyenberg, and Hens, 2008; Waddington, 2004; Wells et al., 2010). This is an offender for whom juvenile offending or delinquency begins and ends during their period of adolescence (Ridge, 2002, 2006; Rowntree, 1901; Ryan, Fauth, and Brooks-Gunn, 2006; Sánchez, 2008). Moffitt argues that most teenagers tend to show some form of antisocial or delinquent behavior during adolescence (Schickedanz, Dreyer, and Halfon, 2015; Schmitz, Wagner, and Menke, 2001; Segretin et al., 2016). It is therefore important to account for these behaviors in childhood to determine whether they will be adolescence-limited offenders or something more long-term (Serbin et al., 2011; Zembe-Mkabile et al., 2015). The other type of offender is the repeat offender, referred to as the life-course-persistent offender (Sinervo and Hill, 2011; Song and Lu, 2002; Sripada et al., 2014). This is an offender who begins offending or showing antisocial or aggressive behavior in adolescence (or even in childhood) and continues into adulthood (State House Uganda, 2017; Stewart, 2005; Torres and Wong, 2013; Townsend, 1979; Twikirize et al., 2014).

Most of the influencing factors for juvenile delinquency tend to be caused by a mix of both genetic and environmental factors (Ziol-Guest, Duncan, and Kalil, 2009; Ziol-Guest et al., 2012). According to Laurence Steinberg's book "*Adolescence*," the two largest predictors of juvenile delinquency are parenting style and peer group association (Ansell, 2016; Ashiabi, 2000; Ashworth, Hill, and Walker, 1994; Bäckman, and Nilsson, 2007; Bhargava et al., 2004). Additional factors that may lead a teenager into juvenile delinquency include poor or low socioeconomic status, poor school readiness or performance or failure, and peer rejection (Bloom and Canning, 2001; Bourdillon and Boyden, 2011; Boyden and James, 2014; Bruch and Touraine, 1940). Delinquent activity, especially the involvement in youth gangs, may also be caused by a desire for protection against violence or financial hardship (Duncan and Rodgers, 1988; Evans, 2004; Farah et al., 2006). Juvenile offenders can view the delinquent activity as a means of gaining access to resources to protect against such threats (Chamberlain et al., 2016; Chiputwa, Spielman, and Qaim, 2015). Research by Carrie Dabb indicates that even changes in the weather can increase the likelihood of children exhibiting deviant behavior (Corcoran and Chaudry, 1997; Deaton, 2006; Dreyer, 2013; Duncan and Magnuson, 2013). Family factors that may influence offending include the level of parental supervision, the way parents discipline a child, parental conflict or separation, criminal activity by parents or siblings, parental abuse or neglect, and the quality of the parent-child relationship (Lichter, Shanahan, and Gardner, 2002; Lipina, 2016; Lipina et al., 2013). Hence, parenting style is one of the largest predictors of juvenile delinquency (Lopez and Velasco, 2011; Lyytikäinen et al., 2006; Magnuson and Votruba-Drzal, 2008).

There are four categories of parenting styles that describe the attitudes and behaviors that parents express while raising their children (Jones, Vargas, and Villar, 2008; Kendig, Mattingly, and Bianchi, 2014; Kim et al., 2013). The first is authoritative parenting which is characterized by warmth and support in addition to a discipline (Duncan et al., 1998; Evans and Kim, 2007; Hannum, Liu, and Alvarado-Urbina, 2017). The second is indulgent parenting which is characterized by warmth and regard towards their children but lack structure and discipline (Evans and Kim, 2013; Hart, 2008; Hatcher et al., 2019). The third is authoritarian parenting which is characterized by high discipline without warmth, thus leading to often hostile demeanor and harsh correction (Evans and Kutcher, 2011; Hill and Sandfort, 1995; Hobcraft, 1998; Hobcraft and Kiernan, 2001). The 4th is neglectful parenting which is both non-responsive and non-demanding (Evans and Schamberg, 2009; Holzer et al., 2008; Hong, 2015). The child is not engaged either affectionately or disciplinary by the parent (Jain and Vaachani, 2006; Jarjoura, Triplett, and Brinker, 2002; Javanbakht et al., 2015). According to research done by Laura E. Berk, the style of parenting would be most beneficial for a child (Duncan, Kalil, and Ziol-Guest, 2008; Evans, 2016; Fierman et al., 2016). Based on studies conducted by Diana Baumrind (1971) is the authoritative child-rearing style because it combines acceptance with discipline to render healthy development for the child (Jones, Vargas, and Villar, 2007; Kalil, Duncan, and Ziol-Guest, 2016; Kaplinsky, 2005; Kapoor, 1993). Children brought up by single parents are more likely to live in poverty and engage in delinquent behavior than those who live with both parents (Kim et al., 2015; Krason, 2015; Lesner, 2018; Mazza et al., 2017). However, according to research done by Graham and Bowling; once the attachment a child feels towards their parent(s) and the level of parental supervision is taken into account, children in single-parent families are no more likely to offend than others (McLoyd, Aikens, and

Burton, 2007; Mickelson, 2002; Miller and Chen, 2013; Miller et al., 2011). It was seen that when a child has low parental supervision they are much more likely to offend. Negative peer group association is more likely when adolescents are left unsupervised (Ministry of Finance, 2014; Morrow, 2013; Muñoz, Álvarez-Verdejo, and García-Fernández, 2016; Nikulina and Widom, 2014). A lack of supervision is also connected to poor relationships between children and parents (Nikulina, Widom, and Czaja, 2011; Okiror, 2015; Penn, 2004; Ratcliffe and McKernan, 2010). Children who are often in conflict with their parents may be less willing to discuss their activities with them (Ridge, 2002; Rowntree, 1901; Ryan, Fauth, and Brooks-Gunn, 2006; Sánchez, 2008). The conflict between a child's parents is also much more closely linked to offending than being raised by a lone parent (Ridge, 2006; Schickedanz, Dreyer, and Halfon, 2015; Schmitz, Wagner, and Menke, 2001).

Adolescents with siblings who have committed crimes are more likely to be influenced by their siblings and become delinquent if the sibling is older, of the same sex or gender, and maintains a good relationship with the child (Segretin et al., 2016; Serbin et al., 2011). Cases, where a younger criminal sibling influences an older one, are rare (Sinervo and Hill, 2011; Song and Lu, 2002; Sripada et al., 2014; State House Uganda, 2017). An aggressive more hostile sibling is less likely to influence a younger sibling in the direction of delinquency, if anything, the more strained the relationship between the siblings, the less they will want to influence each other (Stewart, 2005; Torres and Wong, 2013; Townsend, 1979; Twikirize et al., 2014; Vallas, Fremstad, and Ekman, 2015). Children resulting from unintended pregnancies are more likely to exhibit delinquent behavior. They also have lower mother-child relationship quality (Van den Waeyenberg, and Hens, 2008; Waddington, 2004; Wells et al., 2010). Peer rejection in childhood is also a large predictor of juvenile delinquency (Zembe-Mkabile et al., 2015; Ziol-Guest, Duncan, and Kalil, 2009; Ziol-Guest et al., 2012). This rejection can affect the child's ability to be socialized properly and often leads them to gravitate towards anti-social peer groups (Ansell, 2016; Dreyer, 2013; Evans, 2016; Evans and Kim, 2013; Jones, Vargas, and Villar, 2007; Mbabazi and Pyeong, 2014; Schickedanz, Dreyer, and Halfon, 2015). Association with anti-social groups often leads to the promotion of violent, aggressive, and deviant behavior (Ashiabi, 2000; Duncan and Magnuson, 2013; Fierman et al., 2016). Robert Vargas's "Being in 'Bad' Company," explains that adolescents who can choose between groups of friends are less susceptible to peer influence that could lead them to commit illegal acts (Hart, 2008; Kalil, Duncan, and Ziol-Guest, 2016; Kaplinsky, 2005; McLaughlin and Rank, 2018; Schmitz, Wagner, and Menke, 2001). Aggressive adolescents who have been rejected by peers are also more likely to have a "hostile attribution bias," which leads people to interpret the actions of others (whether they be hostile or not) as purposefully hostile and aggressive towards them (Ashworth, Hill, and Walker, 1994; Lichter, Shanahan, and Gardner, 2002; Duncan, Kalil, and Ziol-Guest, 2013). This often leads to an impulsive and aggressive reaction (Hatcher et al., 2019; Kapoor, 1993; McLoyd, Aikens, and Burton, 2007).

Conformity plays a significant role in the vast impact that peer group influence has on an individual (Bäckman, and Nilsson, 2007; Bhargava et al., 2004; Lipina, 2016; Evans and Cassells, 2014). Aronson, Wilson, and Akert (2013) point to the research experiment conducted by Solomon Asch (1956), to ascertain whether a group could influence an individual's behavior (Evans and Kutcher, 2011; Mickelson, 2002; Segretin et al., 2016; Jones, Vargas, and Villar, 2008). The experiment was executed by asking a participant to determine which line in the set of three lines matched the length of an original line. Confederates knew the purpose of the experiment and were directed to answer the questions incorrectly during certain phases of the experiment. These confederates answered the question before the participant. The confederates answered the first few questions correctly, as did the participant. Eventually, all of the confederates started to answer incorrectly. The purpose of the experiment was to see if the group would influence the participant to answer incorrectly. Asch found that 76% of the participants confirmed and answered incorrectly when influenced by the group. According to these findings, it was concluded that a peer group that is involved in deviant behavior can influence an adolescent to engage in similar activities (Bloom and Canning, 2001; Lipina et al., 2013). Once the adolescent becomes part of the group, they will be susceptible to groupthink (Fujiura and Yamaki, 2000; Hill and Sandfort, 1995; Kendig, Mattingly, and Bianchi, 2014).

A common contributor to juvenile delinquency rates is a phenomenon referred to as the school-to-prison pipeline (Miller and Chen, 2013; Miller et al., 2011). In recent years, school disciplinary measures have become increasingly policed. 67% of high school students attend schools with police officers (Bourdillon and Boyden, 2011; Lopez and Velasco, 2011; Garrett, Ng'andu, and Ferron, 1994). This rise in police presence is often attributed to the implementation of zero-tolerance policies (Hobcraft, 1998; Kim et al., 2013). Based on the "broken windows" theory of criminology and the

Gun-Free Schools Act, zero-tolerance policies stress the use of specific, consistent, and harsh punishment to deal with in school infractions (Muñoz, Álvarez-Verdejo, and García-Fernández, 2016; Sripada et al., 2014). Often measures such as suspension or expulsion are assigned to students who deviant regardless of the reason or past disciplinary history (Boyden and James, 2014; Lyytikäinen et al., 2006; Duncan et al., 2012). This use of punishment often has been linked with increasing high school dropout rates and future arrests (Hobcraft and Kiernan, 2001; Kim et al., 2015; Nikulina and Widom, 2014). It was found in a 2018 study that students who received a suspension were less likely to graduate and more likely to be arrested or on probation (Bruch and Touraine, 1940; Magnuson and Votruba-Drzal, 2008; Evans and Fuller-Rowell, 2013). As stated in research by Matthew Theriot, the increased police presence in the school and use of tougher punishment methods leads student actions to be criminalized and in turn referred to juvenile justice systems (Guest and Biasini, 2001; Evans and Schamberg, 2009; Krason, 2015; Lesner, 2018). The Center on Youth Justice at the Vera Institute of Justice found that "for similar students attending similar schools, a single suspension or expulsion doubles the risk that a student will repeat a grade (Nikulina, Widom, and Czaja, 2011; State House Uganda, 2017; Stewart, 2005; Torres and Wong, 2013). Being retained a grade, especially while in middle or high school, is one of the strongest predictors of dropping out (Chamberlain et al., 2016). In a national longitudinal study, it was reported that youth with a prior suspension were 68% more likely to drop out of school (Duncan et al., 1998; Mazza et al., 2017).

The School to Prison Pipeline disproportionately affects minority students (Chiputwa, Spielman, and Qaim, 2015; Evans and Kim, 2007; Okiror, 2015; Townsend, 1979). According to data compiled by the United States Government Accountability Office, 39% of students who received a suspension in the 2013–2014 school year were Black, even though Black students accounted for only about 15% of public-school students (Corcoran and Chaudry, 1997; Deaton, 2006; Kim et al., 2016; Twikirize et al., 2014). This over-representation applied to both boys and girls of African descent (Evans, 2004; Jain and Vaachani, 2006; Ministry of Finance, 2014; Vallas, Fremstad, and Ekman, 2015). Compared to White students, black students were expelled or suspended 3 times as frequently (Duncan and Rodgers, 1988; Holzer et al., 2008). Juvenile delinquency is the unlawful activities by minors in their teen or pre-teen years (Farah et al., 2006). It is influenced by four main risk factors namely; personality, background, state of mind, and drugs (Duncan, Kalil, and Ziol-Guest, 2008; Morrow, 2013; Song and Lu,

2002; Ziol-Guest et al., 2012). Gender is another risk factor in regards to influencing delinquent behavior (Hannum, Liu, and Alvarado-Urbina, 2017; Penn, 2004; Ratcliffe; Van den Waeyenberg, and Hens, 2008; Sinervo and Hill, 2011). The predictors of different types of delinquency vary across females and males for various reasons, but a common underlying reason for this is socialization (Hong, 2015; Jarjoura, Triplett, and Brinker, 2002; Ridge, 2002; Waddington, 2004; Ziol-Guest, Duncan, and Kalil, 2009). Different predictors of delinquency emerge when analyzing distinct offending types across gender, but overall it is evident that males commit more crimes than females (Javanbakht et al., 2015; Wells et al., 2010). Across all offenses, females are less likely to be involved in delinquent acts than males (Rowntree, 1901; Ryan, Fauth, and Brooks-Gunn, 2006; Sánchez, 2008; Ridge, 2006). Females not only commit fewer offenses, but they also commit less serious offenses (Serbin et al., 2011; Zembe-Mkabile et al., 2015).

Socialization plays a key role in the gender gap in delinquency because male and female juveniles are often socialized differently (Duncan et al., 2012; Evans and Fuller-Rowell, 2013; Guest and Biasini, 2001). Girls' and boys' experiences are heavily mediated by gender, which alters their interactions in society (Kendig, Mattingly, and Bianchi, 2014; Kim et al., 2013). Males and females are differently controlled and bonded, suggesting that they will not make the same choices and may follow different paths of delinquency (Segretin et al., 2016; Serbin et al., 2011). Social bonds are important for both males and females, but different aspects of the bond are relevant for each gender (Bäckman, and Nilsson, 2007; Bhargava et al., 2004; Lipina, 2016; Evans and Cassells, 2014). The degree of involvement in social settings is a significant predictor of male's violent delinquency but is not significant for females (Duncan et al., 1998; Evans and Kim, 2007; Hannum, Liu, and Alvarado-Urbina, 2017). Males tend to be more connected with their peer relationships which in effect has a stronger influence on their behavior (Javanbakht et al., 2015; Jones, Vargas, and Villar, 2007; Kalil, Duncan, and Ziol-Guest, 2016). Association with delinquent peers is one of the strongest correlates of juvenile delinquency, and much of the gender gap can be accounted for by the fact that males are more likely to have friends that support delinquent behavior (Bhargava et al., 2004; Bloom and Canning, 2001; Bourdillon and Boyden, 2011; Boyden and James, 2014). Delinquent peers are positively and significantly related to delinquency in males, but delinquent peers are negatively and insignificantly related to delinquency for females (Bourdillon and Boyden, 2011; Lopez and Velasco, 2011; Garrett, Ng'andu, and Ferron, 1994).

Gender differences continue to be identified in juvenile delinquent populations (Hart, 2008; Kalil, Duncan, and Ziol-Guest, 2016; Kaplinsky, 2005; McLaughlin and Rank, 2018; Schmitz, Wagner, and Menke, 2001). For example, for females; familial functioning relationships have shown to be more important (Javanbakht et al., 2015; Wells et al., 2010). Female juveniles tend to be more strongly connected with their families, the disconnect or the lack of socialization between their family members can significantly predict their likelihood of committing crimes as juveniles and even as adults (Jones, Vargas, and Villar, 2007; Kalil, Duncan, and Ziol-Guest, 2016; Kaplinsky, 2005; Kapoor, 1993). When the family is disrupted, females are more likely to engage in delinquent behavior than males (Duncan, Kalil, and Ziol-Guest, 2008; Morrow, 2013; Song and Lu, 2002; Ziol-Guest et al., 2012). Boys, however, tend to be less connected to their family and are not as affected by these relationships (Hatcher et al., 2019; Evans and Kutcher, 2011; Hill and Sandfort, 1995). When it comes to minor offenses such as fighting, vandalism, shoplifting, and the carrying of weapons, gender differences are limited because they are most common among both males as well as females (Vallas, Fremstad, and Ekman, 2015; Van den Waeyenberg, and Hens, 2008; Waddington, 2004; Wells et al., 2010). Elements of the social bond, social disorganization, routine activities, opportunity, and attitudes towards violence are also related to delinquent behavior among both males and females (Boyden and James, 2014; Lyytikäinen et al., 2006; Duncan et al., 2012).

Individual psychological or behavioral risk factors that may make offending more likely include low intelligence, impulsiveness or the inability to delay gratification, aggression, lack of empathy, and restlessness (Duncan, Kalil, and Ziol-Guest, 2013; Evans and Cassells, 2014; Guest and Biasini, 2001; Duncan et al., 1998). Other risk factors that may be evident during childhood and adolescence include aggressive or troublesome behavior, language delays or impairments, lack of emotional control (learning to control one's anger), and cruelty to animals (Kendig, Mattingly, and Bianchi, 2014; Kim et al., 2013). Children with low intelligence are more likely to do badly in school (Segretin et al., 2016; Serbin et al., 2011). This may increase the chances of offending because low educational attainment, a low attachment to school, and low educational aspirations are all risk factors for offending in themselves (Bäckman, and Nilsson, 2007; Bhargava et al., 2004; Lipina, 2016; Evans and Cassells, 2014). Children who perform poorly at school are also more likely to be truant, and the status offense of truancy is linked to further offending (Duncan et al., 1998; Evans and Kim, 2007; Hannum,

Liu, and Alvarado-Urbina, 2017). Impulsiveness is seen by some as the key aspect of a child's personality that predicts offending (Javanbakht et al., 2015; Jones, Vargas, and Villar, 2007; Kalil, Duncan, and Ziol-Guest, 2016). However, it is not clear whether these aspects of personality are a result of "deficits in the executive functions of the brain" or a result of parental influences or other social factors (Bhargava et al., 2004; Bloom and Canning, 2001; Bourdillon and Boyden, 2011; Boyden and James, 2014). In any event, studies of adolescent development show that teenagers are more prone to risk-taking, which may explain the high disproportionate rate of offending among adolescents (Bourdillon and Boyden, 2011; Lopez and Velasco, 2011; Garrett, Ng'andu, and Ferron, 1994). Indeed, some have argued that perhaps the most effective way of preventing and dealing with juvenile delinquency is to tackle the social problem of child poverty (Hart, 2008; Kalil, Duncan, and Ziol-Guest, 2016; Kaplinsky, 2005; McLaughlin and Rank, 2018; Schmitz, Wagner, and Menke, 2001).

CHAPTER 3 SUMMARY

Benchmarking child poverty is a priority for policymakers because it allows them to respond in ways that are informed and coherent. However, the difficulty of measuring child poverty and benchmarking means that often policy is made on account of supposition rather than in proven fact. That is why child poverty persists despite the various interventions that have been adopted to deal with it. This chapter has shown that children in poverty are likely to suffer from poor health, live in unsuitable housing, be poorly educated, come from families with low incomes, and have negative experiences with the juvenile justice system. All these factors are associated with each other and may even sustain each other. In the next chapter, we specifically focus on the measures that have been adopted to understand and categorize child poverty.

Chapter 4

Measurement of Childhood Poverty

CONTENTS

It is very difficult to effectively deal with child poverty and its consequences if you have very little idea of what it comprises. The previous chapter has highlighted some of the indicators of child poverty (education, health, housing, income, and criminality). However, those indicators are not precise measures. It is from that background that this chapter highlights some of the key measures of child poverty or general poverty that have been adopted internationally. These include absolute poverty, relative poverty, the capability approach, the child development index (CDI), and a host of other localized measures. By the end of this chapter, the reader should have an idea of how child poverty is measured internationally.

4.1. ABSOLUTE INDICATORS OF CHILDHOOD POVERTY

Absolute poverty refers to a condition where a person does not have the minimum amount of income needed to meet the minimum requirements for one or more basic living needs over an extended period (Javanbakht et al., 2015; Wells et al., 2010). This includes things like food, weight, access to water, toilet facilities, shelter, healthcare, information, and other services (Jones, Vargas, and Villar, 2007; Kalil, Duncan, and Ziol-Guest, 2016; Kaplinsky, 2005; Kapoor, 1993). Living in absolute poverty is harmful and can endanger lives (Duncan, Kalil, and Ziol-Guest, 2008; Morrow, 2013; Song and Lu, 2002; Ziol-Guest et al., 2012). The standards set for absolute poverty are the same across countries (Hatcher et al., 2019; Evans and Kutcher, 2011; Hill and Sandfort, 1995). When it was established in 1990, the World Bank set the global absolute poverty line as living on less than $1 a day (Vallas, Fremstad, and Ekman, 2015; Van den Waeyenberg, and Hens, 2008; Waddington, 2004; Wells et al., 2010).

In simple terms, poverty is not having enough money or access to resources to enjoy a decent standard of living (Boyden and James, 2014; Lyytikäinen et al., 2006; Duncan et al., 2012). This may be that the lack of access to healthcare, education, or water and sanitation facilities (Zembe-Mkabile et al., 2015; Ziol-Guest, Duncan, and Kalil, 2009; Ziol-Guest et al., 2012). Historically, poverty in the UK was defined as either primary and secondary in studies by Seebohm Rowntree in the 20th century (Serbin et al., 2011; Zembe-Mkabile et al., 2015). Primary poverty means not having enough money to meet basic needs, it can also be considered as 'living below the poverty line (Duncan and Rodgers, 1988; Holzer et al., 2008). Secondary poverty is when people earn just enough money to afford the necessities but spend part of it on "coping mechanisms" to deal with financial and work-related stress (high risk or difficult working conditions due to abuse and long hours) and therefore end up struggling to make ends meet (Farah et al., 2006). Being a developed country such as Canada (see Figure 4.1) does not necessarily imply the absence of absolute poverty, although that poverty may be expressed in different ways from that which is experienced by the developing world (Fujiura and Yamaki, 2000; Garrett, Ng'andu, and Ferron, 1994; Duncan et al., 2012; Evans and Fuller-Rowell, 2013).

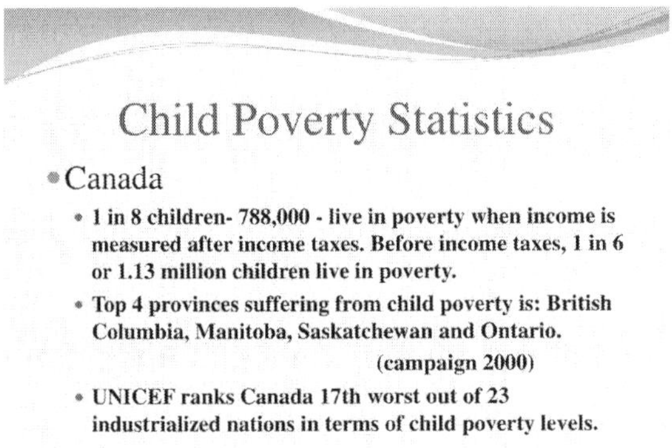

Figure 4.1. Child poverty in Canada.

Source: Slide Serve.

In the end, Rowntree identified low wages as the main cause of poverty in the United Kingdom, rather than the poorest being responsible for their condition (Evans and Kim, 2013; Hart, 2008; Hatcher et al., 2019). This was the most common criticism back then and is ongoing today to some extent (Ansell, 2016; Ashiabi, 2000; Ashworth, Hill, and Walker, 1994; Bäckman, and Nilsson, 2007; Bhargava et al., 2004). Statistics worldwide back this conclusion today, people born into poverty are much more likely to remain poor (Corcoran and Chaudry, 1997; Deaton, 2006; Dreyer, 2013; Duncan and Magnuson, 2013). Some people might escape it, but for the majority, hard work is not the solution when the economic system works against them (McLoyd, Aikens, and Burton, 2007; Mickelson, 2002; Miller and Chen, 2013; Miller et al., 2011). This is what constitutes the cycle of poverty (Lyytikäinen et al., 2006; Magnuson and Votruba-Drzal, 2008; Duncan and Rodgers, 1988). Not having access to healthy food, decent housing, electricity, water means you effectively live in severe, absolute poverty (Bloom and Canning, 2001; Lipina et al., 2013). Moreover, the cost of these essentials is too high for poor families to afford (Mickelson, 2002; Miller and Chen, 2013; Miller et al., 2011). The question then arises as to which one of these is prioritized (Hobcraft, 1998; Kim et al., 2013). That is why finding a definition of relative or absolute poverty is not simple since it does not just involve economics, but it is also affected by society and politics (Ziol-Guest, Duncan, and Kalil, 2009; Ziol-Guest et al., 2012).

Absolute poverty is when household income is below a certain level, which makes it impossible for the person or family to meet the basic needs of life including food, shelter, safe drinking water, education, healthcare, and the like (Bloom and Canning, 2001; Bourdillon and Boyden, 2011; Boyden and James, 2014; Bruch and Touraine, 1940). In this state of poverty, even if the country is growing economically, it does not affect people living below the poverty line (Sinervo and Hill, 2011; Song and Lu, 2002; Sripada et al., 2014). Absolute poverty compares households based on a set income level and this level varies from country to country depending on its overall economic conditions (Duncan, Kalil, and Ziol-Guest, 2008; Evans, 2016; Fierman et al., 2016). In the next section, we provide a contrasting view of poverty which focuses on relative poverty.

4.2. RELATIVE INDICATORS OF CHILDHOOD POVERTY

Relative poverty is when households receive 50% less than average household incomes, so they do have some money but still not enough money to afford anything above the basics (Chiputwa, Spielman, and Qaim, 2015; Evans and Kim, 2007; Okiror, 2015; Townsend, 1979). This type of poverty is, on the other hand, changeable depending on the economic growth of the country (Rowntree, 1901; Ryan, Fauth, and Brooks-Gunn, 2006; Sánchez, 2008; Ridge, 2006). Relative poverty is sometimes described as "relative deprivation" because the people falling under this category are not living in total poverty, but they are not enjoying the same standard of life as everyone else in the country (Hobcraft and Kiernan, 2001; Kim et al., 2015; Nikulina and Widom, 2014). It can be TV, internet, clean clothes, a safe home (a healthy environment, free from abuse or neglect), or even education (Hannum, Liu, and Alvarado-Urbina, 2017; Penn, 2004; Ratcliffe; Van den Waeyenberg, and Hens, 2008; Sinervo and Hill, 2011). Relative poverty can also be permanent, meaning that certain families have no chance of enjoying the same standards of living as other people in the same society currently have access to (Hong, 2015; Jain and Vaachani, 2006; Jarjoura,

Triplett, and Brinker, 2002; Kaplinsky, 2005; Kapoor, 1993; Jones, Vargas, and Villar, 2008). They are basically "trapped" in a low relative income box (Ashworth, Hill, and Walker, 1994; Lichter, Shanahan, and Gardner, 2002; Duncan, Kalil, and Ziol-Guest, 2013). Relative poverty can interact with other factors such as family structure (see Figure 4.2) to increase child poverty (Duncan, Kalil, and Ziol-Guest, 2008; Evans, 2016; Fierman et al., 2016).

Figure 4.2. Relationship between child poverty and family structure.

Source: ASPE.

When the relative approach is used to measure poverty, there is another concept that needs to be explored which persistent poverty (Ansell, 2016; Ashiabi, 2000; Ashworth, Hill, and Walker, 1994; Bäckman, and Nilsson, 2007). This is when households receive 50 or 60% less income than average incomes every 2 out of 3 years. Since long-term poverty has more impactful consequences on economic and social conditions, persistent poverty is an important concept to bear in mind (Schickedanz, Dreyer, and Halfon, 2015; Schmitz, Wagner, and Menke, 2001; Segretin et al., 2016). On the whole, poverty is about exclusion. In its most extreme form, it's the inability to access what you need for a decent life (Mbabazi and Pyeong, 2014; McLaughlin and Rank, 2018; McLoyd, Aikens, and Burton, 2007). Relatively speaking, in more developed countries, it is being excluded from what constitutes normal daily life (Duncan, Kalil, and Ziol-Guest, 2013; Evans and Cassells, 2014; Fujiura and Yamaki, 2000; Garrett, Ng'andu, and Ferron, 1994). These may include things like internet to access jobs or public services, the proper clothes to find that job, paying for education, and access to decent housing (Hong, 2015; Jarjoura, Triplett, and Brinker, 2002; Ridge, 2002; Waddington, 2004; Ziol-Guest, Duncan, and Kalil, 2009). For example, respiratory diseases comprise one of the most common symptoms of poor housing. Relative poverty depends on the level of development of the country (Ridge, 2002, 2006; Rowntree, 1901; Ryan, Fauth, and Brooks-Gunn, 2006; Sánchez, 2008). It is about giving everyone the chance to enjoy the same living standards so that everyone has an equal opportunity to live their life to their full potential (State House Uganda, 2017; Stewart, 2005; Torres and Wong, 2013; Townsend, 1979; Twikirize et al., 2014). In that sense, fighting poverty is about unlocking the huge, untapped economic potential within each country (Nikulina, Widom, and Czaja, 2011).

Relative poverty is the condition in which people lack the minimum amount of income needed to maintain the average standard of living in the society in which they live (Deaton, 2006; Dreyer, 2013; Duncan and Magnuson, 2013; Lichter, Shanahan, and Gardner, 2002; Lipina, 2016; Lopez and Velasco, 2011). Relative poverty is considered the easiest way to measure the level of poverty in an individual country (Jain and Vaachani, 2006; Jarjoura, Triplett, and Brinker, 2002; Javanbakht et al., 2015). Relative poverty is defined relative to the members of a society and, therefore, differs across countries (Nikulina, Widom, and Czaja, 2011; Okiror, 2015; Penn, 2004; Ratcliffe and McKernan, 2010). People are said to be impoverished if they cannot keep up with the standard of living as determined by society (Stewart, 2005; Torres and Wong, 2013; Townsend, 1979; Twikirize et al., 2014; Vallas, Fremstad, and Ekman, 2015). Relative poverty also changes over time (Ridge, 2006; Schickedanz, Dreyer, and Halfon, 2015; Schmitz, Wagner, and Menke, 2001). As the wealth of a society increases, so does the amount of income and resources that the society deems necessary for proper conditions of living (Ashiabi, 2000; Duncan and Magnuson, 2013).

There are several causes of relative poverty (Duncan and Rodgers, 1988; Evans, 2004; Farah et al., 2006). One of those causes is unemployment which has been closely associated with relative poverty (Ansell, 2016; Dreyer, 2013; Evans, 2016; Evans and Kim, 2013; Jones, Vargas, and Villar, 2007; Mbabazi and Pyeong, 2014; Schickedanz, Dreyer, and Halfon, 2015). From 2010–2014, the unemployment rate in the United States was over 8% (Miller and Chen, 2013; Miller et al., 2011). This means that over 18 million Americans over the age of 16 did not have jobs (Evans, 2004; Jain and Vaachani, 2006; Ministry of Finance, 2014; Vallas, Fremstad, and Ekman, 2015). This lack of employment increases the chances of living in poverty

(Serbin et al., 2011). Education can also predict relative poverty (Evans and Kutcher, 2011; Mickelson, 2002; Segretin et al., 2016; Jones, Vargas, and Villar, 2008). The less education you have, the higher your chances of being unemployed (Duncan et al., 1998; Mazza et al., 2017). This in turn increases the likelihood that you will live in poverty (Jones, Vargas, and Villar, 2008; Kendig, Mattingly, and Bianchi, 2014; Kim et al., 2013). That is why some scholars argue that in fighting relative poverty, education is a key component (Kim et al., 2015; Krason, 2015; Lesner, 2018; Mazza et al., 2017). However, the entrenched inequalities in the education provision mean that these types of silos are very hard to overcome (Farah et al., 2006).

Poor health is another critical predictive aspect of relative poverty, particularly in countries like the USA where there is no universal free healthcare system (Lichter, Shanahan, and Gardner, 2002; Lipina, 2016; Lipina et al., 2013). Poor health is not only a cause of poverty, but it is also a consequence of poverty (Evans and Kutcher, 2011; Hill and Sandfort, 1995; Hobcraft, 1998; Hobcraft and Kiernan, 2001). People living in poverty suffer greater levels of physical and mental illness than those who do not (Hobcraft, 1998; Hobcraft and Kiernan, 2001; Evans and Schamberg, 2009; Holzer et al., 2008). Poor health also weakens impoverished communities, which prevents many people from working and earning an income (Mazza et al., 2017; Kim et al., 2016). For example, infectious disease may spread across an impoverished community, killing many. Since these communities do not have access to adequate health care services, they cannot be treated, and the cycle of poverty continues (Van den Waeyenberg, and Hens, 2008; Waddington, 2004; Wells et al., 2010). In the next section, we consider the capability approach to understanding and measuring poverty.

4.3. THE CAPABILITY APPROACH TO CHILDHOOD POVERTY

The capability approach (also referred to as the capabilities approach) is an economic theory conceived in the 1980s as an alternative approach to welfare economics (Ministry of Finance, 2014; Morrow, 2013; Muñoz, Álvarez-Verdejo, and García-Fernández, 2016). In this approach, Amartya Sen and Martha Nussbaum bring together a range of ideas that were previously excluded from (or inadequately formulated in) traditional approaches to the economics of welfare (Sinervo and Hill, 2011; Song and Lu, 2002; Sripada et al., 2014; State House Uganda, 2017). The core focus of the capability approach is on what individuals can do or capable of

(Evans and Schamberg, 2009; Holzer et al., 2008; Hong, 2015). There are many aspects and challenges in assessing capability. Initially, Sen argued for five components in assessing capability (Guest and Biasini, 2001; Evans and Schamberg, 2009; Krason, 2015; Lesner, 2018). First, is the importance of real freedoms in the assessment of a person's advantage (Ridge, 2002; Rowntree, 1901; Ryan, Fauth, and Brooks-Gunn, 2006; Sánchez, 2008). Second, are the individual differences in the ability to transform resources into valuable activities (Hatcher et al., 2019; Kapoor, 1993; McLoyd, Aikens, and Burton, 2007). Third, is the multi-variate nature of activities giving rise to happiness (Evans and Kim, 2007, 2013; Hannum, Liu, and Alvarado-Urbina, 2017; Hart, 2008). Fourth, is a balance of materialistic and nonmaterialistic factors in evaluating human welfare (Chamberlain et al., 2016; Chiputwa, Spielman, and Qaim, 2015). Fifth is a concern for the distribution of opportunities within society (Kim et al., 2016; Mbabazi and Pyeong, 2014; McLaughlin and Rank, 2018). When we consider the possibility of relative poverty in a developed country such as the United Kingdom (see Figure 4.3), we then understand the complexities that the capability approach is trying to incorporate into our understanding of child poverty (Chiputwa, Spielman, and Qaim, 2015; Corcoran and Chaudry, 1997; Lipina et al., 2013).

Figure 4.3. Relative poverty in the United Kingdom.

Source: Department of Works and Pensions via National Statistics 2014 and BBC.

Working in collaboration particularly with Martha Nussbaum, Sudhir Anand, and James Foster; Sen has helped to make the capabilities approach predominant as a paradigm for policy debate in human development (Nikulina and Widom, 2014; Nikulina, Widom, and Czaja, 2011; Okiror, 2015; Penn, 2004; Ratcliffe and McKernan, 2010). Subsequently, his thinking inspired the creation of the UN's Human Development Index (Fujiura and Yamaki, 2000; Hill and Sandfort, 1995; Kendig, Mattingly, and Bianchi, 2014). This is a popular measure of human development, capturing capabilities in health, education, and income (Corcoran and Chaudry, 1997; Deaton, 2006; Kim et al., 2016; Twikirize et al., 2014). In addition, the approach has been operationalized with a high-income country focus by Paul Anand and colleagues (Kim et al., 2015; Krason, 2015; Lesner, 2018). Furthermore, since the creation of the Human Development and Capability Association in the early 2000s; the approach has been extensively discussed by political theorists, philosophers, and a range of social scientists, including those with a particular interest in human health (Bruch and Touraine, 1940; Chamberlain et al., 2016).

The approach emphasizes functional capabilities (Muñoz, Álvarez-Verdejo, and García-Fernández, 2016; Sripada et al., 2014). These are "substantive freedoms," such as the ability to live to old age, engage in economic transactions, or participate in political activities (Lopez and Velasco, 2011; Lyytikäinen et al., 2006; Magnuson and Votruba-Drzal, 2008). The capabilities are construed in terms of the substantive freedoms people have reason to value, instead of utility (in terms of happiness, desire-fulfillment, or choice) or access to resources which include income, commodities, and assets (Bruch and Touraine, 1940; Magnuson and Votruba-Drzal, 2008; Evans and Fuller-Rowell, 2013). Poverty is understood as capability deprivation (Chamberlain et al., 2016). It is noteworthy that the emphasis is not only on how humans function but also on their having the capability, which is a practical choice, "to achieve outcomes that they value and have reason to value" (Ministry of Finance, 2014; Morrow, 2013; Muñoz, Álvarez-Verdejo, and García-Fernández, 2016; Nikulina and Widom, 2014). Everyone could be deprived of such capabilities in many ways, such as by ignorance, government oppression, lack of financial resources, or false consciousness (Duncan et al., 2012; Evans and Fuller-Rowell, 2013; Guest and Biasini, 2001).

This approach to human well-being emphasizes the importance of freedom of choice, individual heterogeneity, and the multi-dimensional nature of welfare (Kim et al., 2016; Mbabazi and Pyeong, 2014; McLaughlin and Rank, 2018). Insignificant respects, the approach is consistent with the handling of choice within conventional microeconomics consumer theory, although its conceptual foundations enable it to acknowledge the existence of claims, like rights, which normatively dominate utility-based claims (Duncan, Kalil, and Ziol-Guest, 2013; Evans and Cassells, 2014; Fujiura and Yamaki, 2000; Garrett, Ng'andu, and Ferron, 1994). In the most basic sense, functioning consists of "beings and doings" (Ansell, 2016; Ashiabi, 2000; Ashworth, Hill, and Walker, 1994; Bäckman, and Nilsson, 2007). As a result, living may be seen as a set of interrelated functioning (Bhargava et al., 2004; Bloom and Canning, 2001; Bourdillon and Boyden, 2011; Boyden and James, 2014). Essentially, functioning is the states and activities constitutive of a person's being (Bruch and Touraine, 1940; Chamberlain et al., 2016). Examples of functioning can vary from elementary things, such as being healthy, having a good job, and being safe, to more complex states, such as being happy, having self-respect, and being calm (Chiputwa, Spielman, and Qaim, 2015; Corcoran and Chaudry, 1997; Lipina et al., 2013). Moreover, Amartya Sen contends that functioning is crucial to an adequate understanding of the capability approach; capability is conceptualized as a reflection of the freedom to achieve valuable functioning (Deaton, 2006; Dreyer, 2013; Duncan and Magnuson, 2013; Lichter, Shanahan, and Gardner, 2002; Lipina, 2016; Lopez and Velasco, 2011).

In other words, functioning is the subjects of the capabilities referred to in the approach: what we are capable, want to be capable, or should be capable to be and do (Lyytikäinen et al., 2006; Magnuson and Votruba-Drzal, 2008; Duncan and Rodgers, 1988). Therefore, a person's chosen combination of functioning, what they are and do, is part of their overall capability set which represents the functioning they were able to do (Evans, 2004; Farah et al., 2006). Yet, functioning can also be conceptualized in a way that signifies an individual's capabilities (Duncan, Kalil, and Ziol-Guest, 2008; Evans, 2016; Fierman et al., 2016). Eating, starving, and fasting would all be considered functioning (Duncan, Kalil, and Ziol-Guest, 2013; Evans and Cassells, 2014; Guest and Biasini, 2001; Duncan et al., 1998). However, the functioning of fasting differs significantly from that of starving because fasting, unlike starving, involves a choice and is understood as choosing to starve despite the presence of other options (Fujiura and Yamaki, 2000; Garrett, Ng'andu, and Ferron, 1994; Duncan et al., 2012; Evans and Fuller-Rowell, 2013). Consequently, an understanding of what constitutes functioning is inherently tied together with an understanding of capabilities, as defined by this approach (Evans and Kim, 2007, 2013; Hannum, Liu, and Alvarado-Urbina, 2017; Hart, 2008).

Capabilities are the alternative combinations of functioning that are feasible for a person to achieve (Hatcher et al., 2019; Evans and Kutcher, 2011; Hill and Sandfort, 1995). Formulations of capability have two parts: functioning and opportunity freedom (Hobcraft, 1998; Hobcraft and Kiernan, 2001; Evans and Schamberg, 2009; Holzer et al., 2008). This represents the substantive freedom to pursue different functioning combinations (Hong, 2015; Jain and Vaachani, 2006; Jarjoura, Triplett, and Brinker, 2002; Kaplinsky, 2005; Kapoor, 1993; Jones, Vargas, and Villar, 2008). Ultimately, capabilities denote a person's opportunity and ability to generate valuable outcomes, taking into account relevant personal characteristics and external factors (Javanbakht et al., 2015; Jones, Vargas, and Villar, 2007; Kalil, Duncan, and Ziol-Guest, 2016). The important part of this definition is the "freedom to achieve," because if freedom had only instrumental value (valuable as a means to achieve an end) and no intrinsic value (valuable in and of itself) to a person's well-being, then the value of the capability set as a whole would simply be defined by the value of a person's actual combination of functioning (Kendig, Mattingly, and Bianchi, 2014; Kim et al., 2013). Such a definition would not acknowledge the entirety of what a person is capable of doing and their resulting current state due to the nature of the options available to them (Kim et al., 2015; Krason, 2015; Lesner, 2018). Consequently, the capability set outlined by this approach is not merely concerned with achievements (Mazza et al., 2017; Kim et al., 2016). Rather, freedom of choice, in and of itself, is of direct importance to a person's quality of life (Mbabazi and Pyeong, 2014; McLaughlin and Rank, 2018; McLoyd, Aikens, and Burton, 2007). In addition to being the result of capabilities, some functioning is also a prerequisite for capabilities (Mickelson, 2002; Miller and Chen, 2013; Miller et al., 2011). In other words, there is a dual role of some functioning as both ends and instruments (Ministry of Finance, 2014; Morrow, 2013; Muñoz, Álvarez-Verdejo, and García-Fernández, 2016). Examples of functioning that are a direct requirement for capabilities are good nourishment, mental, and physical health, and education (Nikulina and Widom, 2014; Nikulina, Widom, and Czaja, 2011; Okiror, 2015; Penn, 2004; Ratcliffe and McKernan, 2010).

An extension of the capabilities approach was published in 2013 in "*Freedom, Responsibility, and Economics of the Person*" (Ridge, 2002, 2006; Rowntree, 1901; Ryan, Fauth, and Brooks-Gunn, 2006; Sánchez, 2008). This book explores the interconnected concepts of person, responsibility, and freedom in economics, moral philosophy, and politics (Schickedanz, Dreyer, and Halfon, 2015; Schmitz, Wagner, and Menke, 2001; Segretin et al., 2016). Such literature tries to reconcile the rationality and morality of individuals (Serbin et al., 2011; Zembe-Mkabile et al., 2015). It presents a methodological reflection (phenomenology versus Kantian thought) to re-humanize the person, through actions, and through the values and norms that lead to corresponding rights and obligations that must be ordered (Sinervo and Hill, 2011; Song and Lu, 2002; Sripada et al., 2014). The book extends the capabilities approach in a critical form (State House Uganda, 2017; Stewart, 2005; Torres and Wong, 2013; Townsend, 1979; Twikirize et al., 2014). In particular, it considers freedom concerning responsibility, that is, the capacity of people to apply moral constraints to themselves (Vallas, Fremstad, and Ekman, 2015; Van den Waeyenberg, and Hens, 2008; Waddington, 2004; Wells et al., 2010). By contrast, Sen's capability approach considers freedom as purely functional rationality of choice (Ziol-Guest, Duncan, and Kalil, 2009; Ziol-Guest et al., 2012). The next section explores the development and use of the child development index (CDI) which borrows many ideas from the capability approach.

4.4. USE OF THE CHILD DEVELOPMENT INDEX (CDI)

The CDI is an index combining performance measures specific to children (Ansell, 2016; Ashiabi, 2000; Ashworth, Hill, and Walker, 1994; Bäckman, and Nilsson, 2007; Bhargava et al., 2004). This may incorporate education, health, and nutrition which are then amalgamated to produce a score on a scale of 0 to 100 (Bloom and Canning, 2001; Bourdillon and Boyden, 2011; Boyden and James, 2014; Bruch and Touraine, 1940). A zero score would be the best (Duncan and Rodgers, 1988; Evans, 2004; Farah et al., 2006). The higher the score, the worse children are faring (Chamberlain et al., 2016; Chiputwa, Spielman, and Qaim, 2015). The CDI was developed by Save the Children UK in 2008 through the contributions of Terry McKinley, Director of the Centre for Development Policy and Research at the School of Oriental and African Studies (SOAS), University of London, with support from Katerina Kyril. The indicators which make up the index were chosen because they are easily available, commonly understood, and indicative of child wellbeing (Corcoran and Chaudry, 1997; Deaton, 2006; Dreyer, 2013; Duncan and Magnuson, 2013). Perhaps the CDI reflects the diversity and range in poverty indicators across nations, even where all the members of the cluster are considered to be middle-income or high-income countries (see Figure 4.4).

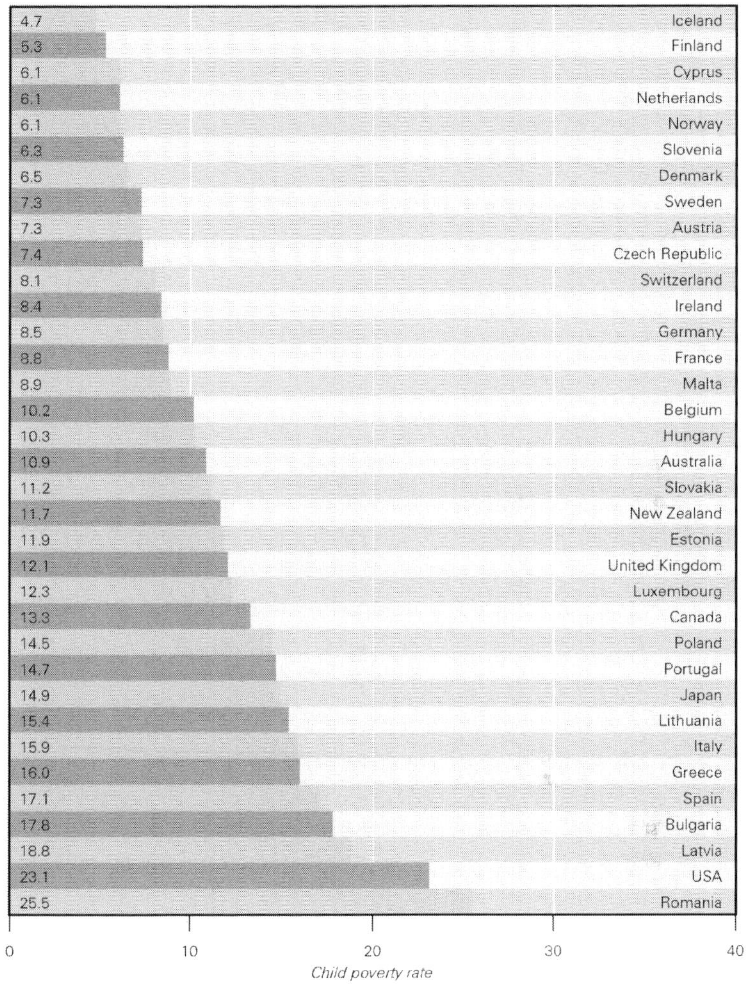

Figure 4.4. The variances in child poverty rates among wealthier nations.

Source: UNICEF via seen this.

Health is an important contributor to the CDI (Lichter, Shanahan, and Gardner, 2002; Lipina, 2016; Lipina et al., 2013). For example, the analysts will consider the under-five mortality rate (Lopez and Velasco, 2011; Lyytikäinen et al., 2006; Magnuson and Votruba-Drzal, 2008). This is the probability of dying between birth and 5 years of age, expressed as a percentage on a scale of 0 to 340 deaths per 1,000 live births (Jones, Vargas, and Villar, 2008; Kendig, Mattingly, and Bianchi, 2014; Kim et al., 2013). Hence, a zero score in this component equals an under-five mortality rate of 0 deaths per 1,000 live births, and a score of 100 equals our upper bound of 340 deaths per 1,000 live births (Duncan et al., 1998; Evans and Kim, 2007; Hannum, Liu, and Alvarado-Urbina, 2017). The upper bound is higher than any country has ever reached (Evans and Kim, 2013; Hart, 2008; Hatcher et al., 2019). Niger came the closest in the 1990s with 320 under-five deaths per 1,000 live births (Evans and Kutcher, 2011; Hill and Sandfort, 1995; Hobcraft, 1998; Hobcraft and Kiernan, 2001). Nutrition is the second consideration when compiling the CDI (Evans and Schamberg, 2009; Holzer et al., 2008; Hong, 2015). In this case, the analyst will consider the percentage of under-fives who are moderately or severely underweight (Jain and Vaachani, 2006; Jarjoura, Triplett, and Brinker, 2002; Javanbakht et al., 2015). The common definition of moderately or severely underweight, which we use here, is being below two standard deviations of the median weight for age of the reference population (Duncan, Kalil, and Ziol-Guest, 2008; Evans, 2016; Fierman et al., 2016). The last component of the CDI is education (Jones, Vargas, and Villar, 2007; Kalil, Duncan, and Ziol-Guest, 2016; Kaplinsky, 2005; Kapoor, 1993). Analysts will consider the percentage of primary-school-age children who are not enrolled in school (Kim et al., 2015; Krason, 2015; Lesner, 2018; Mazza et al., 2017). For our measure of education deprivation, we use the opposite of the Net Primary Enrolment rate-i.e., 100-the NER (McLoyd, Aikens, and Burton, 2007; Mickelson, 2002; Miller and Chen, 2013; Miller et al., 2011). This gives us the percentage of primary-school-age children who are not enrolled (Ministry of Finance, 2014; Morrow, 2013; Muñoz, Álvarez-Verdejo, and García-Fernández, 2016; Nikulina and Widom, 2014).

The CDI tells us about how children are faring around the world (Nikulina, Widom, and Czaja, 2011; Okiror, 2015; Penn, 2004; Ratcliffe and McKernan, 2010). For example, it may explain whether some countries are making good progress in improving child well-being (Ridge, 2002; Rowntree, 1901; Ryan, Fauth, and Brooks-Gunn, 2006; Sánchez, 2008). It can be used for comparative analysis between and among nations. The CDI answers these questions (Ridge, 2006; Schickedanz, Dreyer, and Halfon, 2015; Schmitz, Wagner, and Menke, 2001). The index measures child well-being over three periods from 1990 (Segretin et al., 2016; Serbin et al., 2011). Japan is in the first place, scoring just 0.4. Niger in Africa is in 137th place, with the highest score, 58, in 2000–2006 (Sinervo and Hill, 2011; Song and Lu, 2002; Sripada et al., 2014; State House Uganda, 2017). Overall, child well-being has improved by 34% since 1990, but progress is slow (Stewart, 2005; Torres and Wong, 2013; Townsend, 1979; Twikirize et al., 2014;

Vallas, Fremstad, and Ekman, 2015). Children are doing worse in Sub-Saharan Africa than in any other region (Van den Waeyenberg, and Hens, 2008; Waddington, 2004; Wells et al., 2010). Africa scores 35 in the Index, reflecting the high level of deprivation in primary schooling, child health, and child nutrition (Zembe-Mkabile et al., 2015; Ziol-Guest, Duncan, and Kalil, 2009; Ziol-Guest et al., 2012). It is also making the slowest progress, improving child well-being by only 20% over 1990–2006 (Ansell, 2016; Dreyer, 2013; Evans, 2016; Evans and Kim, 2013; Jones, Vargas, and Villar, 2007; Mbabazi and Pyeong, 2014; Schickedanz, Dreyer, and Halfon, 2015). However, progress has been very mixed because some countries in Africa have done incredibly well, while others did spectacularly badly (Ashiabi, 2000; Duncan and Magnuson, 2013; Fierman et al., 2016). Countries like Malawi cut child deprivation in half, enrolling more than 90% of primary school children (Hart, 2008; Kalil, Duncan, and Ziol-Guest, 2016; Kaplinsky, 2005; McLaughlin and Rank, 2018; Schmitz, Wagner, and Menke, 2001). However, some of the poorest children in Africa live in countries suffering from conflict and poor governance; such as Zimbabwe and the Democratic Republic of Congo (Ashworth, Hill, and Walker, 1994; Lichter, Shanahan, and Gardner, 2002; Duncan, Kalil, and Ziol-Guest, 2013). Slow progress in reducing child mortality and malnutrition is a particular problem since one in six babies born in Africa will not live to see their 5th birthday (Hatcher et al., 2019; Kapoor, 1993; McLoyd, Aikens, and Burton, 2007). Rich and poor countries worldwide must urgently choose to tackle this problem (Bäckman, and Nilsson, 2007; Bhargava et al., 2004; Lipina, 2016; Evans and Cassells, 2014).

East Asia has made considerable progress in child well-being in recent years, improving it by 45% over 1990–2006, reducing deprivation to a score of just 8.5 (Evans and Kutcher, 2011; Mickelson, 2002; Segretin et al., 2016; Jones, Vargas, and Villar, 2008). Only one other developing region, Latin America, scores better (Bloom and Canning, 2001; Lipina et al., 2013). Asia has the best level of primary school enrollment and has managed to halve its child mortality rate between 1990 and 2006 (Fujiura and Yamaki, 2000; Hill and Sandfort, 1995; Kendig, Mattingly, and Bianchi, 2014). Much of this progress is because of China's significant improvement, where almost two-thirds of the region's children live (Miller and Chen, 2013; Miller et al., 2011). China has made tremendous progress in increasing people's incomes (Bourdillon and Boyden, 2011; Lopez and Velasco, 2011; Garrett, Ng'andu, and Ferron, 1994). Nonetheless, 417,000 children under the age of 5 years still died in China in 2006 alone (Hobcraft, 1998; Kim et al., 2013).

Countries like Malaysia and Thailand did even better in all three of the areas the CDI measures (Muñoz, Álvarez-Verdejo, and García-Fernández, 2016; Sripada et al., 2014). However, as in other regions of the world, government policy plays an important role in children's lives (Boyden and James, 2014; Lyytikäinen et al., 2006; Duncan et al., 2012). For example, Myanmar saw almost no improvement at all (Bruch and Touraine, 1940; Magnuson and Votruba-Drzal, 2008; Evans and Fuller-Rowell, 2013). And in many countries, the poorest, most isolated groups are being left behind (Hobcraft and Kiernan, 2001; Kim et al., 2015; Nikulina and Widom, 2014).

South Asia has a high level of deprivation, scoring 26.4 (Guest and Biasini, 2001; Evans and Schamberg, 2009; Krason, 2015; Lesner, 2018). This is three times worse than East Asia (Nikulina, Widom, and Czaja, 2011; State House Uganda, 2017; Stewart, 2005; Torres and Wong, 2013). It is also making slow progress, improving child well-being by just 32% between 1990 and 2006, compared to East Asia's 45% improvement (Chamberlain et al., 2016). This is because India (where almost three-quarters of the region's children live) made the least progress of any country in South Asia; just a 27% improvement (Duncan et al., 1998; Mazza et al., 2017). In this region, child nutrition is a substantial obstacle because almost 1 in 2 children is underweight (Chiputwa, Spielman, and Qaim, 2015; Evans and Kim, 2007; Okiror, 2015; Townsend, 1979). The region's enrollment indicator improved by 59% while its nutrition indicator improved by only 14% (Corcoran and Chaudry, 1997; Deaton, 2006; Kim et al., 2016; Twikirize et al., 2014). Higher levels of economic growth in the region are not widely translating into reduced child deprivation (Evans, 2004; Jain and Vaachani, 2006; Ministry of Finance, 2014; Vallas, Fremstad, and Ekman, 2015).

The Latin America and the Caribbean region made substantial progress in improving child well-being in the 1990s, scoring 6.8 in the index of child deprivation (Duncan and Rodgers, 1988; Holzer et al., 2008). This is the lowest of any developing country region (Farah et al., 2006). It made the most percentage improvement of any region in the world, reducing child deprivation by 57% over the period, 1990–2006 (Duncan, Kalil, and Ziol-Guest, 2008; Morrow, 2013; Song and Lu, 2002; Ziol-Guest et al., 2012). This improvement was largely driven by reductions in child mortality and increases in primary school enrollment (Hannum, Liu, and Alvarado-Urbina, 2017; Penn, 2004; Ratcliffe; Van den Waeyenberg, and Hens, 2008; Sinervo and Hill, 2011). The region's child mortality rate is now the lowest of any developing region (Hong, 2015; Jarjoura, Triplett, and Brinker, 2002; Ridge, 2002; Waddington, 2004; Ziol-Guest, Duncan, and Kalil, 2009). The region's poorer countries, like Peru and El Salvador, have started to catch up with the levels of child well-being seen in better-off countries in the region (Javanbakht et al., 2015; Wells et al., 2010).

The Middle East and North Africa region score 11.2 in this index, worse than East Asia but only a third as bad as Sub-Saharan Africa (Rowntree, 1901; Ryan, Fauth, and Brooks-Gunn, 2006; Sánchez, 2008; Ridge, 2006). The region has reduced its level of child deprivation by 41% between 1990 and 2006 (Serbin et al., 2011; Zembe-Mkabile et al., 2015). However, there is considerable variation within the region (Duncan et al., 2012; Evans and Fuller-Rowell, 2013; Guest and Biasini, 2001). Yemen is doing poorly, with a large increase in malnutrition over the period (Ansell, 2016; Ashiabi, 2000; Ashworth, Hill, and Walker, 1994; Bäckman, and Nilsson, 2007). Moreover, in several countries, such as Djibouti and Jordan, progress has stalled in some areas (Ansell, 2016; Ashiabi, 2000; Ashworth, Hill, and Walker, 1994; Bäckman, and Nilsson, 2007; Bhargava et al., 2004). In addition, the region includes Iraq, Lebanon, and the occupied Palestinian territory where child deprivation has increased (Ansell, 2016; Dreyer, 2013; Evans, 2016; Evans and Kim, 2013; Jones, Vargas, and Villar, 2007; Mbabazi and Pyeong, 2014; Schickedanz, Dreyer, and Halfon, 2015). In contrast, several large countries such as Morocco, Egypt, and Algeria have made substantial improvements (Ashiabi, 2000; Duncan and Magnuson, 2013; Fierman et al., 2016). Again, little improvement has been made in reducing child malnutrition in the region as a whole (Ashworth, Hill, and Walker, 1994; Lichter, Shanahan, and Gardner, 2002; Duncan, Kalil, and Ziol-Guest, 2013).

The region containing Central and Eastern Europe and the Commonwealth of Independent States, for which data are much sparser in the early 1990s, saw an improvement of almost 15% in its index score between 1995 and 1999; and 2000–2006 (Bäckman, and Nilsson, 2007; Bhargava et al., 2004; Lipina, 2016; Evans and Cassells, 2014). Its score stands at 9.2, slightly worse than East Asia and slightly better than the Middle East and North Africa (Bhargava et al., 2004; Bloom and Canning, 2001; Bourdillon and Boyden, 2011; Boyden and James, 2014). Turkey, with a large child population, made the most progress in the region, reducing its score from 20 in the early 1990s to 7 for 2000–2006 (Bloom and Canning, 2001; Bourdillon and Boyden, 2011; Boyden and James, 2014; Bruch and Touraine, 1940). The CDI shows that there is a low level of deprivation in developed countries in the three basic areas of child rights that it measures (Bloom and Canning, 2001; Lipina et al., 2013). On a scale of 0–100, these countries score 2.1, the lowest regional Index score worldwide (Bourdillon and Boyden, 2011;

Lopez and Velasco, 2011; Garrett, Ng'andu, and Ferron, 1994). There is still some variation between these countries, however (Boyden and James, 2014; Lyytikäinen et al., 2006; Duncan et al., 2012). For example, the United States has a child mortality rate that is twice Japan's and worse even than that of Cuba's (Bruch and Touraine, 1940; Chamberlain et al., 2016). This chapter closes with a review of some localized and informal measures of child poverty that can be used as operational guides in the absence of national and international standards.

4.5. LOCALIZED MEASURES OF CHILDHOOD POVERTY

In the absence of suitable national and international standards, communities may develop their localized measures of child poverty (Bruch and Touraine, 1940; Magnuson and Votruba-Drzal, 2008; Evans and Fuller-Rowell, 2013). The success or failure of these measures will depend on the extent to which research and consultation have taken place before adopting them (Chamberlain et al., 2016; Chiputwa, Spielman, and Qaim, 2015). In some cases, the community may even have to experiment with the measures before they can become fully accepted (Chiputwa, Spielman, and Qaim, 2015; Corcoran and Chaudry, 1997; Lipina et al., 2013). When developing these measures, the community will bear in mind the principles and guidance that are provided by existing national and international law or convention (Chiputwa, Spielman, and Qaim, 2015; Evans and Kim, 2007; Okiror, 2015; Townsend, 1979). They will also take into consideration the local customs and perspectives of the frontline communities (Corcoran and Chaudry, 1997; Deaton, 2006; Dreyer, 2013; Duncan and Magnuson, 2013). For example, the United Nations (UN) Convention on the Rights of the Child contains 54 articles covering almost every aspect of the rights and wellbeing of children (Corcoran and Chaudry, 1997; Deaton, 2006; Kim et al., 2016; Twikirize et al., 2014). It is a comprehensive legal text negotiated and agreed to by 192 heads of state (Deaton, 2006; Dreyer, 2013; Duncan and Magnuson, 2013; Lichter, Shanahan, and Gardner, 2002; Lipina, 2016; Lopez and Velasco, 2011).

There is a substantial body of research and statistics that indicate that being wealthy does not necessarily indicate greater performance on the poverty indices (Duncan and Rodgers, 1988; Evans, 2004; Farah et al., 2006). Indeed, there are cases of relative poverty that exist in some of the most advanced nations (Duncan and Rodgers, 1988; Holzer et al., 2008). By developing localized measures of poverty, it is possible to tie performance to targets that make sense to local people (Duncan, Kalil, and Ziol-Guest, 2013; Evans and Cassells, 2014; Fujiura and Yamaki, 2000; Garrett, Ng'andu, and Ferron, 1994). Approaches that take into account local conditions are seen to be preferable to the homogenous approaches that have been used in the past with less-than-ideal results (Duncan, Kalil, and Ziol-Guest, 2013; Evans and Cassells, 2014; Guest and Biasini, 2001; Duncan et al., 1998). Indeed, some developing nations see the poverty rankings as yet another sign that the hegemony that once dominated them still exists (Duncan, Kalil, and Ziol-Guest, 2008; Evans, 2016; Fierman et al., 2016). Others question the notion of child poverty because it has become so attached to Western and European notions of superiority (Duncan et al., 2012; Evans and Fuller-Rowell, 2013; Guest and Biasini, 2001). As we can see in Figure 4.5, relative poverty exists in industrialized nations. Moreover, the nature of relative poverty means that it can never be eliminated since it occurs.

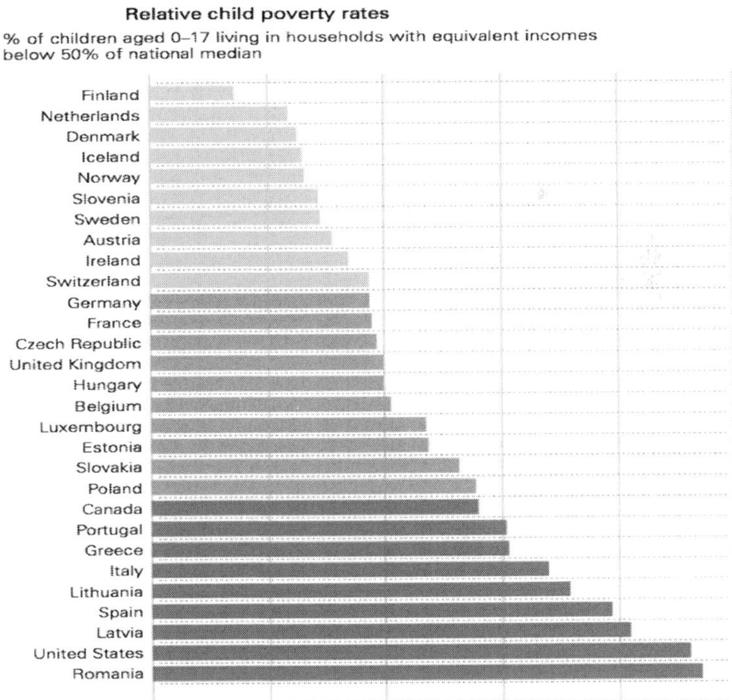

Figure 4.5. Relative poverty in the most developed nations.

Source: The Globalist.

Typically, the localized measure will begin by identifying a social problem such as poverty (Duncan et al., 1998; Evans and Kim, 2007; Hannum, Liu, and Alvarado-Urbina, 2017). This can then be reconstructed and re-conceived into very local terms (Duncan et al., 1998; Mazza et al., 2017). From that element, the policy planners can work out some of the underlying factors that either cause or sustain that social problem (Evans and Kim, 2007, 2013; Hannum, Liu, and Alvarado-Urbina, 2017; Hart, 2008). Moreover, those factors that prevent an effective response can also be included (Evans and Kim, 2013; Hart, 2008; Hatcher et al., 2019). All these factors can then be developed into individualized indicators or a unified indicator of child poverty (Evans and Kutcher, 2011; Hill and Sandfort, 1995; Hobcraft, 1998; Hobcraft and Kiernan, 2001). The local index of child poverty will also have to explain what it means to be poor and not to be poor in very precise terms (Evans and Kutcher, 2011; Mickelson, 2002; Segretin et al., 2016; Jones, Vargas, and Villar, 2008). This will then allow for a comparative analysis and even benchmarking performance of the various members of the community or even segments of the local population (Evans and Schamberg, 2009; Holzer et al., 2008; Hong, 2015). Some countries have found these localized measures to be so successful that they end up sharing them with other localities (Evans, 2004; Farah et al., 2006). Ultimately, these can lead to the development of a composite national or regional or even continental index of child poverty (Evans, 2004; Jain and Vaachani, 2006; Ministry of Finance, 2014; Vallas, Fremstad, and Ekman, 2015).

CHAPTER 4 SUMMARY

The measurement of child poverty can be in both absolute and relative terms. The former has the advantage of consistency, while the latter has the advantage of context. Given the merits and demerits of measuring absolute and relative poverty, most jurisdictions use them in combination. The capability approach stems out of the acknowledgment of the complex and multi-faceted aspects of poverty, including health, education, income, opportunity, and choice. Indeed, the capability approach has been used to develop a number of life quality indices which help in comparing levels of child poverty as well as their impact on communities. At the same time, local communities have also come up with their own internalized measures that are uniquely relevant to them. Having understood some of the factors that contribute to child poverty, the next chapter tries to establish causation beyond mere associations.

Chapter 5

Causes of Childhood Poverty

CONTENTS

Although researchers are reluctant to make absolute claims about causation, there have emerged certain factors that are strongly associated with child poverty. These can be within a generation, across generations, in micro and macro systems, inherited deprivation from parents, and even poor policy formulation. This chapter attempts to shed light on how these factors and contextual issues might be linked to child poverty or even cause it. In so doing, this chapter lays the foundation for dealing with child poverty by addressing each of these issues. Indeed, by the end of this chapter, the reader should have an idea of how policy measures have been used to tackle gaps and problems in all these areas.

5.1. INTRA-GENERAL CAUSES OF CHILDHOOD POVERTY

Even within a single generation, inequalities might mean that child poverty continues to rise despite the general prosperity of a community (Farah et al., 2006). Certainly, we have seen this trend in developed countries that are still dealing with the problem despite their vast resources and seemingly sound social support systems (Fujiura and Yamaki, 2000; Garrett, Ng'andu, and Ferron, 1994; Duncan et al., 2012; Evans and Fuller-Rowell, 2013). The world is falling short in its promise and commitment to ensure that every child enjoys a safe and nurturing childhood (Fujiura and Yamaki, 2000; Hill and Sandfort, 1995; Kendig, Mattingly, and Bianchi, 2014). The Convention on the Rights of the Child, which came to force in 1989, provides that children, regardless of their location, have the right to a childhood in which they can learn, play, be healthy, and develop (Guest and Biasini, 2001; Evans and Schamberg, 2009; Krason, 2015; Lesner, 2018). However, 15 years after the adoption of the Convention and after more than 15 years of market-led economic growth, governments, and the international community are still far from fulfilling children's rights and creating a world fit for children (Hannum, Liu, and Alvarado-Urbina, 2017; Penn, 2004; Ratcliffe; Van den Waeyenberg, and Hens, 2008; Sinervo and Hill, 2011).

Over half of the children in the developing world live in poverty (Hart, 2008; Kalil, Duncan, and Ziol-Guest, 2016; Kaplinsky, 2005; McLaughlin and Rank, 2018; Schmitz, Wagner, and Menke, 2001). There have been attempts to create minimum standards to protect children (Hatcher et al., 2019; Evans and Kutcher, 2011; Hill and Sandfort, 1995). However, these standards are largely ignored by the developing world, where regimes are more focused on entrenching themselves into power (Hatcher et al., 2019;

Kapoor, 1993; McLoyd, Aikens, and Burton, 2007). One of the problems is the piecemeal approach to development which leaves certain countries perpetually on the bottom heap (Hobcraft and Kiernan, 2001; Kim et al., 2015; Nikulina and Widom, 2014). There is a lack of coherence and consistency in development economics and the hegemony that rules the world today such that the poorer nations never really get a chance to master their own destiny (Hobcraft, 1998; Hobcraft and Kiernan, 2001; Evans and Schamberg, 2009; Holzer et al., 2008). One of the biggest victims of this failure are children who have to put up with substandard livelihoods (Hobcraft, 1998; Kim et al., 2013). Even children living in a highly industrialized and well-organized country such as Germany may still be susceptible to child poverty (see Figure 5.1). That suggestions other problems apart from income inequality across nations.

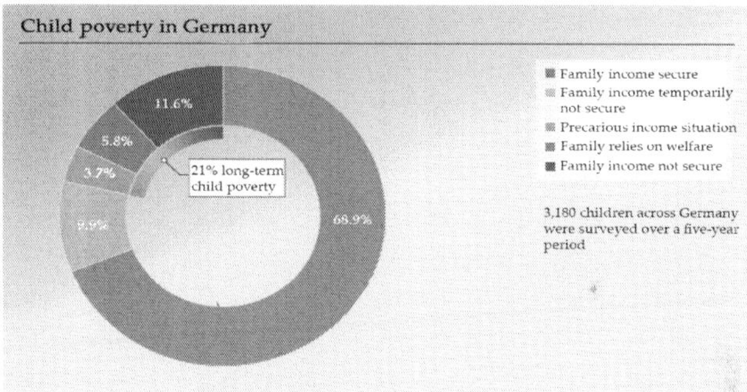

Figure 5.1. Child poverty in Germany.

Source: Bertelsmann Foundation via DW.

While some nations have transformed into economic, political, and social powerhouses over the last 50 years; others have markedly declined (Hong, 2015; Jain and Vaachani, 2006; Jarjoura, Triplett, and Brinker, 2002; Kaplinsky, 2005; Kapoor, 1993; Jones, Vargas, and Villar, 2008). This is particularly true of Sub-Saharan countries where a series of bad governments have sowed the seeds of habitual violence and instability (Hong, 2015; Jarjoura, Triplett, and Brinker, 2002; Ridge, 2002; Waddington, 2004; Ziol-Guest, Duncan, and Kalil, 2009). The colonial legacy of dependency means that many of the policy formulations in the developing world are poor imitations of what has been done in the developed world (Jain and Vaachani, 2006; Jarjoura, Triplett, and Brinker, 2002; Javanbakht et al., 2015). The unequal access to trade under the supposedly "free trade" regime means that these poorer countries rarely get a good price for their largely agricultural produce (Javanbakht et al., 2015; Jones, Vargas, and Villar, 2007; Kalil, Duncan, and Ziol-Guest, 2016).

In the meantime, those industrialized nations can secure a significant markup on the technologies that they habitually export to the developing world (Javanbakht et al., 2015; Wells et al., 2010). Worse still, some of the industrialized nations have sowed the seeds of discomfort and regime instability in the developing world for their geopolitical reasons (Jones, Vargas, and Villar, 2007; Kalil, Duncan, and Ziol-Guest, 2016; Kaplinsky, 2005; Kapoor, 1993). This has meant that development has taken a heavy toll to the extent that the life of a child born in the poorest nations is in no way comparative to one born in the richest (Jones, Vargas, and Villar, 2008; Kendig, Mattingly, and Bianchi, 2014; Kim et al., 2013). Regardless of their talent, character, effort, and ambition; these children are doomed to failure right from birth and up to their death (Kendig, Mattingly, and Bianchi, 2014; Kim et al., 2013). The next section focuses on some transgenerational causes of child poverty.

5.2. TRANSGENERATIONAL CAUSES OF CHILDHOOD POVERTY

Children can inherit unfair and deprived social circumstances which limit their ability to prosper (Kim et al., 2015; Krason, 2015; Lesner, 2018). The consequences of child poverty also mean that these children carry the same burdens to their offspring (Kim et al., 2015; Krason, 2015; Lesner, 2018; Mazza et al., 2017). The creates entire generations of people that are living in abject poverty with no realistic prospect of escaping their predicament (Kim et al., 2016; Mbabazi and Pyeong, 2014; McLaughlin and Rank, 2018). Children exposed to family poverty have been found to have higher morbidity and mortality rates, poorer mental health and cognitive outcomes, and reduced life chances across a wide range of life domains (Lichter, Shanahan, and Gardner, 2002; Lipina, 2016; Lipina et al., 2013). Throughout extensive studies, half the families in the study experienced poverty on at least one occasion (Mbabazi and Pyeong, 2014; McLaughlin and Rank, 2018; McLoyd, Aikens, and Burton, 2007). Only a very small minority of families experienced persistent poverty over decades (McLoyd, Aikens, and Burton, 2007; Mickelson, 2002; Miller and Chen, 2013; Miller et al., 2011). Logistic regressions with time lag show that family poverty predicts subsequent adversities and adverse events predict subsequent poverty (Mickelson, 2002; Miller and Chen, 2013; Miller et al., 2011). For ethnic minorities (see Figure 5.2), the risk of falling into child poverty is higher than those for the dominant race in a given community (Miller and Chen, 2013; Miller et al., 2011).

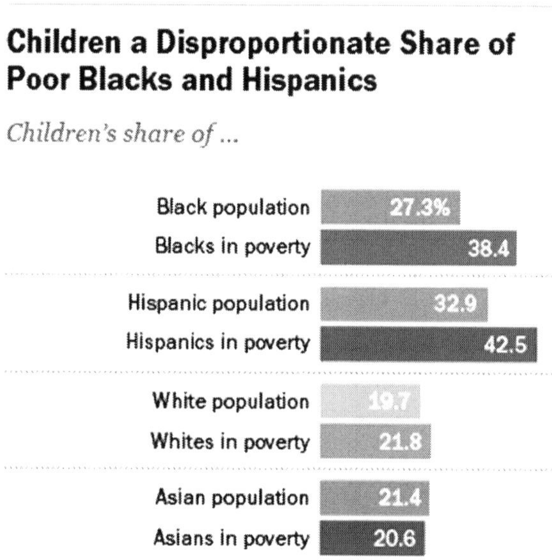

Figure 5.2. Child poverty among ethnic minorities in the USA.

Source: US Census Bureau, "Income and Poverty in the United States" (2013).

It is common for families to move in and out of poverty, as their circumstances are affected by such adversities as unemployment and marital breakdown (Mazza et al., 2017; Kim et al., 2016). There is, however, very little known about the extent to which poverty is experienced by children over their early life course, particularly in community samples (Lopez and Velasco, 2011; Lyytikäinen et al., 2006; Magnuson and Votruba-Drzal, 2008). Poverty affects about 20% of families at any time point (Lyytikäinen et al., 2006; Magnuson and Votruba-Drzal, 2008; Duncan and Rodgers, 1988). Experiences of poverty and adversity are common and may vary greatly over the child's early life course (Ministry of Finance, 2014; Morrow, 2013; Muñoz, Álvarez-Verdejo, and García-Fernández, 2016). In assessing the health consequences of poverty, it is important to distinguish the timing and chronicity of early life course experiences of poverty and adversity (Ministry of Finance, 2014; Morrow, 2013; Muñoz, Álvarez-Verdejo, and García-Fernández, 2016; Nikulina and Widom, 2014). The adverse consequences of poverty are many and varied (Muñoz, Álvarez-Verdejo, and García-Fernández, 2016; Sripada et al., 2014).

With occasional exceptions, economically disadvantaged persons are at increased risk of worse mental and physical health (Nikulina and Widom, 2014; Nikulina, Widom, and Czaja, 2011; Okiror, 2015; Penn, 2004; Ratcliffe and McKernan, 2010). They are more likely to have higher mortality rates for most diseases (Nikulina, Widom, and Czaja, 2011; Okiror, 2015; Penn, 2004; Ratcliffe and McKernan, 2010). Socioeconomically disadvantaged families have children who are more likely to have developmental delays as well as higher rates of morbidity and mortality (Nikulina, Widom, and Czaja, 2011; State House Uganda, 2017; Stewart, 2005; Torres and Wong, 2013). Children reared in economically disadvantaged families are not only more likely to have poorer health in childhood, but their health as adults also appears to be adversely affected, independent of their economic standing in adulthood (Ridge, 2002, 2006; Rowntree, 1901; Ryan, Fauth, and Brooks-Gunn, 2006; Sánchez, 2008). There is also evidence that life stress and adversity are linked to poverty and may contribute to the poor health of the economically disadvantaged (Ridge, 2002; Rowntree, 1901; Ryan, Fauth, and Brooks-Gunn, 2006; Sánchez, 2008).

Despite the documented impact of poverty and adversity on child and subsequent adult health, there is little known about the pattern of child exposure to poverty and adversity over the early life course (Ridge, 2006; Schickedanz, Dreyer, and Halfon, 2015; Schmitz, Wagner, and Menke, 2001). Further, little is known about the early-life adversities experienced by children from socioeconomically disadvantaged families, and the extent to which these adversities persist after the child leaves home (Rowntree, 1901; Ryan, Fauth, and Brooks-Gunn, 2006; Sánchez, 2008; Ridge, 2006). There is a need to know whether both poverty and life adversities are inter-generationally transmitted (Schickedanz, Dreyer, and Halfon, 2015; Schmitz, Wagner, and Menke, 2001; Segretin et al., 2016). Efforts to specifically document the intra and intergenerational transmission of poverty in economically-developed countries are few (Segretin et al., 2016; Serbin et al., 2011). In any event, past studies may not provide an accurate indication of what is happening in the current period (Serbin et al., 2011; Zembe-Mkabile et al., 2015). Prospective longitudinal studies of the intergenerational transmission of poverty may take 20–30 years to provide data (Serbin et al., 2011; Zembe-Mkabile et al., 2015). For example, the most detailed data on the intergenerational transmission of poverty comes from the Panel Study of Income Dynamics (PSID), which commenced in

1968 (Sinervo and Hill, 2011; Song and Lu, 2002; Sripada et al., 2014). The PSID found that poverty is not a rare event, with one-third of US children experiencing at least a year of living in poverty (Sinervo and Hill, 2011; Song and Lu, 2002; Sripada et al., 2014; State House Uganda, 2017). The PSID also found that most families living in poverty experienced temporary periods of poverty, moving out of poverty once their circumstances changed (State House Uganda, 2017; Stewart, 2005; Torres and Wong, 2013; Townsend, 1979; Twikirize et al., 2014). Only some 5% of children in this population sample experienced persistent poverty, defined as living in poverty for 10 years or more (Stewart, 2005; Torres and Wong, 2013; Townsend, 1979; Twikirize et al., 2014; Vallas, Fremstad, and Ekman, 2015).

Socioeconomic status in general, and poverty in particular, are associated with a wide number of structural (human capital) and behavioral or social (social capital) characteristics (Vallas, Fremstad, and Ekman, 2015; Van den Waeyenberg, and Hens, 2008; Waddington, 2004; Wells et al., 2010). Many of these characteristics may contribute to the persistence of intergenerational poverty (Van den Waeyenberg, and Hens, 2008; Waddington, 2004; Wells et al., 2010). The structural factors involve income and assets, patterns of marriage and employment (or unemployment), levels of education, and skill attainment (Zembe-Mkabile et al., 2015; Ziol-Guest, Duncan, and Kalil, 2009; Ziol-Guest et al., 2012). The behavioral and social factors include a wide range of behavior (e.g., lifestyle, patterns of parenting), as well as aspirations and attitudes-for example, to having children, child-rearing, and child care (Ziol-Guest, Duncan, and Kalil, 2009; Ziol-Guest et al., 2012). To the extent that there is an intergenerational transmission of poverty, there is also likely to be the intergenerational transmission of the many related structural and behavioral characteristics associated with poverty (Zembe-Mkabile et al., 2015; Ziol-Guest, Duncan, and Kalil, 2009; Ziol-Guest et al., 2012). While there are only a limited number of studies tracking the intergenerational transmission of poverty, their findings are broadly consistent (Van den Waeyenberg, and Hens, 2008; Waddington, 2004; Wells et al., 2010). These studies confirm that children reared in poverty, are more likely to themselves experience poverty in adulthood (Vallas, Fremstad, and Ekman, 2015; Van den Waeyenberg, and Hens, 2008; Waddington, 2004; Wells et al., 2010).

Three long-term trends are contributing to increases in the proportion of the population living in poverty (Stewart, 2005; Torres and Wong, 2013; Townsend, 1979; Twikirize et al., 2014; Vallas, Fremstad, and Ekman, 2015). If these trends continue then the proportion of populations living in poverty in developed economies can be expected to increase, irrespective of the capacity of some individuals to improve their social and economic circumstances (State House Uganda, 2017; Stewart, 2005; Torres and Wong, 2013; Townsend, 1979; Twikirize et al., 2014). These trends involve changes in family composition, changes like labor markets, and the aging of the population (Sinervo and Hill, 2011; Song and Lu, 2002; Sripada et al., 2014). In developed countries, the poor are largely comprised of three groups: single mothers, the under-employed or unemployed, and (aged) pensioners (Sinervo and Hill, 2011; Song and Lu, 2002; Sripada et al., 2014; State House Uganda, 2017). While some factors contributing to poverty are increasing over time, there is little known about how these factors might impact the early life course (Serbin et al., 2011; Zembe-Mkabile et al., 2015). There is a high level of persistence in family poverty across the child's early life course and generations (Serbin et al., 2011; Zembe-Mkabile et al., 2015). There is a high level of persistence in life adversities (stressful life events) across the child's early life course and generations (Segretin et al., 2016; Serbin et al., 2011). Poverty over the child's early life course predicts subsequent adversities, but adversities do not predict subsequent poverty (Schickedanz, Dreyer, and Halfon, 2015; Schmitz, Wagner, and Menke, 2001; Segretin et al., 2016). The next section focuses on the micro and macro systems that foster child poverty.

5.3. MICRO AND MACRO SYSTEMS OF CHILDHOOD POVERTY

Child poverty can occur at and be a consequence of micro and macro structures within society (Rowntree, 1901; Ryan, Fauth, and Brooks-Gunn, 2006; Sánchez, 2008; Ridge, 2006). Macrosociology is a large-scale approach to sociology, emphasizing the analysis of social systems and populations at the structural level, often at a necessarily high level of theoretical abstraction (Ridge, 2006; Schickedanz, Dreyer, and Halfon, 2015; Schmitz, Wagner, and Menke, 2001). Though macro sociology does concern itself with individuals, families, and other constituent aspects of a society, it does so about a larger social system of which such elements are a part (Ridge, 2002, 2006; Rowntree, 1901; Ryan, Fauth, and Brooks-Gunn, 2006; Sánchez, 2008). The approach is also able to analyze generalized collectivities, such as "the city" and "the church" (Ridge, 2002; Rowntree, 1901; Ryan, Fauth, and Brooks-Gunn, 2006; Sánchez, 2008). In contrast, micro-sociology focuses on the individual social agency (Nikulina, Widom, and Czaja,

2011; State House Uganda, 2017; Stewart, 2005; Torres and Wong, 2013). Macrosociology, however, deals with broad societal trends that can later be applied to smaller features of society, or vice versa (Nikulina, Widom, and Czaja, 2011; Okiror, 2015; Penn, 2004; Ratcliffe and McKernan, 2010).

To differentiate, macro sociology deals with issues such as war as a whole; the distress of Third-World countries; poverty on a national/international level; and environmental deprivation, whereas microsociology analyzes issues such as the individual features of war (e.g., camaraderie, one's pleasure in violence, etc.); the role of women in third-world countries; poverty's effect on "the family"; and how immigration impacts a country's environment (Nikulina and Widom, 2014; Nikulina, Widom, and Czaja, 2011; Okiror, 2015; Penn, 2004; Ratcliffe and McKernan, 2010). One of the most striking patterns is the interrelationships between different categories of the poor (Muñoz, Álvarez-Verdejo, and García-Fernández, 2016; Sripada et al., 2014). For example, we already know that in the most industrialized nations; the poor are likely to be children, pensioners, people with disabilities, and ethnic minorities (Ministry of Finance, 2014; Morrow, 2013; Muñoz, Álvarez-Verdejo, and García-Fernández, 2016). Although some of these patterns may be reflected in the developing world, they seem to be uniquely relevant to the most industrialized nations (Ministry of Finance, 2014; Morrow, 2013; Muñoz, Álvarez-Verdejo, and García-Fernández, 2016; Nikulina and Widom, 2014). They represent a paradox of deprivation amidst plenty, and they are the foundation of relative poverty, which is increasingly being considered when preparing international statistics (Miller and Chen, 2013; Miller et al., 2011). The European Union has distinguished itself as a beacon of human rights and equality (Mickelson, 2002; Miller and Chen, 2013; Miller et al., 2011). However, even this vast and prosperous region has failed to deal with the problem of child and pensioner poverty (see Figure 5.3). Once again, this highlights the interplay of micro and macro issues that could be sustaining this type of poverty over the long run (McLoyd, Aikens, and Burton, 2007; Mickelson, 2002; Miller and Chen, 2013; Miller et al., 2011).

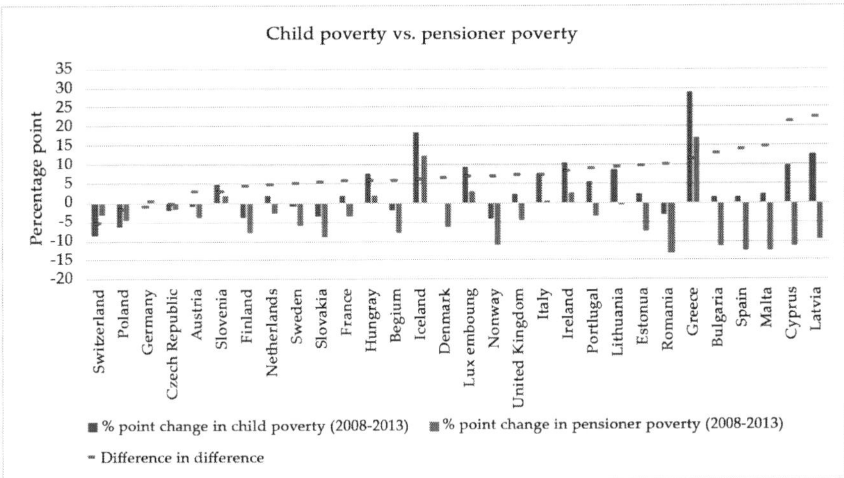

Figure 5.3. Child and pensioner poverty in the European Union.

Source: Statistics Uncovered.

A "society" can be considered as a collective of human populations that are politically autonomous, in which members engage in a broad range of cooperative activities (Mbabazi and Pyeong, 2014; McLaughlin and Rank, 2018; McLoyd, Aikens, and Burton, 2007). The people of Germany, for example, can be deemed "a society," whereas people with German heritage as a whole, including those who populate other countries, would not be considered a society, per se (Mazza et al., 2017; Kim et al., 2016). There are some theoretical strategies within contemporary macro sociology, though four approaches, in particular, have the most influence (Lyytikäinen et al., 2006; Magnuson and Votruba-Drzal, 2008; Duncan and Rodgers, 1988). The first is the Idealist Strategy which attempts to explain the basic features of social life by reference to the creative capacity of the human mind (Lopez and Velasco, 2011; Lyytikäinen et al., 2006; Magnuson and Votruba-Drzal, 2008). Idealists believe that human uniqueness lies in the fact that humans attach symbolic meanings to their actions (Lichter, Shanahan, and Gardner, 2002; Lipina, 2016; Lipina et al., 2013). The second is the Materialist Strategy which attempts to explain the basic features of human social life in terms of the practical, material conditions of their existence, including the nature of a physical environment; the level of technology; and the organization of an economic system (Kim et al., 2016; Mbabazi and Pyeong, 2014; McLaughlin and Rank, 2018). The third is the Functionalist Strategy (or structural functionalism) which essentially states that societies are complex systems of interrelated and interdependent parts, and each part of a society significantly influences the others (Kim et al., 2015; Krason, 2015; Lesner, 2018). Moreover, each part of society exists because it has a specific function to perform in contributing to the society as a whole (Kim et al., 2015; Krason, 2015; Lesner, 2018; Mazza et al., 2017). As such, societies tend toward a state of equilibrium or homeostasis, and if there is a disturbance in any part of the society then the other parts will adjust to restore the stability of the society as a whole (Kendig, Mattingly, and Bianchi, 2014; Kim et al., 2013). The 4th is the Conflict Theoretical Strategy (or conflict theory) which rejects the idea that societies tend toward some basic consensus of harmony in which the features of society work for everyone's good (Jones, Vargas, and Villar, 2008; Kendig, Mattingly, and Bianchi, 2014; Kim et al., 2013). Rather, the basic structure of society is determined by individuals and groups acquiring scarce resources to satisfy their own needs and wants, thus creating endless conflicts (Jones, Vargas, and Villar, 2007; Kalil, Duncan, and Ziol-Guest, 2016; Kaplinsky, 2005; Kapoor, 1993).

At the micro-level, sociologists examine the smallest levels of interaction; even in some cases, just "the self" alone (Javanbakht et al., 2015; Jones, Vargas, and Villar, 2007; Kalil, Duncan, and Ziol-Guest, 2016). Micro-level analyzes might include one-on-one interactions between couples or friends (Javanbakht et al., 2015; Wells et al., 2010). Or perhaps a sociologist is interested in how a person's perception of self is influenced by his or her social context (Jain and Vaachani, 2006; Jarjoura, Triplett, and Brinker, 2002; Javanbakht et al., 2015). In each of these cases, the level of inquiry is micro (Hong, 2015; Jarjoura, Triplett, and Brinker, 2002; Ridge, 2002; Waddington, 2004; Ziol-Guest, Duncan, and Kalil, 2009). When sociologists investigate groups, their inquiry is at the meso level (Hong, 2015; Jain and Vaachani, 2006; Jarjoura, Triplett, and Brinker, 2002; Kaplinsky, 2005; Kapoor, 1993; Jones, Vargas, and Villar, 2008). Sociologists who conduct meso level research might study how norms of workplace behavior vary across professions or how children's sporting clubs are organized, to cite two examples (Hobcraft, 1998; Kim et al., 2013). At the macro level, sociologists examine social structures and institutions (Hobcraft, 1998; Hobcraft and Kiernan, 2001; Evans and Schamberg, 2009; Holzer et al., 2008). Research at the macro level examines large-scale patterns (Hobcraft and Kiernan, 2001; Kim et al., 2015; Nikulina and Widom, 2014). In recent years, sociologists have become increasingly interested in the process and impacts of globalization (Hatcher et al., 2019; Evans and Kutcher, 2011; Hill and Sandfort, 1995). A study of globalization that examines the interrelationships between nations would be an example of a macro-level study (Hatcher et al., 2019; Kapoor, 1993; McLoyd, Aikens, and Burton, 2007). At the meso level, sociologists are likely to examine interactions between gangs or perhaps how different branches of the same gang vary from one area to the next (Hart, 2008; Kalil, Duncan, and Ziol-Guest, 2016; Kaplinsky, 2005; McLaughlin and Rank, 2018; Schmitz, Wagner, and Menke, 2001). At the macro level, we could compare the impact of gang activity across communities or examine the economic impact of gangs on nations (Hannum, Liu, and Alvarado-Urbina, 2017; Penn, 2004; Ratcliffe; Van den Waeyenberg, and Hens, 2008; Sinervo and Hill, 2011). Child poverty as a major social problem is studied at all these levels in a now multi-disciplinary way (Guest and Biasini, 2001; Evans and Schamberg, 2009; Krason, 2015; Lesner, 2018). The next section considers the impact of poverty among adults on children.

5.4. IMPACT OF ADULT POVERTY ON CHILDREN

There is a generalized assumption that poor adults are likely to rear children in poverty, unless there is a drastic and impactful intervention (Fujiura and Yamaki, 2000; Garrett, Ng'andu, and Ferron, 1994; Duncan et al., 2012; Evans and Fuller-Rowell, 2013). In discussions of poverty in the US, child poverty tends to get most of the focus (Farah et al., 2006). In reality, there are good reasons for that focus on children living in poverty; not least because they are the future generation that will determine the fortunes of the nation (Evans, 2004; Jain and Vaachani, 2006; Ministry of Finance, 2014; Vallas, Fremstad, and Ekman, 2015). While the US has more poverty than other rich countries in general, it is a particular outlier on child poverty (Evans, 2004; Farah et al., 2006). In 2016, the US poverty rate for children (defined as the share living on less than half the median income) was 20.9%, compared to 14.2% in Canada, 11.8% in the UK, and 8.9% in Sweden (Evans and Schamberg, 2009; Holzer et al., 2008; Hong, 2015). The USA is just about the only rich country without some kind of per-child cash grant distributed to most parents (Evans and Kutcher, 2011; Mickelson, 2002; Segretin et al., 2016; Jones, Vargas, and Villar, 2008). However, some researchers have started to re-orientate their thinking and concluding that the US poverty discussion focuses too much on children and not enough around childless adults (Evans and Kutcher, 2011; Hill and Sandfort, 1995; Hobcraft, 1998; Hobcraft and Kiernan, 2001). This has policy implications because cash allowances are typically provided to parents and hence excluding those that are child-less (Evans and Kim, 2013; Hart, 2008; Hatcher et al., 2019).

Perhaps that is one of the reasons why child income poverty rates are not yet satisfactory, even in the most developed nations (see Figure 5.4).

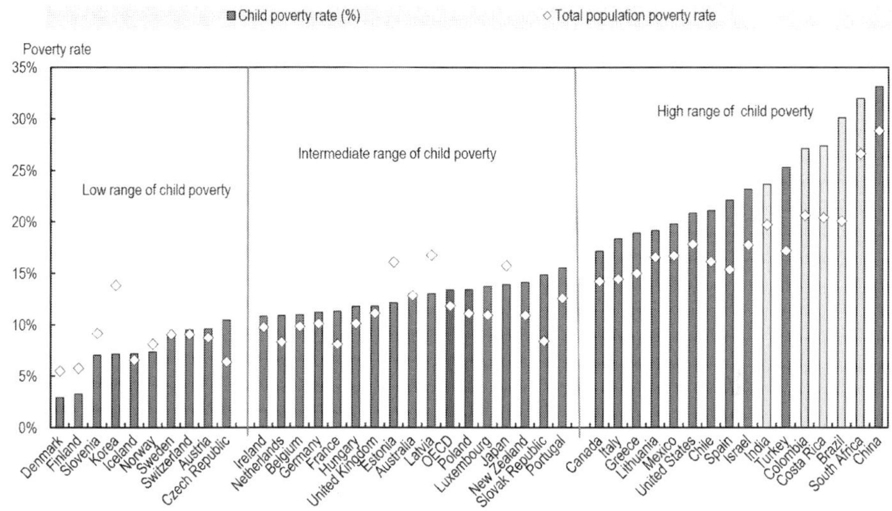

Figure 5.4. Child income poverty rates in 2015 and 2016.

Source: ResearchGate.

Many anti-poverty campaigners argue that offering a simple cash allowance to all parents, as almost all other rich countries do, would be a very good policy (Evans and Kim, 2007, 2013; Hannum, Liu, and Alvarado-Urbina, 2017; Hart, 2008). It is an effective and popular way to cut poverty (Duncan et al., 1998; Evans and Kim, 2007; Hannum, Liu, and Alvarado-Urbina, 2017). Moreover, there are developmental benefits that do not apply as much when supporting adults without children (Duncan et al., 1998; Mazza et al., 2017). There is a gap in not providing support to adults who happen not to have children (Duncan et al., 2012; Evans and Fuller-Rowell, 2013; Guest and Biasini, 2001). First, those adults have other responsibilities to the community which suffers when they are living in abject poverty (Duncan, Kalil, and Ziol-Guest, 2008; Morrow, 2013; Song and Lu, 2002; Ziol-Guest et al., 2012). Secondly, the reality is that the birth rates in developing countries are falling (Duncan, Kalil, and Ziol-Guest, 2008; Evans, 2016; Fierman et al., 2016). This means that only offering cash support to parents will exclude many otherwise deprived people (Duncan, Kalil, and Ziol-Guest, 2013; Evans and Cassells, 2014; Guest and Biasini, 2001; Duncan et al., 1998). One of the options is to consider poverty as a holistic issue that must be dealt with in its entirety rather than skirting around the issue (Duncan, Kalil, and Ziol-Guest, 2013; Evans and Cassells, 2014; Fujiura and Yamaki, 2000; Garrett, Ng'andu, and Ferron, 1994). The Scandinavian countries have adopted this approach by institutionalizing welfare so that everyone within the community feels entitled to support regardless of whether they are rich or poor (Duncan and Rodgers, 1988; Holzer et al., 2008). Of course, others believe that such institutionalized support stifles innovation and may lead to entire generations of people that have never worked and will probably never work (Duncan and Rodgers, 1988; Evans, 2004; Farah et al., 2006). However, that does not detract from the fact that adult poverty can have consequences on the community as a whole and children in particular (Deaton, 2006; Dreyer, 2013; Duncan and Magnuson, 2013; Lichter, Shanahan, and Gardner, 2002; Lipina, 2016; Lopez and Velasco, 2011). This chapter will close with a critique of policy interventions that have failed to address the issue of child poverty.

5.5. INAPPROPRIATE POLICY FORMULATION FOR CHILDHOOD POVERTY

The adoption and implementation of inappropriate policies for child poverty not only become ineffective but can also hamper any future efforts to improve the welfare of a given community (Corcoran and Chaudry, 1997; Deaton, 2006; Kim et al., 2016; Twikirize et al., 2014). There are many policy initiatives and orientations that have been used with mixed success about reducing or eliminating child poverty (Corcoran and Chaudry, 1997; Deaton, 2006; Dreyer, 2013; Duncan and Magnuson, 2013). One of the approaches is increased visibility where issues concerning child poverty are given prominence and precedence (Chiputwa, Spielman, and Qaim, 2015; Evans and Kim, 2007; Okiror, 2015; Townsend, 1979). That means setting an agenda that puts children first and raises community concern if children are in need or otherwise denied their basic rights (Chiputwa, Spielman, and Qaim, 2015; Corcoran and Chaudry, 1997; Lipina et al., 2013). Moreover, the policy framework should be proactive and progressive so that it looks for the best outcomes for children rather than merely focusing on preventing suffering (Chamberlain et al., 2016; Chiputwa, Spielman, and Qaim, 2015). The policy orientation should come right from the highest echelons of the state and then trickle down to the lowest local government entity (Chamberlain et al., 2016). The community as a whole should be socialized in such a way as to take issues of child poverty seriously (Bruch and Touraine, 1940; Magnuson and Votruba-Drzal, 2008; Evans and Fuller-Rowell, 2013). A case in point is community conscientiousness when it comes to the relationship between child poverty and race (see Figure 5.5).

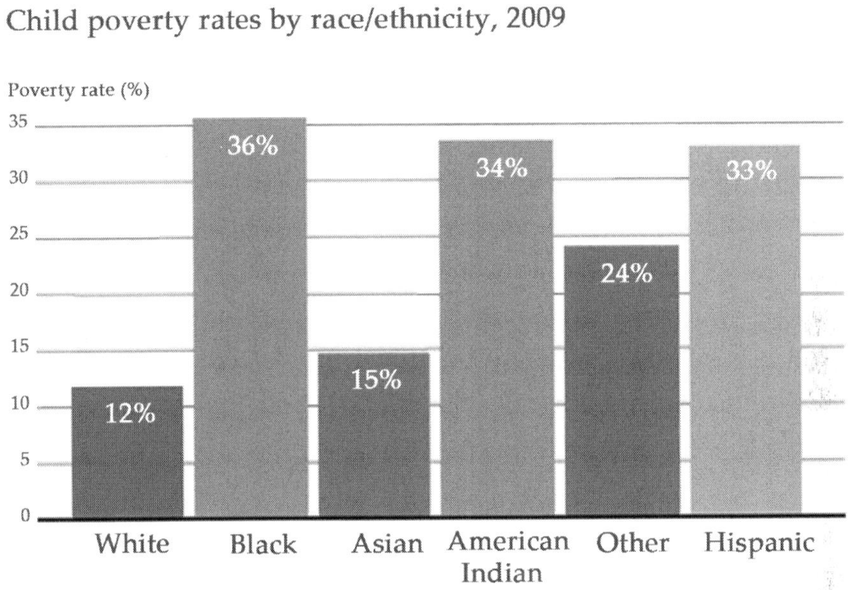

Figure 5.5. Race and the unequal impact of child poverty.

Source: National Center for Children in Poverty via Medium.

Many policy missteps might prevent the government from eliminating child poverty, although this a goal that is often part of a national plan (Bruch and Touraine, 1940; Chamberlain et al., 2016). The first mistake is not providing sufficient resources to deal with problems and hoping that rhetoric alone will be able to deal with entrenched challenges that have failed previous governments (Boyden and James, 2014; Lyytikäinen et al., 2006; Duncan et al., 2012). Another mistake is to import policies without adequately consulting with the local population (Bourdillon and Boyden, 2011; Lopez and Velasco, 2011; Garrett, Ng'andu, and Ferron, 1994). The consequence of such decisions is that the policies which are implemented have very little relevance to the problem that they are supposed to deal with (Bloom and Canning, 2001; Lipina et al., 2013). A case in point is where governments in the developing world adopt either of the two extremes of complete market liberalization or complete command of the social sector (Bloom and Canning, 2001; Bourdillon and Boyden, 2011; Boyden and James, 2014;

Bruch and Touraine, 1940). In the case of complete marketization of the social sector, there is not sufficient supply to meet the demands of children in need (Bhargava et al., 2004; Bloom and Canning, 2001; Bourdillon and Boyden, 2011; Boyden and James, 2014). Where the government adopts a controlled or institutionalized social sector, they may be falling into the trap of utopian planning that does not fully account for the limited funds that are available for the least developed countries (Bäckman, and Nilsson, 2007; Bhargava et al., 2004; Lipina, 2016; Evans and Cassells, 2014). Another important mistake is ignoring the opportunities and resources that already exist in society so that the government ends up taking on undesirable and unaffordable tasks (Ashworth, Hill, and Walker, 1994; Lichter, Shanahan, and Gardner, 2002; Duncan, Kalil, and Ziol-Guest, 2013). The government can be too ambitious and too optimistic about the possibilities (Ashiabi, 2000; Duncan and Magnuson, 2013; Fierman et al., 2016). The result is that so many initiatives are started, but then not completed because yet another priority or new project comes to light (Ansell, 2016; Dreyer, 2013; Evans, 2016; Evans and Kim, 2013; Jones, Vargas, and Villar, 2007; Mbabazi and Pyeong, 2014; Schickedanz, Dreyer, and Halfon, 2015).

CHAPTER 5 SUMMARY

There are many complex factors as to why child poverty exists and why it persists in the world today. Intra-generational causes mean that there is inequality that is experienced by people of the same generation but with very different outcomes. When poverty is transgenerational, it can trap people into undesirable living conditions. This chapter has shown that poverty can exist at the micro, meso, and macro levels; with serious implications regardless of its context. Moreover, the undesirable living conditions or circumstances of parents can have an impact on children. However, the development of inappropriate policy responses has sometimes hindered the success of these interventions against child poverty. The next chapter identifies certain societal factors that are associated with child poverty.

Chapter 6

Societal Factors in Childhood Poverty

CONTENTS

Child poverty is a societal ill and is therefore partly determined by societal factors. A case in point is how racism prevents children from reaching their full potential since they are judged for factors beyond their ability, personality, and effort. Immigrant children have to deal with the negative effects of xenophobia which can harm them in all spheres of their lives. This chapter also explores the plight of sexual minorities that are living in poverty, and yet receiving very little moral and practical support from their communities. Similarly, the class system can prevent children from reaching their full potential through adherence to prejudices and artificial societal barriers to success. This chapter will close with an overview of how disability can create and exacerbate child poverty. By the end of the chapter, the reader will have an idea of how some of the societal ills mentioned end up contributing to child poverty.

6.1. RACISM AND CHILDHOOD POVERTY

Racism is the belief that groups of humans possess different behavioral traits corresponding to physical appearance and can be divided based on the superiority of one race over another (Ansell, 2016; Ashiabi, 2000; Ashworth, Hill, and Walker, 1994; Bäckman, and Nilsson, 2007). It may also mean prejudice, discrimination, or antagonism directed against other people because they are of a different race or ethnicity (Ansell, 2016; Ashiabi, 2000; Ashworth, Hill, and Walker, 1994; Bäckman, and Nilsson, 2007; Bhargava et al., 2004). Modern variants of racism are often based on social perceptions of biological differences between peoples (Serbin et al., 2011; Zembe-Mkabile et al., 2015). These views can take the form of social actions, practices or beliefs, or political systems in which different races are ranked as inherently superior or inferior to each other, based on presumed shared inheritable traits, abilities, or qualities (Hobcraft and Kiernan, 2001; Kim et al., 2015; Nikulina and Widom, 2014). In terms of political systems (e.g., apartheid) that support the expression of prejudice or aversion in discriminatory practices or laws, racist ideology may include associated social aspects such as nativism, xenophobia, otherness, segregation, hierarchical ranking, and supremacism (Jones, Vargas, and Villar, 2008; Kendig, Mattingly, and Bianchi, 2014; Kim et al., 2013). One of the problems when dealing with the impact of racism is that it is so well hidden in official reports, a case in point being the Strathcona report on inequalities (see Figure 6.1).

Figure 6.1. Example of a regional poverty status report in Strathcona.

Source: First call and Sparc BC via Slide Player.

While the concepts of race and ethnicity are considered to be separate in contemporary social science, the two terms have a long history of equivalence in popular usage and older social science literature (Duncan et al., 1998; Evans and Kim, 2007; Hannum, Liu, and Alvarado-Urbina, 2017). "Ethnicity" is often used in a sense close to one traditionally attributed to "race": the division of human groups based on qualities assumed to be essential or innate to the group, such as shared ancestry or shared behavior (Van den Waeyenberg, and Hens, 2008; Waddington, 2004; Wells et al., 2010). Therefore, racism and racial discrimination are often used to describe discrimination on an ethnic or cultural basis, independent of whether these differences are described as racial (Javanbakht et al., 2015; Jones, Vargas, and Villar, 2007; Kalil, Duncan, and Ziol-Guest, 2016). According to a United Nations (UN) convention on racial discrimination, there is no distinction between the terms "racial" and "ethnic" discrimination (Stewart, 2005; Torres and Wong, 2013; Townsend, 1979; Twikirize et al., 2014; Vallas, Fremstad, and Ekman, 2015). The UN convention further concludes that superiority based on racial differentiation is scientifically false, morally condemnable, socially unjust and dangerous (Sinervo and Hill, 2011; Song and Lu, 2002; Sripada et al., 2014). The Convention also declared that there is no justification for racial discrimination, anywhere, in theory or in practice (Evans and Kim, 2007, 2013; Hannum, Liu, and Alvarado-Urbina, 2017; Hart, 2008). Racism is a relatively modern concept, arising in the European age of imperialism, the subsequent growth of capitalism, and especially the Atlantic slave trade, of which it was a major driving force (Evans and Kim, 2013; Hart, 2008; Hatcher et al., 2019). It was also a major force behind racial segregation especially in the United States in the 19th and early 20th centuries and South Africa under apartheid; 19th and 20th century racism in Western culture is particularly well documented and constitutes a reference point in studies and discourses about racism (Lichter, Shanahan, and Gardner, 2002; Lipina, 2016; Lipina et al., 2013).

Racism has played a role in genocides such as the Holocaust, the Armenian genocide, and genocide of Serbs, and colonial projects including the European colonization of the Americas, Africa, and Asia as well as the Soviet deportations of indigenous minorities (Chamberlain et al., 2016). Indigenous peoples have been and are often subject to racist attitudes (Hannum, Liu, and Alvarado-Urbina, 2017; Penn, 2004; Ratcliffe; Van den Waeyenberg, and Hens, 2008; Sinervo and Hill, 2011). Sociologists, in general, recognize "race" as a social construct (Duncan, Kalil, and Ziol-Guest, 2008; Morrow, 2013; Song and Lu, 2002; Ziol-Guest et al., 2012). This means that, although the concepts of race and racism are based on observable biological characteristics, any conclusions drawn about race based on those observations are heavily influenced by cultural ideologies (Bourdillon and Boyden, 2011; Lopez and Velasco, 2011; Garrett, Ng'andu, and Ferron, 1994). Racism, as an ideology, exists in a society at both the individual and institutional level (Ridge, 2006; Schickedanz, Dreyer, and Halfon, 2015; Schmitz, Wagner, and Menke, 2001). While much of the research and work on racism during the last half-century or so has concentrated on "white racism" in the Western world, historical accounts of race-based social practices can be found across the globe (Muñoz, Álvarez-Verdejo, and García-Fernández, 2016; Sripada et al., 2014). Thus, racism can be broadly defined to encompass individual and group prejudices and acts of discrimination that result in material and cultural advantages conferred on a majority or a dominant social group (Ansell, 2016; Ashiabi, 2000; Ashworth, Hill, and Walker, 1994; Bäckman, and Nilsson, 2007). So-called "white racism" focuses on societies in which white populations are the majority of the dominant social group (Hong, 2015; Jarjoura, Triplett, and Brinker, 2002; Ridge, 2002; Waddington, 2004; Ziol-Guest, Duncan, and Kalil, 2009). In studies of these majority white societies, the aggregate of material and cultural advantages is usually termed "white privilege" (Evans, 2004; Jain and Vaachani, 2006; Ministry of Finance, 2014; Vallas, Fremstad, and Ekman, 2015).

Race and race relations are prominent areas of study in sociology and economics (Javanbakht et al., 2015; Wells et al., 2010). Much of the sociological literature focuses on white racism (Fujiura and Yamaki, 2000; Garrett, Ng'andu, and Ferron, 1994; Duncan et al., 2012; Evans and Fuller-Rowell, 2013). Some of the earliest sociological works on racism were penned by sociologist W. E. B. Du Bois, the first African American to earn a doctoral degree from Harvard University. Du Bois wrote that the problem of the 20th century is the problem of the color line (Bloom and Canning, 2001; Lipina et al., 2013).

Wellman (1993) defines racism as culturally sanctioned beliefs, which, regardless of intentions involved, defend the advantages whites have because of the subordinated position of racial minorities (Nikulina, Widom, and Czaja, 2011; State House Uganda, 2017; Stewart, 2005; Torres and Wong, 2013).In both sociology and economics, the outcomes of racist actions are often measured by the inequality in income, wealth, net worth, and access to other cultural resources (such as education), between racial groups (Lyytikäinen et al., 2006; Magnuson and Votruba-Drzal, 2008; Duncan and Rodgers, 1988).

In sociology and social psychology, racial identity and the acquisition of that identity is often used as a variable in racism studies (Jain and Vaachani, 2006; Jarjoura, Triplett, and Brinker, 2002; Javanbakht et al., 2015). Racial ideologies and racial identity affect individuals' perception of race and discrimination (Bäckman, and Nilsson, 2007; Bhargava et al., 2004; Lipina, 2016; Evans and Cassells, 2014).

Cazenave and Maddern (1999) define racism as "a highly organized system of 'race'-based group privilege that operates at every level of society and is held together by a sophisticated ideology of color or 'race' supremacy (Evans and Schamberg, 2009; Holzer et al., 2008; Hong, 2015).

Racial centrality (the extent to which a culture recognizes individuals' racial identity) appears to affect the degree of discrimination African American young adults perceive whereas racial ideology may buffer the detrimental emotional effects of that discrimination (Ridge, 2002; Rowntree, 1901; Ryan, Fauth, and Brooks-Gunn, 2006; Sánchez, 2008). Sellers and Shelton (2003) found that a relationship between racial discrimination and emotional distress was moderated by racial ideology and social beliefs (Nikulina and Widom, 2014; Nikulina, Widom, and Czaja, 2011; Okiror, 2015; Penn, 2004; Ratcliffe and McKernan, 2010). In practical terms, those that are discriminated against are poorer and get less desirable access to social services (Schickedanz, Dreyer, and Halfon, 2015; Schmitz, Wagner, and Menke, 2001; Segretin et al., 2016). In the next section, we consider how xenophobia blights the prospects of immigrant children and eventually leads them into poverty.

6.2. XENOPHOBIA AND POVERTY AMONG IMMIGRANT CHILDREN

Xenophobia is the fear or hatred of that which is perceived to be foreign or strange (Jones, Vargas, and Villar, 2007; Kalil, Duncan, and Ziol-Guest, 2016; Kaplinsky, 2005; Kapoor, 1993).

It is an expression of perceived conflict between an in-group and an outgroup and it may manifest itself in suspicion of the out-group's activities by the in-group, the in-group's desire to eliminate the out-group's presence, and the in-group's fear of losing its religious, national, ethnic or racial identity (Duncan and Rodgers, 1988; Holzer et al., 2008). A 1997 review article on xenophobia holds the view that it is an element of a political struggle about who has the right to be cared for by the state and society: a fight for the collective good of the modern state (Hong, 2015; Jain and Vaachani, 2006; Jarjoura, Triplett, and Brinker, 2002; Kaplinsky, 2005; Kapoor, 1993; Jones, Vargas, and Villar, 2008).

According to one source, xenophobia can also be exhibited as an "uncritical exaltation of another culture" which is ascribed "an unreal, stereotyped, and exotic quality" (Chamberlain et al., 2016; Chiputwa, Spielman, and Qaim, 2015). An early example of xenophobic sentiment in Western culture is the Ancient Greek denigration of foreigners as "barbarians," the belief that the Greek people and culture were superior to all others, and the subsequent conclusion that barbarians were naturally meant to be enslaved (Farah et al., 2006). Because child poverty closely aligns with general poverty (see Figure 6.2), it is important to consider how the plight of impoverished immigrant children impacts immigrants as a group and the community as a whole.

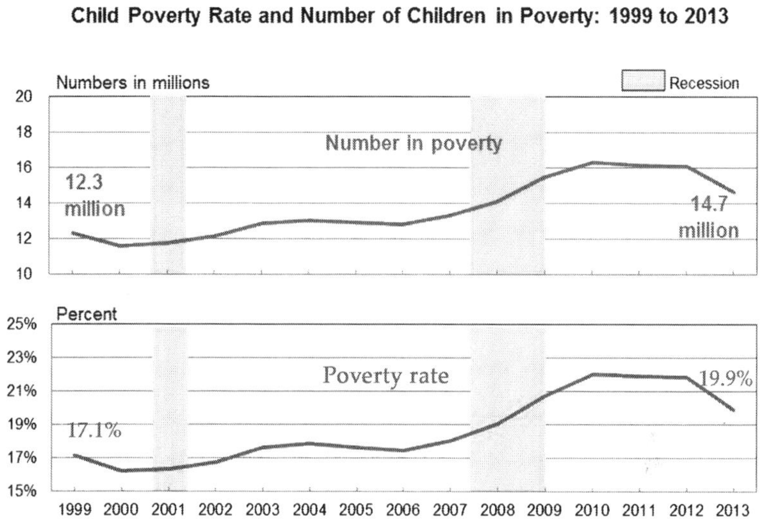

Figure 6.2. Comparison of child population and children in poverty 1999 to 2013.

Source: Census Bureau.

Many countries are struggling with the effects and after-effects of xenophobia, which is often underpinned by racism that severely impacts immigrant children (Duncan, Kalil, and Ziol-Guest, 2013; Evans and Cassells, 2014; Fujiura and Yamaki, 2000; Garrett, Ng'andu, and Ferron, 1994). A case in point is how there was a time when South America was considered to be a beacon of good race relations when in fact the reality is very different (Sinervo and Hill, 2011; Song and Lu, 2002; Sripada et al., 2014; State House Uganda, 2017). For example, racism in Mexico has a long history (Hobcraft, 1998; Kim et al., 2013). Historically, Mexicans with light skin tones had absolute control over dark-skinned Amerindians due to the structure of the Spanish colonial caste system (Miller and Chen, 2013; Miller et al., 2011). When a Mexican of a darker-skinned tone marries one of a lighter skinned-tone, it is common for them to say that they are 'making the race better' (Chiputwa, Spielman, and Qaim, 2015; Corcoran and Chaudry, 1997; Lipina et al., 2013). This can be interpreted as a self-attack on their ethnicity (Bruch and Touraine, 1940; Chamberlain et al., 2016). Despite improving the economic and social conditions of Indigenous Mexicans, discrimination against Indigenous Mexicans continues to this day, and there are few laws to protect Indigenous Mexicans from discrimination (Evans, 2004; Farah et al., 2006). Violent attacks against indigenous Mexicans are moderately common and many times go unpunished (Ashiabi, 2000; Duncan and Magnuson, 2013; Fierman et al., 2016). In Venezuela, like other South American countries, economic inequality often breaks along ethnic and racial lines (Segretin et al., 2016; Serbin et al., 2011). A 2013 Swedish academic study stated that Venezuela was the most racist country in the Americas, followed by the Dominican Republic (Vallas, Fremstad, and Ekman, 2015; Van den Waeyenberg, and Hens, 2008; Waddington, 2004; Wells et al., 2010).

As in most countries, many people in the US continue to be xenophobic against other races (Deaton, 2006; Dreyer, 2013; Duncan and Magnuson, 2013; Lichter, Shanahan, and Gardner, 2002; Lipina, 2016; Lopez and Velasco, 2011). In the view of a network of scores of US civil rights and human rights organizations, discrimination permeates all aspects of life in the United States and extends to all communities of color (Duncan et al., 2012; Evans and Fuller-Rowell, 2013; Guest and Biasini, 2001). Discrimination against racial, ethnic, and religious minorities is widely acknowledged especially in the case of Indians, Muslims, Sikhs as well as other ethnic groups (Ashworth, Hill, and Walker, 1994; Lichter, Shanahan, and Gardner, 2002; Duncan, Kalil, and Ziol-Guest, 2013). This has also led to a rise in so-called reverse racism cases, which generally are not reported or accepted due to mainstream American politics (Evans and Kutcher, 2011; Hill and Sandfort, 1995; Hobcraft, 1998; Hobcraft and Kiernan, 2001). Members of every major American ethnic and religious minority have perceived discrimination in their dealings with other minority racial and religious groups (Hart, 2008; Kalil, Duncan, and Ziol-Guest, 2016; Kaplinsky, 2005; McLaughlin and Rank, 2018; Schmitz, Wagner, and Menke, 2001). Philosopher Cornel West has stated that racism is an integral element within the very fabric of American culture and society. It is embedded in the country's first collective definition, enunciated in its subsequent laws, and imbued in its dominant way of life (Zembe-Mkabile et al., 2015; Ziol-Guest, Duncan, and Kalil, 2009; Ziol-Guest et al., 2012). A 2019 survey by the Pew Research Center suggested that 76% of black and Asian respondents had experienced some form of discrimination, at least from time to time (Ministry of Finance, 2014; Morrow, 2013; Muñoz, Álvarez-Verdejo, and García-Fernández, 2016). Immigrant children are often on the receiving end of racist views and xenophobic policy (Ansell, 2016; Ashiabi, 2000; Ashworth, Hill, and Walker, 1994; Bäckman, and Nilsson, 2007; Bhargava et al., 2004). The next section considers poverty among sexual minorities.

6.3. POVERTY AND SEXUAL MINORITIES

Sexual minorities are the heart of many issues of intersectionality, and child poverty is just another manifestation of the social injustice that they face in many communities (Kim et al., 2016; Mbabazi and Pyeong, 2014; McLaughlin and Rank, 2018). A sexual minority is a group whose sexual identity, orientation, or practices differ from the majority of the surrounding society (Mazza et al., 2017; Kim et al., 2016). Primarily used to refer to LGB or non-heterosexual individuals; it can also refer to transgender, non-binary (including the third gender) or intersex individuals (Rowntree, 1901; Ryan, Fauth, and Brooks-Gunn, 2006; Sánchez, 2008; Ridge, 2006). Variants such as GSM ("Gender and Sexual Minorities"), GSSM ("Gender, Sexual, and Sexuality Minorities") GSRM ("Gender, Sexual, and Romantic Minorities"), and GSD ("Gender and Sexual Diversity") have been considered in academia (Guest and Biasini, 2001; Evans and Schamberg, 2009; Krason, 2015; Lesner, 2018). However, it is SGM ("Sexual and Gender Minority") that has gained the most advancement since 2014 (Hobcraft, 1998; Hobcraft and Kiernan, 2001; Evans and Schamberg, 2009; Holzer et al., 2008). In 2015 the NIH announced the formation of the Sexual and Gender Minority Research Office (Hatcher et al., 2019; Evans and Kutcher, 2011; Hill and Sandfort, 1995). Regions such as Sub-Saharan Africa which have high levels of child poverty (see Figure 6.3), but also simultaneously suppress sexual minorities; the link between this type of minority status and poverty is under-investigated (Nikulina, Widom, and Czaja, 2011; Okiror, 2015; Penn, 2004; Ratcliffe and McKernan, 2010).

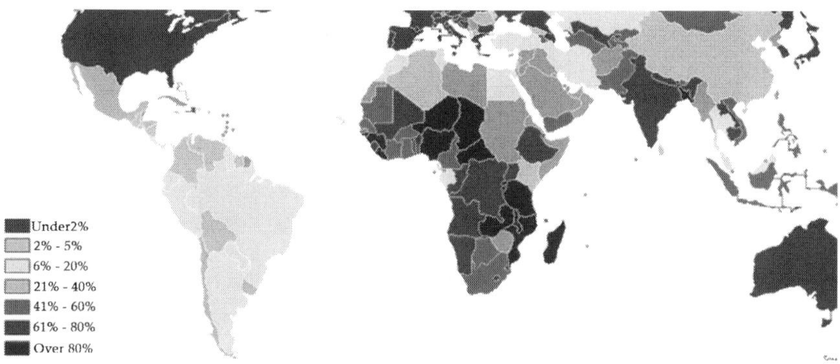

Figure 6.3. Africa lags in many indicators of child poverty.

Source: Study.com.

Numerous professional and academic institutions have adopted this term (Ansell, 2016; Dreyer, 2013; Evans, 2016; Evans and Kim, 2013; Jones, Vargas, and Villar, 2007; Mbabazi and Pyeong, 2014; Schickedanz, Dreyer, and Halfon, 2015). Sexual and gender minority is an umbrella term that encompasses populations included in the acronym "LGBTI" (lesbian, gay, bisexual, transgender, and intersex), and those whose sexual orientation or gender identity varies (Kim et al., 2015; Krason, 2015; Lesner, 2018; Mazza et al., 2017). It includes those who may not self-identify as LGBTI (e.g., queer, questioning, two-spirit, asexual, men who have sex with men, gender variant), or those who have a specific medical condition affecting reproductive development (Corcoran and Chaudry, 1997; Deaton, 2006; Kim et al., 2016; Twikirize et al., 2014). Examples of the latter include individuals with differences or disorders of sex development, who sometimes identify as intersex (State House Uganda, 2017; Stewart, 2005; Torres and Wong, 2013; Townsend, 1979; Twikirize et al., 2014).

Social issues may lead to possible health and psychological issues, especially in youth (Bruch and Touraine, 1940; Magnuson and Votruba-Drzal, 2008; Evans and Fuller-Rowell, 2013). It has been found that sexual minorities face increased stress due to stigmas (Duncan and Rodgers, 1988; Evans, 2004; Farah et al., 2006). This stigma-related stress creates elevated coping regulation and social and cognitive processes leading to risk for psychopathology (Ministry of Finance, 2014; Morrow, 2013; Muñoz, Álvarez-Verdejo, and García-Fernández, 2016; Nikulina and Widom, 2014). The Centers for Disease Control and Prevention published their 2015 study of large cohorts of ninth to twelfth-grade students across the US (Duncan, Kalil, and Ziol-Guest, 2008; Evans, 2016; Fierman et al., 2016). Around 100 health behaviors were shown to put LGB students at risk for health consequences. Sexual minority students engage in riskier behaviors when compared with nonsexual minority students (Hatcher et al., 2019; Kapoor, 1993; McLoyd, Aikens, and Burton, 2007). Some literature indicates that LGBT adolescents were victimized more often, had higher rates of psychopathology, left home more frequently, used highly addictive substances more frequently, and were more likely to have more multiple sex partners than heterosexual adolescents (Chiputwa, Spielman, and Qaim, 2015; Evans and Kim, 2007; Okiror, 2015; Townsend, 1979). Based on studies of adolescents, it is concluded that sexual minorities are similar to heterosexual adolescents in developmental needs and concerns (Bhargava et al., 2004; Bloom and Canning, 2001; Bourdillon and Boyden, 2011; Boyden and James, 2014). However, research has suggested that sexual minority youth (more specifically LGBT youth) are more susceptible to psychological and health issues than heterosexual youth (Duncan, Kalil, and Ziol-Guest, 2008; Evans, 2016; Fierman et al., 2016).

Sexual minorities in many countries such as South Africa have sexual-orientation-related health inequities when compared to other countries (Serbin et al., 2011; Zembe-Mkabile et al., 2015). One of the highest prevalence of sexual violence directed toward women of a sexual minority occurs in South Africa (Duncan, Kalil, and Ziol-Guest, 2013; Evans and Cassells, 2014; Guest and Biasini, 2001; Duncan et al., 1998). Women of color who are living in low-income urban areas are notably targeted (Evans and Kutcher, 2011; Mickelson, 2002; Segretin et al., 2016; Jones, Vargas, and Villar, 2008). The perpetrators of sexual violence believe they are "correcting the women," and their actions will cure them of their homosexuality (Lopez and Velasco, 2011; Lyytikäinen et al., 2006; Magnuson and Votruba-Drzal, 2008). Typically, the measures that are taken to control non-heterosexual non-cisgender people include threats to their economic and social wellbeing (Duncan et al., 1998; Mazza et al., 2017). For example, there have been examples of LGBT people losing their jobs or being discriminated against when applying for work (Mbabazi and Pyeong, 2014; McLaughlin and Rank, 2018; McLoyd, Aikens, and Burton, 2007). The way that the social welfare system is conceptualized means that heterosexual married couples with children are prioritized while sexual minorities invariably come at the bottom of the heap (Fujiura and Yamaki, 2000; Hill and Sandfort, 1995; Kendig, Mattingly, and Bianchi, 2014). There have been attempts to make them invisible for purposes of policy formulation which means that sexual minorities do not get a voice (Ziol-Guest, Duncan, and Kalil, 2009; Ziol-Guest et al., 2012). Consequently, some sexual minorities may face child poverty without state support (Kim et al., 2015; Krason, 2015; Lesner, 2018). Others are kicked out of their families and homes at a very young age; meaning that their preparation for the world is stunted (Corcoran and Chaudry, 1997; Deaton, 2006; Dreyer, 2013; Duncan and Magnuson, 2013). It is for this reason, that sexual minorities have experienced child poverty in unique ways (Boyden and James, 2014; Lyytikäinen et al., 2006; Duncan et al., 2012). The next section in this chapter focuses on how the class system fosters child poverty.

6.4. THE CLASS SYSTEM AND CHILDHOOD POVERTY

Class systems tend to divide the populace into those who have and those who do not have (McLoyd, Aikens, and Burton, 2007; Mickelson, 2002; Miller and Chen, 2013; Miller et al., 2011). These divisions then extend to children with some having fairly luxurious lives while others are living in abject poverty (Bloom and Canning, 2001; Bourdillon and Boyden, 2011; Boyden and James, 2014; Bruch and Touraine, 1940). A social class is a set of concepts in the social sciences and political theory centered on models of social stratification which occur in class society (Ridge, 2002, 2006; Rowntree, 1901; Ryan, Fauth, and Brooks-Gunn, 2006; Sánchez, 2008). In a class system, people are grouped into a set of hierarchical social categories (Kendig, Mattingly, and Bianchi, 2014; Kim et al., 2013). The most common of these categories are the upper, middle, and lower classes (Kendig, Mattingly, and Bianchi, 2014; Kim et al., 2013).

"Class" is a subject of analysis for sociologists, political scientists, anthropologists, and social historians (Ridge, 2002, 2006; Rowntree, 1901; Ryan, Fauth, and Brooks-Gunn, 2006; Sánchez, 2008). However, there is not a consensus on a definition of "class" and the term has a wide range of sometimes conflicting meanings (Bloom and Canning, 2001; Bourdillon and Boyden, 2011; Boyden and James, 2014; Bruch and Touraine, 1940). Some people argue that due to social mobility, class boundaries do not exist (McLoyd, Aikens, and Burton, 2007; Mickelson, 2002; Miller and Chen, 2013; Miller et al., 2011). In common parlance, the term "social class" is usually synonymous with "socio-economic class," defined as "people having the same social, economic, cultural, political or educational status," e.g., "the working class"; "an emerging professional class" (Boyden and James, 2014; Lyytikäinen et al., 2006; Duncan et al., 2012). However, academics distinguish social class and socioeconomic status, with the former referring to one's relatively stable sociocultural background and the latter referring to one's current social and economic situation and consequently being more changeable over time (Corcoran and Chaudry, 1997; Deaton, 2006; Dreyer, 2013; Duncan and Magnuson, 2013).

The precise measurements of what determines social class in society have varied over time (Kim et al., 2015; Krason, 2015; Lesner, 2018). Karl Marx thought "class" was defined by one's relationship to the means of production or their relations of production (Ziol-Guest, Duncan, and

Kalil, 2009; Ziol-Guest et al., 2012). His simple understanding of classes in modern capitalist society is the proletariat, those who work but do not own the means of production; and the bourgeoisie, those who invest and live off the surplus generated by the proletariat's operation of the means of production (Fujiura and Yamaki, 2000; Hill and Sandfort, 1995; Kendig, Mattingly, and Bianchi, 2014). This contrasts with the view of the sociologist Max Weber, who argued "class" is determined by economic position, in contrast to "social status" or "Stand" which is determined by social prestige rather than simply just relations of production (Mbabazi and Pyeong, 2014; McLaughlin and Rank, 2018; McLoyd, Aikens, and Burton, 2007). The term "class" is etymologically derived from the Latin classics, which was used by census takers to categorize citizens by wealth to determine military service obligations (Duncan et al., 1998; Mazza et al., 2017). In the late 18th century, the term "class" began to replace classifications such as estates, rank, and orders as the primary means of organizing society into hierarchical divisions (Lopez and Velasco, 2011; Lyytikäinen et al., 2006; Magnuson and Votruba-Drzal, 2008). This corresponded to a general decrease in significance ascribed to hereditary characteristics and an increase in the significance of wealth and income as indicators of position in the social hierarchy (Evans and Kutcher, 2011; Mickelson, 2002; Segretin et al., 2016; Jones, Vargas, and Villar, 2008). It must be noted that even relatively egalitarian societies such as Canada, still experience child poverty (see Figure 6.4).

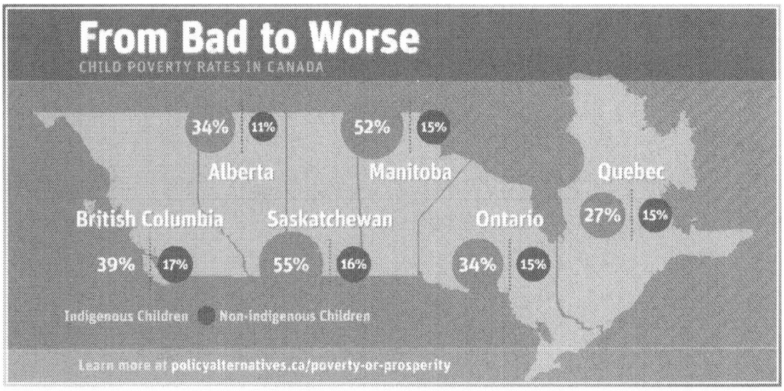

Figure 6.4. Deteriorating child poverty in Canada.

Source: Rebel Youth Magazine.

Definitions of social classes reflect some sociological perspectives, informed by anthropology, economics, psychology, and sociology (Duncan, Kalil, and Ziol-Guest, 2013; Evans and Cassells, 2014; Guest and Biasini,

2001; Duncan et al., 1998). The major perspectives historically have been Marxism and structural functionalism (Serbin et al., 2011; Zembe-Mkabile et al., 2015). The common stratum model of class divides society into a simple hierarchy of working-class, middle class, and upper class (Duncan, Kalil, and Ziol-Guest, 2008; Evans, 2016; Fierman et al., 2016). Within academia, two broad schools of definitions emerge those aligned with 20th-century sociological stratum models of class society and those aligned with the 19th-century historical materialist economic models of the Marxists and anarchists (Bhargava et al., 2004; Bloom and Canning, 2001; Bourdillon and Boyden, 2011; Boyden and James, 2014). Another distinction can be drawn between analytical concepts of social class, such as the Marxist and Weberian traditions, as well as the more empirical traditions such as socioeconomic status approach, which notes the correlation of income, education, and wealth with social outcomes without necessarily implying a particular theory of social structure (Chiputwa, Spielman, and Qaim, 2015; Evans and Kim, 2007; Okiror, 2015; Townsend, 1979).

The upper class is the social class composed of those who are rich, well-born, powerful, or a combination of those (Hatcher et al., 2019; Kapoor, 1993; McLoyd, Aikens, and Burton, 2007). They usually wield the greatest political power. In some countries, wealth alone is sufficient to allow entry into the upper class (Duncan, Kalil, and Ziol-Guest, 2008; Evans, 2016; Fierman et al., 2016). In others, only people who are born or marry into certain aristocratic bloodlines are considered members of the upper class, and those who gain great wealth through commercial activity are looked down upon by the aristocracy as nouveau riche (Ministry of Finance, 2014; Morrow, 2013; Muñoz, Álvarez-Verdejo, and García-Fernández, 2016; Nikulina and Widom, 2014). In the United Kingdom, for example, the upper classes are the aristocracy and royalty, with wealth playing a less important role in class status (Duncan and Rodgers, 1988; Evans, 2004; Farah et al., 2006). Many aristocratic peerages or titles have seats attached to them, with the holder of the title (e.g., Earl of Bristol) and his family being the custodians of the house, but not the owners (Bruch and Touraine, 1940; Magnuson and Votruba-Drzal, 2008; Evans and Fuller-Rowell, 2013). Many of these require high expenditures, so wealth is typically needed (Nikulina, Widom, and Czaja, 2011; Okiror, 2015; Penn, 2004; Ratcliffe and McKernan, 2010). Many aristocratic peerages and their homes are parts of estates, owned, and run by the title holder with amounts of money generated by the land, rents, or other sources of wealth (State House Uganda, 2017; Stewart, 2005; Torres and Wong, 2013; Townsend, 1979; Twikirize et al., 2014). However, in the United States where there is no aristocracy or royalty, the upper-class status belongs to the extremely wealthy, the so-called "super-rich" (Corcoran and Chaudry, 1997; Deaton, 2006; Kim et al., 2016; Twikirize et al., 2014). However, there is some tendency even in the United States for those with old family wealth to look down on those who have earned their money in business, the struggle between new money and old money (Kim et al., 2015; Krason, 2015; Lesner, 2018; Mazza et al., 2017). The upper class is generally contained within the richest 1% or 2% of the population (Ansell, 2016; Dreyer, 2013; Evans, 2016; Evans and Kim, 2013; Jones, Vargas, and Villar, 2007; Mbabazi and Pyeong, 2014; Schickedanz, Dreyer, and Halfon, 2015). Members of the upper class are often born into it and are distinguished by immense wealth, which is passed from generation to generation in the form of estates (Hatcher et al., 2019; Evans and Kutcher, 2011; Hill and Sandfort, 1995). Based on some new social and political theories upper class consists of the wealthiest decile group in society which holds nearly 87% of the whole society's wealth (Hobcraft, 1998; Hobcraft and Kiernan, 2001; Evans and Schamberg, 2009; Holzer et al., 2008). The middle class is the most contested of the three categories, the broad group of people in contemporary society who fall socio-economically between the lower and upper classes (Guest and Biasini, 2001; Evans and Schamberg, 2009; Krason, 2015; Lesner, 2018). One example of the contest of this term is that in the United States "middle class" is applied very broadly and includes people who would elsewhere be considered working class (Rowntree, 1901; Ryan, Fauth, and Brooks-Gunn, 2006; Sánchez, 2008; Ridge, 2006). Middle-class workers are sometimes called "white-collar workers" (Mazza et al., 2017; Kim et al., 2016). Theorists such as Ralf Dahrendorf have noted the tendency toward an enlarged middle class in modern Western societies, particularly with the necessity of an educated workforce in technological economies (Kim et al., 2016; Mbabazi and Pyeong, 2014; McLaughlin and Rank, 2018). Perspectives concerning globalization and neocolonialism, such as dependency theory, suggest this is due to the shift of low-level labor to developing nations and the Third World (Ansell, 2016; Ashiabi, 2000; Ashworth, Hill, and Walker, 1994; Bäckman, and Nilsson, 2007; Bhargava et al., 2004). The middle class is the group of people with typical-everyday jobs that pay significantly more than the poverty line (Ministry of Finance, 2014; Morrow, 2013; Muñoz, Álvarez-Verdejo, and García-Fernández, 2016). Examples of these types of jobs are factory workers, salespeople, teachers, cooks, and nurses (Zembe-Mkabile et al., 2015; Ziol-Guest, Duncan, and Kalil, 2009; Ziol-Guest et al., 2012). There is a new trend by some scholars which assumes that the size of the middle class in every society is the same (Hart, 2008; Kalil, Duncan, and Ziol-Guest, 2016; Kaplinsky, 2005; McLaughlin and Rank, 2018; Schmitz, Wagner, and Menke, 2001). For example, in a paradox of interest theory, the middle class are those who are in 6th–9th decile groups which hold nearly 12% of the whole society's wealth (Evans and Kutcher, 2011; Hill and Sandfort, 1995; Hobcraft, 1998; Hobcraft and Kiernan, 2001).

Lower class (occasionally described as working class) are those employed in low-paying wage jobs with very little economic security (Ashworth, Hill, and Walker, 1994; Lichter, Shanahan, and Gardner, 2002; Duncan, Kalil, and Ziol-Guest, 2013). The term "lower class" also refers to persons with low income (Duncan et al., 2012; Evans and Fuller-Rowell, 2013; Guest and Biasini, 2001). The working class is sometimes separated into those who are employed but lacking financial security or the "working poor" (Deaton, 2006; Dreyer, 2013; Duncan and Magnuson, 2013; Lichter, Shanahan, and Gardner, 2002; Lipina, 2016; Lopez and Velasco, 2011). This is an underclass comprising those who are long-term unemployed or homeless, especially those receiving welfare from the state (Vallas, Fremstad, and Ekman, 2015; Van den Waeyenberg, and Hens, 2008; Waddington, 2004; Wells et al., 2010). The latter is today considered analogous to the Marxist term "lumpenproletariat" (Segretin et al., 2016; Serbin et al., 2011). However, during the time of Marx's writing the lumpenproletariat referred to those in dire poverty; such as the homeless (Ashiabi, 2000; Duncan and Magnuson, 2013; Fierman et al., 2016). Members of the working class are sometimes called blue-collar workers. A person's socioeconomic class has wide-ranging effects (Evans, 2004; Farah et al., 2006). It can impact the schools they can attend, their health, the jobs open to them when they exit the labor market, who they may marry, and their treatment by police and the courts (Bruch and Touraine, 1940; Chamberlain et al., 2016). Angus Deaton and Anne Case have analyzed the mortality rates related to the group of white, middle-aged Americans between the ages of 45 and 54 and its relation to class (Chiputwa, Spielman, and Qaim, 2015; Corcoran and Chaudry, 1997; Lipina et al., 2013). There has been a growing number of suicides and deaths by substance abuse in this particular group of middle-class Americans (Miller and Chen, 2013; Miller et al., 2011). This group also has been recorded to have an increase in reports of chronic pain and poor general health (Hobcraft, 1998; Kim et al., 2013). Deaton and Case concluded from these observations that because of the constant stress that these white, middle-aged Americans feel fighting poverty and wavering between the middle and lower classes, these strains have taken a toll on these people and affected their whole bodies (Sinervo and Hill, 2011; Song and Lu, 2002; Sripada et al., 2014; State House Uganda, 2017).

Lower-class people experience a wide array of health problems as a result of their economic status (Duncan, Kalil, and Ziol-Guest, 2013; Evans and Cassells, 2014; Fujiura and Yamaki, 2000; Garrett, Ng'andu, and Ferron, 1994). They are unable to use health care as often and when they do it is of lower quality, even though they generally tend to experience a much higher rate of health issues (Farah et al., 2006). Lower-class families have higher rates of infant mortality, cancer, cardiovascular disease and disabling physical injuries (Chamberlain et al., 2016; Chiputwa, Spielman, and Qaim, 2015). Additionally, poor people tend to work in much more hazardous conditions, yet generally have much less (if any) health insurance provided for them, as compared to middle- and upper-class workers (Hong, 2015; Jain and Vaachani, 2006; Jarjoura, Triplett, and Brinker, 2002; Kaplinsky, 2005; Kapoor, 1993; Jones, Vargas, and Villar, 2008). The conditions at a person's job vary greatly depending on the class (Duncan and Rodgers, 1988; Holzer et al., 2008). Those in the upper-middle class and middle class enjoy greater freedoms in their occupations (Jones, Vargas, and Villar, 2007; Kalil, Duncan, and Ziol-Guest, 2016; Kaplinsky, 2005; Kapoor, 1993). They are usually more respected, enjoy more diversity, and can exhibit some authority (Mickelson, 2002; Miller and Chen, 2013; Miller et al., 2011). Those in lower classes tend to feel more alienated and have lower work satisfaction overall. The physical conditions of the workplace differ greatly between classes (Schickedanz, Dreyer, and Halfon, 2015; Schmitz, Wagner, and Menke, 2001; Segretin et al., 2016). While middle-class workers may "suffer alienating conditions" or "lack of job satisfaction," blue-collar workers are more apt to suffer alienating, often routine, work with obvious physical health hazards, injury, and even death (Nikulina and Widom, 2014; Nikulina, Widom, and Czaja, 2011; Okiror, 2015; Penn, 2004; Ratcliffe and McKernan, 2010). In the UK, a 2015 government study by the Social Mobility Commission suggested the existence of a "glass floor" in British society preventing those who are less able, but who come from wealthier backgrounds, from slipping down the social ladder (Ridge, 2002; Rowntree, 1901; Ryan, Fauth, and Brooks-Gunn, 2006; Sánchez, 2008). The report proposed a 35% greater likelihood of less able, better-off children becoming high earners than bright poor children (Evans and Schamberg, 2009; Holzer et al., 2008; Hong, 2015). This chapter closes with a look at how disability impacts child poverty rates.

6.5. DISABILITY AND CHILDHOOD POVERTY

Children who have disabilities have a high chance of falling into child poverty, particularly if their parents also have a disability (Bäckman, and Nilsson, 2007; Bhargava et al., 2004; Lipina, 2016; Evans and Cassells, 2014). A disability is any condition that makes it more difficult for a person to do certain activities or interact with the world around them (Jain and Vaachani, 2006; Jarjoura, Triplett, and Brinker, 2002; Javanbakht et al., 2015). These conditions, or impairments, may be cognitive, developmental, intellectual, mental, physical, sensory, or a combination of multiple factors (Lyytikäinen et al., 2006; Magnuson and Votruba-Drzal, 2008; Duncan and Rodgers, 1988). Impairments causing disability may be present from birth or occur during a person's lifetime (Nikulina, Widom, and Czaja, 2011; State House Uganda, 2017; Stewart, 2005; Torres and Wong, 2013). Disability is a contested concept, with different meanings in different communities (Bloom and Canning, 2001; Lipina et al., 2013). The term disability may refer to physical or mental attributes that some institutions, particularly medicine, view as needing to be fixed under the medical model (Fujiura and Yamaki, 2000; Garrett, Ng'andu, and Ferron, 1994; Duncan et al., 2012; Evans and Fuller-Rowell, 2013). A disability may also refer to limitations imposed on people by the constraints of an ableist society under the social model (Javanbakht et al., 2015; Wells et al., 2010). Alternatively, the term may serve to refer to the identity of disabled people (Evans, 2004; Jain and Vaachani, 2006; Ministry of Finance, 2014; Vallas, Fremstad, and Ekman, 2015). Physiological functional capacity (PFC) is a measure of an individual's performance level that gauges one's ability to perform the physical tasks of daily life and the ease with which these tasks are performed (Hong, 2015; Jarjoura, Triplett, and Brinker, 2002; Ridge, 2002; Waddington, 2004; Ziol-Guest, Duncan, and Kalil, 2009). PFC declines with advancing age to result in frailty, cognitive disorders, or physical disorders, all of which may lead to labeling individuals as disabled (Ansell, 2016; Ashiabi, 2000; Ashworth, Hill, and Walker, 1994; Bäckman, and Nilsson, 2007). It is also important to consider how other factors such as family structure (see Figure 6.5) impact the lives of people with disabilities and are also simultaneously poor (Hannum, Liu, and Alvarado-Urbina, 2017; Penn, 2004; Ratcliffe; Van den Waeyenberg, and Hens, 2008; Sinervo and Hill, 2011).

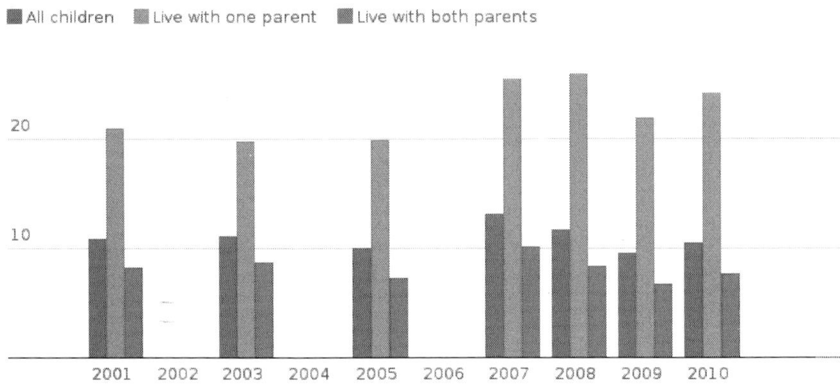

Figure 6.5. Family structures and rates of poverty 2001 through 2010.

Source: Data wrapper.

People with certain types of disabilities struggle to get equal access to some things in society (Muñoz, Álvarez-Verdejo, and García-Fernández, 2016; Sripada et al., 2014). For example, a blind person cannot read printed paper voting ballots and therefore does not have access to voting that requires paper ballots (Ridge, 2006; Schickedanz, Dreyer, and Halfon, 2015; Schmitz, Wagner, and Menke, 2001). Through accommodation (a change that improves access), people with disabilities may lead relatively normal lives (Bourdillon and Boyden, 2011; Lopez and Velasco, 2011; Garrett, Ng'andu, and Ferron, 1994). For example, if voting ballots are available in Braille or on a text-to-speech machine, or if another person reads the ballot to the blind person and recorded the choices, then the blind person would have access to voting. Many different causes of disability often affect basic activities of daily living, such as eating, dressing, transferring, and maintaining personal hygiene; or advanced activities of daily living such as shopping, food preparation, driving, or working (Duncan, Kalil, and Ziol-Guest, 2008; Morrow, 2013; Song and Lu, 2002; Ziol-Guest et al., 2012). For the Americans with Disabilities Act of 1990, the US Equal Employment Opportunity Commission regulations provide a list of conditions that should easily be concluded to be disabilities: deafness, blindness, and intellectual disability (formerly termed mental retardation), partially or completely missing limbs or mobility impairments requiring the use of a wheelchair, autism, cancer, cerebral palsy, diabetes, epilepsy, HIV/AIDS, multiple sclerosis, muscular dystrophy, major depressive disorder, bipolar disorder, post-traumatic stress disorder, obsessive-compulsive disorder, and schizophrenia (Chamberlain et al., 2016). This is not an exhaustive list and many injuries and medical problems cause disability (Lichter, Shanahan, and Gardner, 2002; Lipina, 2016; Lipina et al., 2013). Some causes of disability, such as injuries, may resolve over time and are considered temporary disabilities (Evans and Kim, 2013; Hart, 2008; Hatcher et al., 2019). An acquired disability is the result of impairments that occur suddenly or chronically during the lifespan, as opposed to being born with the impairment (Evans and Kim, 2007, 2013; Hannum, Liu, and Alvarado-Urbina, 2017; Hart, 2008). Invisible disabilities may not be noticeable (Sinervo and Hill, 2011; Song and Lu, 2002; Sripada et al., 2014). Contemporary understandings of disability derive from concepts that arose during the West's scientific Enlightenment; before the Enlightenment, physical differences were viewed through a different lens (Stewart, 2005; Torres and Wong, 2013; Townsend, 1979; Twikirize et al., 2014; Vallas, Fremstad, and Ekman, 2015). There is evidence that humans during prehistory looked after people with disabilities. At the Windover Archeological Site, one of the skeletons that were found was a male about 15 years old, who had spina bifida (Javanbakht et al., 2015; Jones, Vargas, and Villar, 2007; Kalil, Duncan, and Ziol-Guest, 2016). The condition meant that the boy probably paralyzed below the waist, but that he was taken care of in a Hunter-gatherer community (Van den Waeyenberg, and Hens, 2008; Waddington, 2004; Wells et al., 2010). Contemporary concepts of disability are rooted in 18th- and 19th-century developments (Duncan et al., 1998; Evans and Kim, 2007; Hannum, Liu, and Alvarado-Urbina, 2017). Foremost among these was the development of clinical medical discourse, which made the human body visible as a thing to be manipulated, studied, and transformed (Jones, Vargas, and Villar, 2008; Kendig, Mattingly, and Bianchi, 2014; Kim et al., 2013). These worked in tandem with scientific discourses that sought to classify and categorize and, in so doing, became methods of normalization (Hobcraft and Kiernan, 2001; Kim et al., 2015; Nikulina and Widom, 2014).

Studies have illustrated a correlation between disability and poverty (Serbin et al., 2011; Zembe-Mkabile et al., 2015). Notably, jobs offered to disabled people are scarce (Ministry of Finance, 2014; Morrow, 2013; Muñoz, Álvarez-Verdejo, and García-Fernández, 2016; Nikulina and Widom, 2014). In the developed world, there are programs in place that aid intellectually disabled (ID) people to acquire skills they need in the workforce (Van den Waeyenberg, and Hens, 2008; Waddington, 2004; Wells et al., 2010). Such programs include sheltered workshops and adult day care programs (Mbabazi and Pyeong, 2014; McLaughlin and Rank, 2018;

McLoyd, Aikens, and Burton, 2007). Sheltered programs consist of daytime activities such as gardening, manufacturing, and assembling (Javanbakht et al., 2015; Wells et al., 2010). These activities facilitate routine-oriented tasks that in turn allow ID people to gain experience before entering the workforce (Stewart, 2005; Torres and Wong, 2013; Townsend, 1979; Twikirize et al., 2014; Vallas, Fremstad, and Ekman, 2015). Similarly, adult day care programs also include daytime activities (Guest and Biasini, 2001; Evans and Schamberg, 2009; Krason, 2015; Lesner, 2018). However, these activities are based in an educational environment where ID can engage in educational, physical, and communication-based tasks (McLoyd, Aikens, and Burton, 2007; Mickelson, 2002; Miller and Chen, 2013; Miller et al., 2011). This educationally based environment helps facilitate communication, memory, and general living skills (Muñoz, Álvarez-Verdejo, and García-Fernández, 2016; Sripada et al., 2014). In addition, adult day care programs arrange opportunities for their students to engage in community activities (Bourdillon and Boyden, 2011; Lopez and Velasco, 2011; Garrett, Ng'andu, and Ferron, 1994). Such opportunities are arranged by scheduling field trips to public places (Evans and Kim, 2013; Hart, 2008; Hatcher et al., 2019).

Despite, both programs providing essential skills for ID before entering the workforce, researchers have found that ID people prefer to be involved with community-integrated employment (Corcoran and Chaudry, 1997; Deaton, 2006; Kim et al., 2016; Twikirize et al., 2014). Community-integrated employment is job opportunities offered to ID people at minimum wage or a higher rate depending on the position (Jain and Vaachani, 2006; Jarjoura, Triplett, and Brinker, 2002; Javanbakht et al., 2015). Community-integrated employment comes in a variety of occupations ranging from customer service, clerical, janitorial, hospitality, and manufacturing positions (Ashworth, Hill, and Walker, 1994; Lichter, Shanahan, and Gardner, 2002; Duncan, Kalil, and Ziol-Guest, 2013). Within their daily tasks, community-integrated employees work alongside employees who do not have disabilities, but who can assist them with training (Fujiura and Yamaki, 2000; Hill and Sandfort, 1995; Kendig, Mattingly, and Bianchi, 2014). All three options allow ID people to develop and exercise social skills that are vital to everyday life (Lichter, Shanahan, and Gardner, 2002; Lipina, 2016; Lipina et al., 2013). However, it is not guaranteed that community-integrated employees receive the same treatment as employees that do not have ID (Vallas, Fremstad, and Ekman, 2015; Van den Waeyenberg, and Hens, 2008; Waddington, 2004; Wells et al., 2010). According to Lindstrom, Hirano, McCarthy, and Alverson, community-integrated employees are less likely to receive raises

(Bhargava et al., 2004; Bloom and Canning, 2001; Bourdillon and Boyden, 2011; Boyden and James, 2014). In addition, studies conducted in 2013 illustrated only 26% of employees with ID retained full-time status (Duncan and Rodgers, 1988; Holzer et al., 2008).

Furthermore, for many with disabilities, intellectual, and psychical, finding a stable workforce poses many challenges (Chiputwa, Spielman, and Qaim, 2015; Corcoran and Chaudry, 1997; Lipina et al., 2013). According to a study conducted by JARID (Journal of Applied Research and Intellectual Disability), finding a job may be difficult for an ID individual (Hart, 2008; Kalil, Duncan, and Ziol-Guest, 2016; Kaplinsky, 2005; McLaughlin and Rank, 2018; Schmitz, Wagner, and Menke, 2001). Additionally, stabilizing a job is even harder (Nikulina and Widom, 2014; Nikulina, Widom, and Czaja, 2011; Okiror, 2015; Penn, 2004; Ratcliffe and McKernan, 2010). This is largely due to two main factors: production skills and effective social skills (Evans and Kutcher, 2011; Hill and Sandfort, 1995; Hobcraft, 1998; Hobcraft and Kiernan, 2001). This idea is supported by Chadsey-Rusch, who claims that securing employment for the ID, requires adequate production skills and effective social skills (Jones, Vargas, and Villar, 2008; Kendig, Mattingly, and Bianchi, 2014; Kim et al., 2013). However, other underlying factors for job loss include structural factors and the integration between worker and workplace (Segretin et al., 2016; Serbin et al., 2011).

As stated by Kilsby, limited structural factors can affect a multitude of factors in a job (Hatcher et al., 2019; Kapoor, 1993; McLoyd, Aikens, and Burton, 2007). Factors such as a restricted number of hours an ID person is allowed to work (Kim et al., 2015; Krason, 2015; Lesner, 2018; Mazza et al., 2017). This in return, according to Fabian, Wistow, and Schneider leads to a lack of opportunity to develop relationships with coworkers and a chance to better integrate within the workplace (Ridge, 2006; Schickedanz, Dreyer, and Halfon, 2015; Schmitz, Wagner, and Menke, 2001). Nevertheless, those who are unable to stabilize a job often are left discouraged (Schickedanz, Dreyer, and Halfon, 2015; Schmitz, Wagner, and Menke, 2001; Segretin et al., 2016). According to the same study conducted by JARED, many who had participated found that they had made smaller incomes when compared to their co-workers, had an excess of time throughout their days, because they did not have work (Hobcraft and Kiernan, 2001; Kim et al., 2015; Nikulina and Widom, 2014). They also had feelings of hopelessness and failure (Serbin et al., 2011; Zembe-Mkabile et al., 2015).

According to the NOD (National Organization On Disability), not only do the ID people face constant discouragement but many life below the poverty line, because they are unable to find or stabilize employment and because of employee restricting factors placed on ID workers (Duncan, Kalil, and Ziol-Guest, 2013; Evans and Cassells, 2014; Fujiura and Yamaki, 2000; Garrett, Ng'andu, and Ferron, 1994). This then causes the ID people the incapacity to provide for themselves necessities one needs (Bruch and Touraine, 1940; Magnuson and Votruba-Drzal, 2008; Evans and Fuller-Rowell, 2013). Items such as food, medical care, transportation, and housing (Ansell, 2016; Dreyer, 2013; Evans, 2016; Evans and Kim, 2013; Jones, Vargas, and Villar, 2007; Mbabazi and Pyeong, 2014; Schickedanz, Dreyer, and Halfon, 2015). There is a global correlation between disability and poverty, produced by a variety of factors (Hobcraft, 1998; Kim et al., 2013). Disability and poverty may form a vicious circle, in which physical barriers and stigma of disability make it more difficult to get income, which in turn diminishes access to health care and other necessities for a healthy life (Mickelson, 2002; Miller and Chen, 2013; Miller et al., 2011). The World report on disability indicates that half of all disabled people cannot afford health care, compared to a third of abled people (Bloom and Canning, 2001; Lipina et al., 2013). In countries without public services for adults with disabilities, their families may be impoverished (Duncan et al., 2012; Evans and Fuller-Rowell, 2013; Guest and Biasini, 2001).

CHAPTER 6 SUMMARY

This chapter has considered some of the societal factors that create or sustain child poverty. It has shown that racism, xenophobia, discrimination, and the class system can conspire to keep certain children in poverty. In particular, the chapter has highlighted the possibility of intersectionality which reduces opportunities for progress. The next chapter will explore the social construction of child poverty.

Chapter 7

Social Construction of Childhood Poverty

CONTENTS

Some philosophers are of the view that child poverty can be socially constructed, without ignoring its real effects on the community. This chapter summarizes some of the key debates and issues surrounding the social construction of this social problem. These include de-industrialization, globalization, residential segregation, labor market segmentation, and family breakdown. By the end of this chapter, the reader should have an overview of how socially constructed issues impact child poverty.

7.1. DE-INDUSTRIALIZATION AND CHILDHOOD POVERTY

De-industrialization is a process of social and economic change caused by the removal or reduction of industrial capacity or activity in a country or region, especially of heavy industry or manufacturing industry (Kim et al., 2015; Krason, 2015; Lesner, 2018).

There are different interpretations of what de-industrialization is. Many associates the de-industrialization of the United States with the mass closing of automaker plants in the now so-called "Rust Belt" between 1980 and 1990 (Bruch and Touraine, 1940; Chamberlain et al., 2016).

The US Federal Reserve raised interest and exchange rates beginning in 1979, and continuing until 1984, which automatically caused import prices to fall (Ansell, 2016; Ashiabi, 2000; Ashworth, Hill, and Walker, 1994; Bäckman, and Nilsson, 2007; Bhargava et al., 2004). Japan was rapidly expanding productivity during this time, and this decimated the US machine tool sector (Bäckman, and Nilsson, 2007; Bhargava et al., 2004; Lipina, 2016; Evans and Cassells, 2014). The second wave of de-industrialization occurred between 2001 and 2009, culminating in the automaker bailout of GM and Chrysler, from which the US did not recover (Javanbakht et al., 2015; Jones, Vargas, and Villar, 2007; Kalil, Duncan, and Ziol-Guest, 2016). De-industrialization has been implicated in the increasing poverty rates among working families (see Figure 7.1).

Research has pointed to investment in patents rather than in new capital equipment as a contributing factor (Ansell, 2016; Ashiabi, 2000; Ashworth, Hill, and Walker, 1994; Bäckman, and Nilsson, 2007). At a more fundamental level, Cairncross, and Lever offer four possible definitions of deindustrialization.

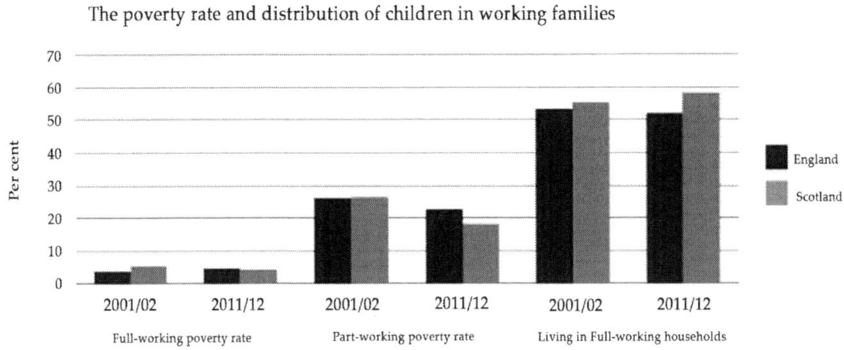

Figure 7.1. Poverty and the distribution of children in working families.

Source: Joseph Rowntree Foundation.

First, is a straightforward long-term decline in the output of manufactured goods or employment in the manufacturing sector (Chiputwa, Spielman, and Qaim, 2015; Evans and Kim, 2007; Okiror, 2015; Townsend, 1979). Second is a shift from manufacturing to the service sectors, so that manufacturing has a lower share of total employment (Ridge, 2002, 2006; Rowntree, 1901; Ryan, Fauth, and Brooks-Gunn, 2006; Sánchez, 2008). Such a shift may occur even if manufacturing employment is growing in absolute terms (Ridge, 2002; Rowntree, 1901; Ryan, Fauth, and Brooks-Gunn, 2006; Sánchez, 2008). Third, is when manufactured goods comprise a declining share of external trade, so that there is a progressive failure to achieve a sufficient surplus of exports over imports to maintain an economy in external balance (Sinervo and Hill, 2011; Song and Lu, 2002; Sripada et al., 2014; State House Uganda, 2017). Fourth, is when there is a continuing state of balance of trade deficit (as described in the third definition above) that accumulates to the extent that a country or region is unable to pay for necessary imports to sustain further production of goods, thus initiating a further downward spiral of economic decline (Duncan et al., 1998; Mazza et al., 2017). Consequently, families and their children may fall into poverty after de-industrialization (Evans, 2004; Jain and Vaachani, 2006; Ministry of Finance, 2014; Vallas, Fremstad, and Ekman, 2015). The next section focuses on the role of globalization in child poverty.

7.2. GLOBALIZATION AND CHILDHOOD POVERTY

Globalization is the process of interaction and integration among people, companies, and governments worldwide (Ziol-Guest, Duncan, and Kalil, 2009; Ziol-Guest et al., 2012). As a complex and multifaceted phenomenon, globalization is considered by some as a form of capitalist expansion which entails the integration of local and national economies into a global, unregulated market economy (Duncan and Rodgers, 1988; Evans, 2004; Farah et al., 2006). Globalization has grown due to advances in transportation and communication technology (Corcoran and Chaudry, 1997; Deaton, 2006; Dreyer, 2013; Duncan and Magnuson, 2013). With the increased global interactions comes the growth of international trade, ideas, and culture. Globalization is primarily an economic process of interaction and integration that's associated with social and cultural aspects (Duncan, Kalil, and Ziol-Guest, 2008; Evans, 2016; Fierman et al., 2016). However, conflicts and diplomacy are also large parts of the history of globalization, and modern globalization (Nikulina, Widom, and Czaja, 2011; State House Uganda, 2017; Stewart, 2005; Torres and Wong, 2013). Economically, globalization involves goods, services, the economic resources of capital, technology, and data (Evans and Kim, 2007, 2013; Hannum, Liu, and Alvarado-Urbina, 2017; Hart, 2008). Also, the expansions of global markets liberalize the economic activities of the exchange of goods and funds (Ashiabi, 2000; Duncan and Magnuson, 2013; Fierman et al., 2016).

The removal of cross-border trade barriers has made the formation of global markets more feasible (Chamberlain et al., 2016). The steam locomotive, steamship, jet engine, and container ships are some of the advances in the means of transport while the rise of the telegraph and its modern offspring, the Internet, and mobile phones show development in telecommunications infrastructure (Rowntree, 1901; Ryan, Fauth, and Brooks-Gunn, 2006; Sánchez, 2008; Ridge, 2006). All of these improvements have been major factors in globalization and have generated further interdependence of economic and cultural activities around the globe (Serbin et al., 2011; Zembe-Mkabile et al., 2015). Vulnerable groups such as single parents (see Figure 7.2) continue to face the risk of poverty in the era of globalization. This is true even if that globalization is meant to create job opportunities (Lyytikäinen et al., 2006; Magnuson and Votruba-Drzal, 2008; Duncan and Rodgers, 1988).

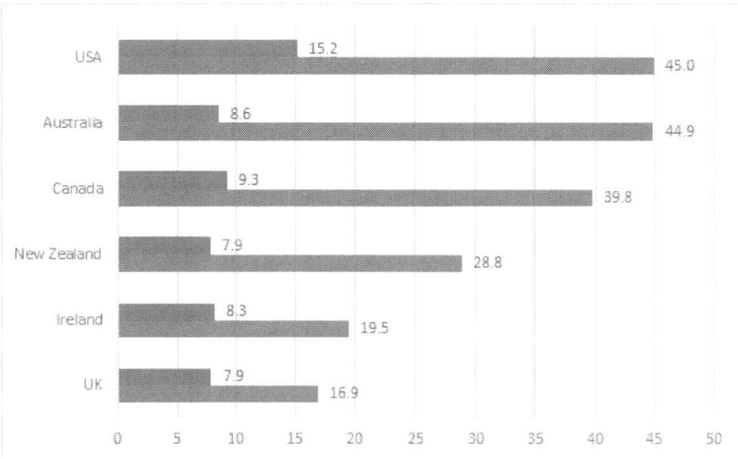

Figure 7.2. Single parent employment and child poverty in selected countries.

Source: Utopia.

Since the 1980s, modern globalization has spread rapidly through the expansion of capitalism and neoliberal ideologies (Farah et al., 2006). The implementation of neoliberal policies has allowed for the privatization of public industry, deregulation of laws or policies that interfered with the free flow of the market, as well as cut-backs to governmental social services (Jones, Vargas, and Villar, 2007; Kalil, Duncan, and Ziol-Guest, 2016; Kaplinsky, 2005; Kapoor, 1993). These neoliberal policies were introduced to many developing countries in the form of structural adjustment programs (SAPs) that were implemented by the World Bank and the International Monetary Fund (IMF) (Fujiura and Yamaki, 2000; Garrett, Ng'andu, and Ferron, 1994; Duncan et al., 2012; Evans and Fuller-Rowell, 2013). These programs require that the country receiving monetary aid would open its markets to capitalism, privatize public industry, allow free trade, cut social services like healthcare and education and allow the free movement of giant multinational corporations (Boyden and James, 2014; Lyytikäinen et al., 2006; Duncan et al., 2012). These programs allowed the World Bank and the IMF to become global financial market regulators that would promote neoliberalism and the creation of free markets for multinational corporations on a global scale (Evans, 2004; Farah et al., 2006). Indigenous workers and industries have been negatively affected by globalization because it imports cheaper alternatives (Hannum, Liu, and Alvarado-Urbina, 2017; Penn, 2004; Ratcliffe; Van den Waeyenberg, and Hens, 2008; Sinervo and

Hill, 2011). Hence, globalization has been associated with high domestic unemployment and industrial strife as the local communities adjust to the new realities of them being subject to external competition (Duncan, Kalil, and Ziol-Guest, 2008; Morrow, 2013; Song and Lu, 2002; Ziol-Guest et al., 2012). The children of those parents that have been left behind will inevitably face poverty (Ministry of Finance, 2014; Morrow, 2013; Muñoz, Álvarez-Verdejo, and García-Fernández, 2016). The next section considers how residential segregation fosters child poverty.

7.3. RESIDENTIAL SEGREGATION AND CHILDHOOD POVERTY

Residential segregation in the United States is the physical separation of two or more groups into different neighborhoods (Mazza et al., 2017; Kim et al., 2016). This is a form of segregation that sorts population groups into various neighborhood contexts and shapes the living environment at the neighborhood level (Bloom and Canning, 2001; Bourdillon and Boyden, 2011; Boyden and James, 2014; Bruch and Touraine, 1940). While it has traditionally been associated with racial segregation, it generally refers to any kind of sorting based on some criteria populations such as race, ethnicity, and income (Duncan, Kalil, and Ziol-Guest, 2008; Evans, 2016; Fierman et al., 2016). While overt segregation is illegal in the United States, housing patterns show significant and persistent segregation for certain races and income groups (Lopez and Velasco, 2011; Lyytikäinen et al., 2006; Magnuson and Votruba-Drzal, 2008). The history of American social and public policies, like Jim Crow laws and Federal Housing Administration's early redlining policies, set the tone for segregation in housing (State House Uganda, 2017; Stewart, 2005; Torres and Wong, 2013; Townsend, 1979; Twikirize et al., 2014). Trends in residential segregation are attributed to suburbanization, discrimination, and personal preferences (Evans and Kutcher, 2011; Mickelson, 2002; Segretin et al., 2016; Jones, Vargas, and Villar, 2008).

Residential segregation produces negative socioeconomic outcomes for minority groups (Hong, 2015; Jarjoura, Triplett, and Brinker, 2002; Ridge, 2002; Waddington, 2004; Ziol-Guest, Duncan, and Kalil, 2009). Public policies for housing attempt to promote integration and mitigate these negative effects (Nikulina, Widom, and Czaja, 2011; Okiror, 2015; Penn, 2004; Ratcliffe and McKernan, 2010). Race-based residential segregation in American cities dates from the rapid urbanization which occurred in the last years of the 19th and the first years of the 20th century (Miller and Chen, 2013; Miller et al., 2011). Before that time, the African-Americans who lived in cities lived in scattered locations (Hong, 2015; Jain and Vaachani, 2006; Jarjoura, Triplett, and Brinker, 2002; Kaplinsky, 2005; Kapoor, 1993; Jones, Vargas, and Villar, 2008). Even interventions such as education (see Figure 7.3), may not fully overcome some of the embedded inequalities that are reproduced in segregated communities (Hatcher et al., 2019; Evans and Kutcher, 2011; Hill and Sandfort, 1995).

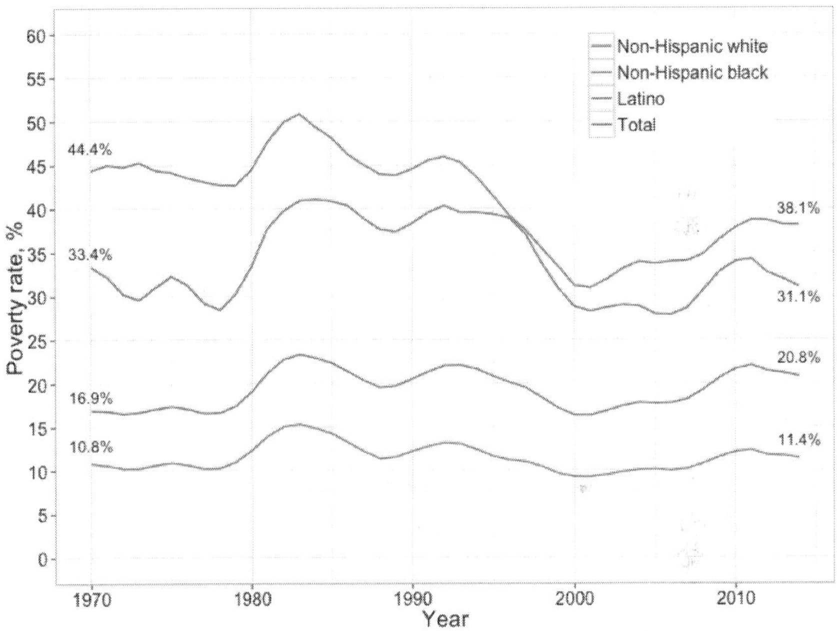

Figure 7.3. The positive impact of educational reform on child poverty rates.

Source: Education Next.

The development of segregated residential neighborhoods was associated with massive influxes of European immigrants and African-Americans (Deaton, 2006; Dreyer, 2013; Duncan and Magnuson, 2013; Lichter, Shanahan, and Gardner, 2002; Lipina, 2016; Lopez and Velasco, 2011). These groups had limited funds and job opportunities and ended up clustered in neighborhoods with poor housing (Duncan, Kalil, and Ziol-Guest, 2013; Evans and Cassells, 2014; Guest and Biasini, 2001; Duncan et al., 1998). These neighborhoods were characterized by social unrest and diseases such as typhoid and tuberculosis (Evans and Schamberg, 2009;

Holzer et al., 2008; Hong, 2015). Progressive social reformers attempted to ameliorate these conditions, but were unsuccessful, particularly concerning African-Americans (Kim et al., 2016; Mbabazi and Pyeong, 2014; McLaughlin and Rank, 2018). Around 1910 they turned to efforts to contain the problems in segregated neighborhoods (Sinervo and Hill, 2011; Song and Lu, 2002; Sripada et al., 2014). The first ordinance establishing segregated neighborhoods was passed in Baltimore in 1910 (Zembe-Mkabile et al., 2015; Ziol-Guest, Duncan, and Kalil, 2009; Ziol-Guest et al., 2012). Overt ordinances were struck down in *Buchanan v. Warley*, 245 US 60 (1917). However, the practice continued and became deeply ingrained in urban culture, resulting in limited housing for an expanding population and development of the African-American ghetto with poor overcrowded housing and numerous social ills (Zembe-Mkabile et al., 2015; Ziol-Guest, Duncan, and Kalil, 2009; Ziol-Guest et al., 2012). In large part, residential discrimination was driven by school segregation which was legal until *Brown v. Board of Education* was decided in 1954 but has persisted due to continuing segregated residential patterns in most American cities to the present (Sinervo and Hill, 2011; Song and Lu, 2002; Sripada et al., 2014). The next section examines the impact of labor market segmentation on child poverty.

7.4. LABOR MARKET SEGMENTATION AND CHILDHOOD POVERTY

Labor market segmentation is the division of the labor market according to a principle such as occupation, geography, and industry (Kim et al., 2016; Mbabazi and Pyeong, 2014; McLaughlin and Rank, 2018). One type of segmentation is to define groups "with little or no crossover capability," such that members of one segment cannot easily join another segment (Evans and Schamberg, 2009; Holzer et al., 2008; Hong, 2015). This can result in different segments, for example, men and women, receiving different wages for the same work (Duncan, Kalil, and Ziol-Guest, 2013; Evans and Cassells, 2014; Guest and Biasini, 2001; Duncan et al., 1998). 19th-century Irish political economist John Elliott Cairnes referred to this phenomenon as that of "non-competing groups" (Deaton, 2006; Dreyer, 2013; Duncan and Magnuson, 2013; Lichter, Shanahan, and Gardner, 2002; Lipina, 2016; Lopez and Velasco, 2011). A related concept is that of a dual labor market (DLM), that splits the aggregate labor market between a primary sector and a secondary sector (Hatcher et al., 2019; Evans and Kutcher, 2011; Hill and

Sandfort, 1995). The theory of labor market segmentation contrasts with neo-classical economic theory, which posits the existence of a unified market for labor, consisting of buyers and sellers in open competition (Hong, 2015; Jain and Vaachani, 2006; Jarjoura, Triplett, and Brinker, 2002; Kaplinsky, 2005; Kapoor, 1993; Jones, Vargas, and Villar, 2008). The labor market thus functions as do other markets (Nikulina, Widom, and Czaja, 2011; Okiror, 2015; Penn, 2004; Ratcliffe and McKernan, 2010). In this model, the difference between different workers' wages and conditions arise from individual differences in their human capital (skills, experience, or formal education) or tastes (Miller and Chen, 2013; Miller et al., 2011). On the latter, as part of the theory of compensating wage differentials, those who prefer risky or dirty jobs receive higher compensation than those who take safe or clean ones (Hong, 2015; Jarjoura, Triplett, and Brinker, 2002; Ridge, 2002; Waddington, 2004; Ziol-Guest, Duncan, and Kalil, 2009). Put another way, differences in compensation for labor arise only on the supply side (Duncan et al., 1998; Evans and Kim, 2007; Hannum, Liu, and Alvarado-Urbina, 2017). Single parents (see Figure 7.4) often suffer the brunt of the poverty-related problems arising out of labor market segmentation (Evans and Kutcher, 2011; Mickelson, 2002; Segretin et al., 2016; Jones, Vargas, and Villar, 2008).

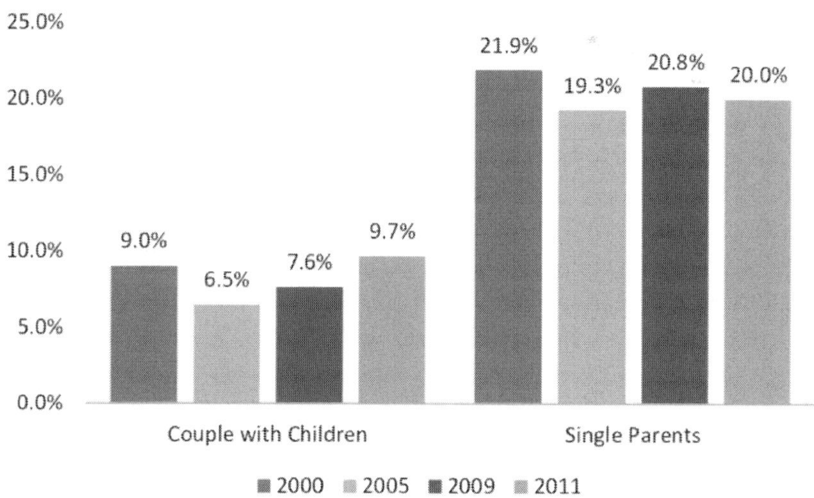

Figure 7.4. Comparison of child poverty among single and non-single parents.

Source: ResearchGate.

The theory of labor market segmentation posits that differences on the demand side imply differences in compensation that are not explained by individual worker characteristics (State House Uganda, 2017; Stewart, 2005; Torres and Wong, 2013; Townsend, 1979; Twikirize et al., 2014). Labor markets are not perfect markets (Lopez and Velasco, 2011; Lyytikäinen et al., 2006; Magnuson and Votruba-Drzal, 2008). Non-market institutions such as craft unions and professional associations affect employer strategies, producing different results for workers with similar characteristics (Duncan, Kalil, and Ziol-Guest, 2008; Evans, 2016; Fierman et al., 2016). All workers should be subject to the same employment standards, such as minimum wages, maximum hour laws, occupational safety, security, and health laws, regardless of the sector (Bloom and Canning, 2001; Bourdillon and Boyden, 2011; Boyden and James, 2014; Bruch and Touraine, 1940).

Modern labor market segmentation theory arose in the early 1960s. It changed the view of many economists who had seen the labor market as a market of individuals with different characteristics of: e.g., education and motivation (Mazza et al., 2017; Kim et al., 2016). This perspective was intended to help explain the demand-side of the market, and the nature and strategy of employers (Hobcraft, 1998; Hobcraft and Kiernan, 2001; Evans and Schamberg, 2009; Holzer et al., 2008). The idea of non-competing groups developed under the general label of labor market segmentation theory (Chamberlain et al., 2016; Chiputwa, Spielman, and Qaim, 2015). The market segmentation model was developed to accommodate the differences in job markets (Kendig, Mattingly, and Bianchi, 2014; Kim et al., 2013). For example, lawyers, and fashion designers work in different markets (Ministry of Finance, 2014; Morrow, 2013; Muñoz, Álvarez-Verdejo, and García-Fernández, 2016). Such markets arise from the division of labor, increasing differentiation and specialization (Duncan, Kalil, and Ziol-Guest, 2008; Morrow, 2013; Song and Lu, 2002; Ziol-Guest et al., 2012). These workers are unable to switch between occupations because they require different skills and investment in training and qualifications (Hannum, Liu, and Alvarado-Urbina, 2017; Penn, 2004; Ratcliffe; Van den Waeyenberg, and Hens, 2008; Sinervo and Hill, 2011). For example, nurses, and doctors form separate occupational labor markets even though they work side by side in the same organizations (Evans, 2004; Farah et al., 2006). The poor may be sometimes left behind by the labor segmentation such that they are unable to provide necessities for their families (Boyden and James, 2014;

Lyytikäinen et al., 2006; Duncan et al., 2012). This chapter will close by considering how the breakdown of families impacts child poverty rates.

7.5. FAMILY BREAKDOWN AND CHILDHOOD POVERTY

Marital breakdown refers to the common process whereby the relationship between a married couple erodes, such that they cannot ordinarily restore their relationship (Fujiura and Yamaki, 2000; Garrett, Ng'andu, and Ferron, 1994; Duncan et al., 2012; Evans and Fuller-Rowell, 2013). There are many stages to the process, and each individual goes through the stages at different rates. It is a complex process involving psychology, personal finance, and often religion (Jones, Vargas, and Villar, 2007; Kalil, Duncan, and Ziol-Guest, 2016; Kaplinsky, 2005; Kapoor, 1993). It is the breach of domestic anticipation, often leading to a divorce or dissolution of the marital relationship (Farah et al., 2006). Often there are children, in-laws, and other individuals involved in the process (Lyytikäinen et al., 2006; Magnuson and Votruba-Drzal, 2008; Duncan and Rodgers, 1988). At the end of the process, there may be no relationship left, or there may be a long-term relationship at a distance (Serbin et al., 2011; Zembe-Mkabile et al., 2015).

Every marital breakdown is therefore different in this regard (Rowntree, 1901; Ryan, Fauth, and Brooks-Gunn, 2006; Sánchez, 2008; Ridge, 2006). Family disruption is a term referring to events that disrupt the structure of individual families (Chamberlain et al., 2016) (Ashiabi, 2000; Duncan and Magnuson, 2013; Fierman et al., 2016). These events include divorce, legal separation, and parental death, out-of-home placement, and deployment (Evans and Kim, 2007, 2013; Hannum, Liu, and Alvarado-Urbina, 2017; Hart, 2008). Some studies suggest that juveniles who have experienced more family disruptions are at a higher risk of delinquency, drug use, negative personality traits, anxiety, academic hardship, lack of social mobility, lack of personality development, and depression in adulthood (Nikulina, Widom, and Czaja, 2011; State House Uganda, 2017; Stewart, 2005; Torres and Wong, 2013). A significant proportion of the populace still believes that family breakdown is a critical cause of child poverty (see Figure 7.5).

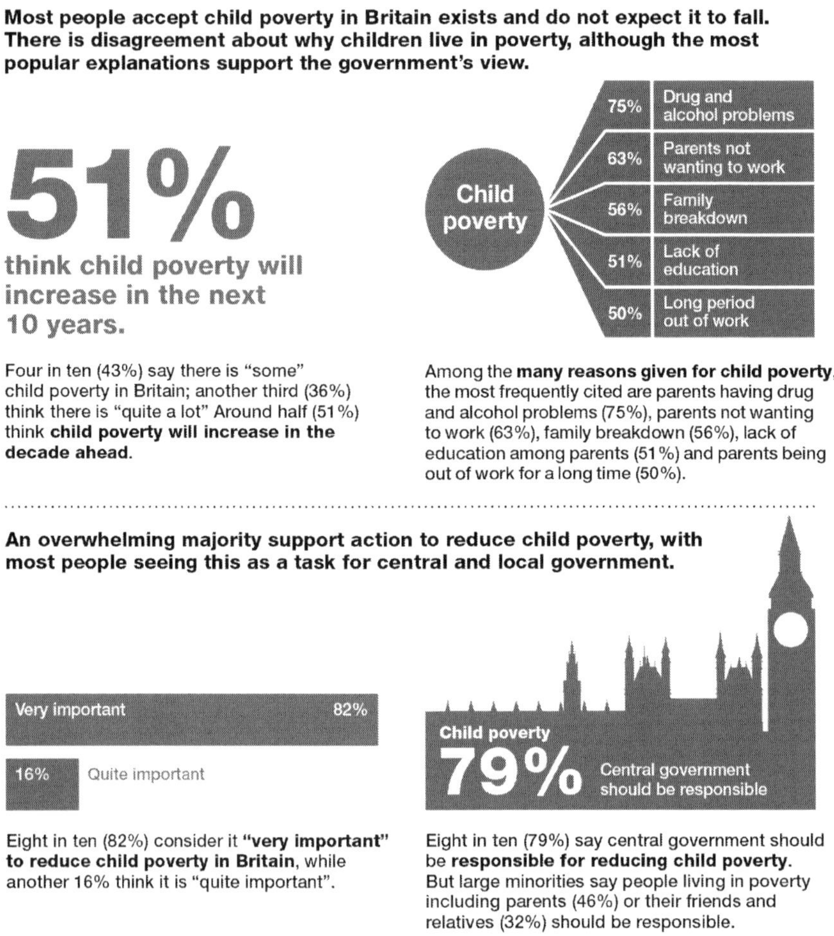

Figure 7.5. Community attitudes to child poverty in the UK.

Source: SAGE Research Methods.

Studies have associated family disruption with delinquency and drug use (Duncan, Kalil, and Ziol-Guest, 2008; Evans, 2016; Fierman et al., 2016). According to a study conducted in 1999 by the Office of Juvenile Justice and Delinquency Prevention (OJJDP) that studied the relationship between family types and levels of delinquency/drug use, the greater number of times children live through a divorce, the more delinquent they become (Corcoran and Chaudry, 1997; Deaton, 2006; Dreyer, 2013; Duncan and Magnuson, 2013). Family transitions put the children at an increased risk for conflict and behavioral problems (Duncan and Rodgers, 1988; Evans, 2004; Farah et al., 2006). The data suggests that these constant changes stir up emotions that lead to wrongdoings (Ziol-Guest, Duncan, and Kalil, 2009; Ziol-Guest et al., 2012). Dysfunctional families pervade all strata of society regardless of social, financial, or intellectual status (Duncan et al., 1998; Mazza et al., 2017). Nevertheless, until recently; the concept of a dysfunctional family was not taken seriously by professionals (therapists, social workers, teachers, counselors, clergy, etc.), especially among the middle and upper classes (Sinervo and Hill, 2011; Song and Lu, 2002; Sripada et al., 2014; State House Uganda, 2017). Any intervention would have been seen as violating the sanctity of marriage and increasing the probability of divorce, which was socially unacceptable at the time (Ridge, 2002; Rowntree, 1901; Ryan, Fauth, and Brooks-Gunn, 2006; Sánchez, 2008). Historically, children of dysfunctional families were expected to obey their parents (ultimately the father), and cope with the situation alone (Ridge, 2002, 2006; Rowntree, 1901; Ryan, Fauth, and Brooks-Gunn, 2006; Sánchez, 2008). The financial stability of dysfunctional families is always in question, and therefore, these disruptions contribute to child poverty (Chiputwa, Spielman, and Qaim, 2015; Evans and Kim, 2007; Okiror, 2015; Townsend, 1979).

CHAPTER 7 SUMMARY

Poverty is a social problem because it impacts many aspects of social life. For example, de-industrialization increased unemployment and poverty, while globalization has the same effect through the importation of goods and people. Over time, this leads to inequality that is manifested in the form of residential segregation. At the micro-level, issues such as labor market segmentation can be combined with a family breakdown to leave children in poverty. The last chapter in this book will explain the universality of child poverty and how that impacts our responses to it.

Chapter 8

Universality of Childhood Poverty

CONTENTS

As this book has shown, poverty can exist in both developing and developed countries. Child poverty is even more universal than child poverty. This book will highlight this fact concerning the vicious cycle of poverty as well as identify some policy implications of this reality.

8.1. CHILDHOOD POVERTY AMONG DEVELOPED NATIONS

Child poverty still exists in the developed nations that have developed clear policies on this issue (Ansell, 2016; Ashiabi, 2000; Ashworth, Hill, and Walker, 1994; Bäckman, and Nilsson, 2007). First of all, credit has to be given for their ability to deal with absolute poverty using interventions such as the New Deal and the Welfare State in the Nordic countries (Javanbakht et al., 2015; Jones, Vargas, and Villar, 2007; Kalil, Duncan, and Ziol-Guest, 2016). However, relative poverty exists because communities cannot be entirely equal (Bäckman, and Nilsson, 2007; Bhargava et al., 2004; Lipina, 2016; Evans and Cassells, 2014). Some might argue that complete equality has not always brought positive results, judging from the experiences of those that lived under communist and socialist governments (Ansell, 2016; Ashiabi, 2000; Ashworth, Hill, and Walker, 1994; Bäckman, and Nilsson, 2007; Bhargava et al., 2004). However, the challenge for these developed countries is to reduce the gap between the rich and poor as much as possible (Bruch and Touraine, 1940; Chamberlain et al., 2016). Figure 8.1 shows an illustration example of child poverty across the USA, despite it being the richest nation on earth.

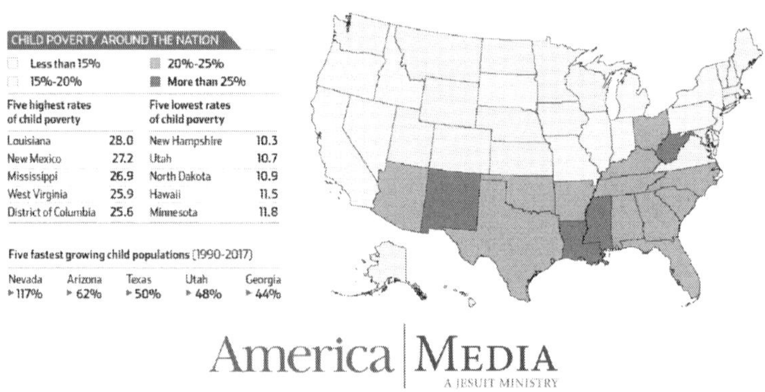

Figure 8.1. Poverty by states in the USA.

Source: America Media.

8.2. CHILDHOOD POVERTY AMONG MIDDLE-INCOME COUNTRIES

Middle-income countries are in a slightly different situation since they aspire to offer social support to all their citizenry but do not have the funds to be able to achieve that goal. However, middle-income countries also engage in long-term investment schemes that are meant to build human capital. They can be suitable contexts for experimentation in terms of identifying new imaginative ways of providing social welfare in a much more sustainable way. Some middle-income countries like India are facing high levels of inequality while others like China are not performing well on the human development index. Eradicating poverty might be one of the pathways for these countries to achieve industrialized status. As Figure 8.2 child relative income poverty states were a problem as recently as 2014.

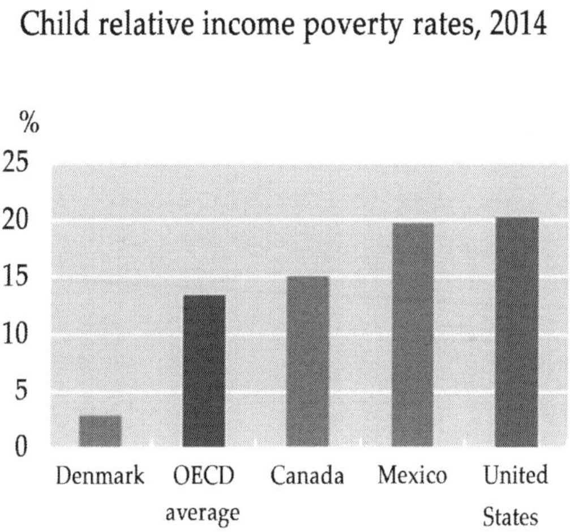

Figure 8.2. Child relative income poverty rates in 2014.

Source: Foundation for Economic Education.

8.3. CHILDHOOD POVERTY AMONG DEVELOPING COUNTRIES

There is no doubt that child poverty remains a very serious problem in developing countries (Kim et al., 2015; Krason, 2015; Lesner, 2018). Children are more than twice as likely as adults to live in extreme poverty, according to a new analysis from the World Bank Group and UNICEF (Duncan et al., 2012; Evans and Fuller□Rowell, 2013; Guest and Biasini, 2001). Meanwhile, developing countries do not have the kind of resources that can support an institutionalized welfare system (Bloom and Canning, 2001; Lipina et al., 2013). That means that any interventions against child poverty are sporadic and blatantly ineffective (Mickelson, 2002; Miller and Chen, 2013; Miller et al., 2011). Research indicates that in 2013, about 19.5% of children in developing countries were living in households that survived on an average of US$1.90 a day or less per person, compared to just 9.2% of adults (Hobcraft, 1998; Kim et al., 2013). Globally, almost 385 million children were living in extreme poverty (Ansell, 2016; Dreyer, 2013; Evans, 2016; Evans and Kim, 2013; Jones, Vargas, and Villar, 2007; Mbabazi and Pyeong, 2014; Schickedanz, Dreyer, and Halfon, 2015). Unlike countries like the USA, which are capable of a multiplicity of complex responses to child poverty (see Figure 8.3), developing countries are unable to fund such priorities (Bruch and Touraine, 1940; Magnuson and Votruba-Drzal, 2008; Evans and Fuller-Rowell, 2013).

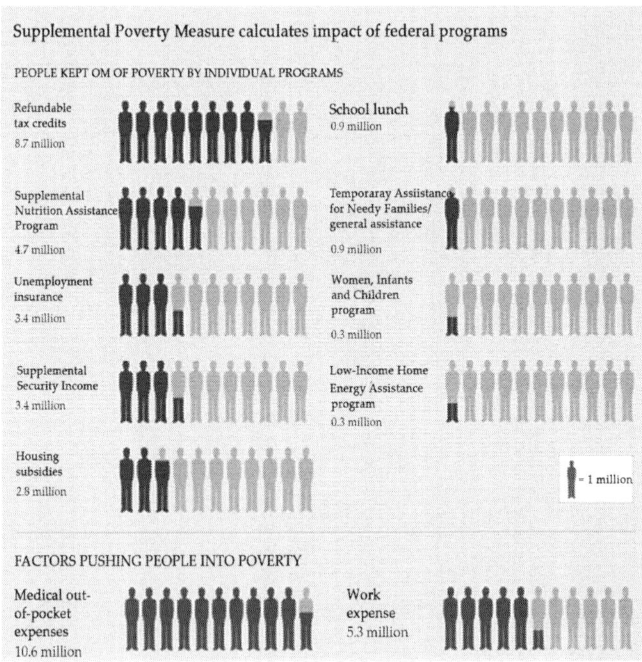

Figure 8.3. Supplemental poverty measures in the USA.

Source: Center for American Progress.

The vast majority of these children living in extreme poverty are in the developing world (Duncan, Kalil, and Ziol-Guest, 2013; Evans and Cassells, 2014; Fujiura and Yamaki, 2000; Garrett, Ng'andu, and Ferron, 1994). Children are disproportionately affected, as they make up around a third of the population studied, but half of the extremely poor (Serbin et al., 2011; Zembe-Mkabile et al., 2015). The youngest children are the most at risk, with more than one-fifth of children under the age of five in the developing world living in extremely poor households (Hobcraft and Kiernan, 2001; Kim et al., 2015; Nikulina and Widom, 2014). Sub-Saharan Africa has both the highest rates of children living in extreme poverty at just under 50%, and the largest share of the world's extremely poor children, at just over 50% (Schickedanz, Dreyer, and Halfon, 2015; Schmitz, Wagner, and Menke, 2001; Segretin et al., 2016). South Asia has the second-highest share at nearly 36%, with over 30% of extremely poor children living in India alone (Ridge, 2006; Schickedanz, Dreyer, and Halfon, 2015; Schmitz, Wagner, and Menke, 2001). More than four out of five children in extreme poverty live in rural areas (Kim et al., 2015; Krason, 2015; Lesner, 2018; Mazza et al., 2017). In addition, the report reveals that even at higher thresholds, poverty also affects children disproportionately (Hatcher et al., 2019; Kapoor, 1993; McLoyd, Aikens, and Burton, 2007). About 45% of children are living in households subsisting on less than $3.10 a day per person, compared with nearly 27% of adults (Segretin et al., 2016; Serbin et al., 2011).

UNICEF and the World Bank Group are calling on governments to routinely measure child poverty at the national and subnational level and focus on children in national poverty reduction plans as part of efforts to end extreme poverty by 2030 (Jones, Vargas, and Villar, 2008; Kendig, Mattingly, and Bianchi, 2014; Kim et al., 2013). Developing countries are encouraged to strengthen child-sensitive social protection systems, including cash transfer programs that directly help poor families to pay for food, health care, education, and other services that protect children from the impact of poverty and improve their chances of breaking the cycle in their own lives (Evans and Kutcher, 2011; Hill and Sandfort, 1995; Hobcraft, 1998; Hobcraft and Kiernan, 2001). Additionally, they should prioritize investments in education, health, clean water, sanitation, and infrastructure that benefit the poorest children, as well as those that help prevent people from falling back into poverty after setbacks like droughts, disease, or economic instability (Nikulina and Widom, 2014; Nikulina, Widom, and Czaja, 2011; Okiror, 2015; Penn, 2004; Ratcliffe and McKernan, 2010). All this should occur in a context where policy decisions are shaped so that economic growth benefits the poorest children (Hart, 2008; Kalil, Duncan, and Ziol-Guest, 2016; Kaplinsky, 2005; McLaughlin and Rank, 2018; Schmitz, Wagner, and Menke, 2001). The next section briefly looks at the impact of the vicious cycle of poverty.

8.4. THE VICIOUS CYCLE OF POVERTY

In economics, the cycle of poverty is the set of factors or events by which poverty, once started, is likely to continue unless there is outside intervention (Chiputwa, Spielman, and Qaim, 2015; Corcoran and Chaudry, 1997; Lipina et al., 2013). Families trapped in the cycle of poverty, have either limited or no resources (Duncan and Rodgers, 1988; Holzer et al., 2008). Many disadvantages collectively work in a circular process making it virtually impossible for individuals to break the cycle (Bhargava et al., 2004; Bloom and Canning, 2001; Bourdillon and Boyden, 2011; Boyden and James, 2014). This occurs when poor people do not have the resources necessary to get out of poverty, such as financial capital, education, or connections (Vallas, Fremstad, and Ekman, 2015; Van den Waeyenberg, and Hens, 2008; Waddington, 2004; Wells et al., 2010). In other words, impoverished individuals do not have access to economic and social resources as a result of their poverty (Lichter, Shanahan, and Gardner, 2002; Lipina, 2016; Lipina et al., 2013). This lack may increase their poverty (Fujiura and Yamaki, 2000; Hill and Sandfort, 1995; Kendig, Mattingly, and Bianchi, 2014). This could mean that the poor remain poor throughout their lives (Ashworth, Hill, and Walker, 1994; Lichter, Shanahan, and Gardner, 2002; Duncan, Kalil, and Ziol-Guest, 2013). The poverty cycle can be called the "development trap" or "poverty trap" when it is applied to countries (Jain and Vaachani, 2006; Jarjoura, Triplett, and Brinker, 2002; Javanbakht et al., 2015). In the case of localities like Scotland (see Figure 8.4), the poor remain poor while the rich become richer.

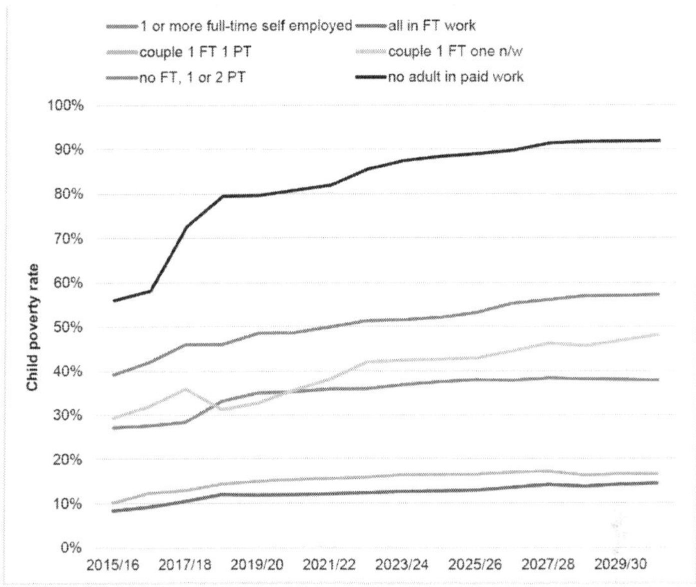

Figure 8.4. Child poverty patterns in Scotland.

Source: The Scottish Government.

Ruby K. Payne distinguishes between situational poverty, which can generally be traced to a specific incident within the lifetimes of the person or family members in poverty, and generational poverty, which is a cycle that passes from generation to generation and goes on to argue that generational poverty has its own distinct culture and belief patterns (Corcoran and Chaudry, 1997; Deaton, 2006; Kim et al., 2016; Twikirize et al., 2014). Measures of social mobility examine how frequently poor people become wealthier, and how often children are wealthier or achieve higher income than their parents (Evans and Kim, 2013; Hart, 2008; Hatcher et al., 2019). Chronic general poverty can be created or sustained for large numbers of people through general economic conditions, which tend to be self-sustaining (Bourdillon and Boyden, 2011; Lopez and Velasco, 2011; Garrett, Ng'andu, and Ferron, 1994). Metrics for these conditions include the following: First, there is a low gross domestic product or overall low productivity, failing to produce enough wealth for the population as a whole to escape poverty (Muñoz, Álvarez-Verdejo, and García-Fernández, 2016; Sripada et al., 2014). Second, there is high unemployment, creating poverty for the unemployed and putting downward pressure on wages (McLoyd, Aikens, and Burton, 2007; Mickelson, 2002; Miller and Chen, 2013; Miller et al., 2011). Third, there is high-income inequality, creating poverty by allocating wealth unevenly (Guest and Biasini, 2001; Evans and Schamberg, 2009; Krason, 2015; Lesner, 2018). Lastly, there is low social mobility, perpetuating poverty for a given person or family (Stewart, 2005; Torres and Wong, 2013; Townsend, 1979; Twikirize et al., 2014; Vallas, Fremstad, and Ekman, 2015). Children are the worst affected by the vicious cycle of poverty since they are inherently vulnerable and cannot independently generate an income for themselves (Javanbakht et al., 2015; Wells et al., 2010).

CHAPTER 8 SUMMARY

This chapter has explained the universality of child poverty and some of the explanations for its existence. We have seen that poverty exists in virtually all nations regardless of their development status. The vicious cycle of poverty keeps many in perpetual poverty. Given the harm that it brings to the community, child poverty should always be a matter of concern to all policymakers and implementers.

Chapter 9

Concluding Remarks

This book has explored child poverty as one of the prevailing social evils. The book has shown that child poverty is far from being a problem for "third world countries." It is a social problem that can afflict even the most developed nations if it is ignored. Child poverty affects some of the most vulnerable members of the community. Therefore, interventions ought to be a matter of course. However, the book has also demonstrated some of the limitations that countries face when trying to create a fairer society. I hope you have enjoyed reading the book and will explore the other books in the series.

Bibliography

1. Ansell, N., (2016). 'Once upon a time': Orphanhood, childhood studies and the depoliticization of childhood poverty in Southern Africa. *Childhood, 23*(2), 162–177.
2. Ashiabi, G. S., (2000). Some correlates of childhood poverty in Ghana. *Journal of Children and Poverty, 6*(2), 155–168.
3. Ashworth, K., Hill, M., & Walker, R., (1994). Patterns of childhood poverty: New challenges for policy. *Journal of Policy Analysis and Management, 13*(4), 658–680.
4. Bäckman, O., & Nilsson, A., (2007). *Childhood Poverty and Labor Market Exclusion*. Institute for Futures Studies, Working Paper: 13.
5. Bhargava, P., Mathur, K., & Rajagopal, S., (2004). *Understanding Childhood Poverty in Rajasthan*. Childhood Poverty Research and Policy Center.
6. Bloom, D., & Canning, D., (2001). Cumulative causality, economic growth, and the demographic transition. In: Kelley, B. N, A. C., & Sinding, S. W., (eds.), *Population Matters: Demographic Change, Economic Growth, and Poverty in the Developing World*. Oxford: Oxford University Press.
7. Bourdillon, M., & Boyden, J., (2011). *Childhood Poverty: Multidisciplinary Approaches*. Springer.
8. Boyden, J., & James, Z., (2014). Schooling, childhood poverty and international development: Choices and challenges in a longitudinal study. *Oxford Review of Education, 40*(1), 10–29.

9. Bruch, H., & Touraine, G., (1940). Obesity in childhood: V. The family frame of obese children. *Psychosomatic Medicine.*
10. Chamberlain, L. J., Hanson, E. R., Klass, P., Schickedanz, A., Nakhasi, A., Barnes, M. M., & Navsaria, D., (2016). Childhood poverty and its effect on health and well-being: Enhancing training for learners across the medical education continuum. *Academic Pediatrics, 16*(3), S155–S162.
11. Chiputwa, B., Spielman, D. J., & Qaim, M., (2015). Food standards, certification, and poverty among coffee farmers in Uganda. *World Development, 66*(1), 400–412.
12. Corcoran, M. E., & Chaudry, A., (1997). The dynamics of childhood poverty. *The Future of Children*, 40–54.
13. Deaton, A., (2006). *Measuring Poverty*. Oxford: Oxford University Press.
14. Dreyer, B. P., (2013). To create a better world for children and families: the case for ending childhood poverty. *Academic Pediatrics, 13*(2), 83–90.
15. Duncan, G. J., & Magnuson, K., (2013). The long reach of early childhood poverty. In: *Economic Stress, Human Capital, and Families in Asia* (pp. 57–70). Springer, Dordrecht.
16. Duncan, G. J., & Rodgers, W. L., (1988). Longitudinal aspects of childhood poverty. *Journal of Marriage and the Family*, 1007–1021.
17. Duncan, G. J., Kalil, A., & Ziol-Guest, K. M., (2013). Early childhood poverty and adult achievement, employment, and health. *Family Matters, 93*, 27–35.
18. Duncan, G. J., Kalil, A., & Ziol-Guest, K., (2008). *Economic Costs of Early Childhood Poverty*. Issue Paper: 4.
19. Duncan, G. J., Magnuson, K., Kalil, A., & Ziol-Guest, K., (2012). The importance of early childhood poverty. *Social Indicators Research, 108*(1), 87–98.
20. Duncan, G. J., Yeung, W. J., Brooks-Gunn, J., & Smith, J. R., (1998). How much does childhood poverty affect the life chances of children? *American Sociological Review*, 406–423.
21. Evans, G. W., & Cassells, R. C., (2014). Childhood poverty, cumulative risk exposure, and mental health in emerging adults. *Clinical Psychological Science,* 2(3), 287–296.

22. Evans, G. W., & Fuller-Rowell, T. E., (2013). Childhood poverty, chronic stress, and young adult working memory: The protective role of self-regulatory capacity. *Developmental Science, 16*(5), 688–696.

23. Evans, G. W., & Kim, P., (2007). Childhood poverty and health: Cumulative risk exposure and stress dysregulation. *Psychological Science, 18*(11), 953–957.

24. Evans, G. W., & Kim, P., (2013). Childhood poverty, chronic stress, self-regulation, and coping. *Child Development Perspectives, 7*(1), 43–48.

25. Evans, G. W., & Kutcher, R., (2011). Loosening the link between childhood poverty and adolescent smoking and obesity: The protective effects of social capital. *Psychological Science, 22*(1), 3–7.

26. Evans, G. W., & Schamberg, M. A., (2009). Childhood poverty, chronic stress, and adult working memory. *Proceedings of the National Academy of Sciences, 106*(16), 6545–6549.

27. Evans, G. W., (2004). The environment of childhood poverty. *American Psychologist, 59*(2), 77.

28. Evans, G. W., (2016). Childhood poverty and adult psychological well-being. *Proceedings of the National Academy of Sciences, 113*(52), 14949–14952.

29. Farah, M. J., Shera, D. M., Savage, J. H., Betancourt, L., Giannetta, J. M., Brodsky, N. L., & Hurt, H., (2006). Childhood poverty: Specific associations with neurocognitive development. *Brain Research, 1110*(1), 166–174.

30. Fierman, A. H., Beck, A. F., Chung, E. K., Tschudy, M. M., Coker, T. R., Mistry, K. B., & Flanagan, P. J., (2016). Redesigning health care practices to address childhood poverty. *Academic Pediatrics, 16*(*3*), S136–S146.

31. Fujiura, G. T., & Yamaki, K., (2000). Trends in the demography of childhood poverty and disability. *Exceptional Children, 66*(2), 187–199.

32. Garrett, P., Ng'andu, N., & Ferron, J., (1994). Is rural residency a risk factor for childhood poverty? *1 Rural Sociology, 59*(1), 66–83.

33. Guest, K. C., & Biasini, F. J., (2001). Middle childhood, poverty, and adjustment: Does social support have an impact? *Psychology in the Schools, 38*(6), 549–560.

34. Hannum, E., Liu, R., & Alvarado-Urbina, A., (2017). Evolving approaches to the study of childhood poverty and education. *Comparative Education, 53*(1), 81–114.

35. Hart, J., (2008). Business as usual? *The Global Political Economy of Childhood Poverty*.

36. Hatcher, A. M., Gibbs, A., Jewkes, R., McBride, R. S., Peacock, D., & Christofides, N., (2019). Effect of childhood poverty and trauma on adult depressive symptoms among young men in peri-urban South African settlements. *Journal of Adolescent Health, 64*(1), 79–85.

37. Hill, M. S., & Sandfort, J. R., (1995). Effects of childhood poverty on productivity later in life: Implications for public policy. *Children and Youth Services Review, 17*(1, 2), 91–126.

38. Hobcraft, J., & Kiernan, K., (2001). Childhood poverty, early motherhood, and adult social exclusion. *The British Journal of Sociology, 52*(3), 495–517.

39. Hobcraft, J., (1998). *Intergenerational and Life-Course Transmission of Social Exclusion: Influences and Childhood Poverty, Family Disruption and Contact with the Police*. LSE STICERD Research Paper No. CASE015.

40. Holzer, H. J., Whitmore, S. D., Duncan, G. J., & Ludwig, J., (2008). The economic costs of childhood poverty in the United States. *Journal of Children and Poverty, 14*(1), 41–61.

41. Hong, Z., (2015). *The Price of China's Economic Development: Power, Capital, and the Poverty Rights*. Lexington: The University Press of Kentucky.

42. http://www.crisismagazine.com/2015/perpetuating-anti-poverty-programs-dont-work (accessed on 23 March 2021).

43. http://www.statehouse.go.ug/media/news/2017/03/21/get-rid-poverty-through-modern-agriculture%E2%80%9D-%E2%80%93-president-museveni (accessed on 23 March 2021).

44. https://www.americanprogress.org/issues/poverty/report/2015/01/28/105520/a-fair-shot-for-workers-with-disabilities/ (accessed on 23 March 2021).

45. Jain, S., & Vaachani, S., (2006). *Multinational Corporation and Global Poverty Reduction*. Massachusetts: Edward Elgar.

46. Jarjoura, G. R., Triplett, R. A., & Brinker, G. P., (2002). Growing up poor: Examining the link between persistent childhood poverty and

delinquency. *Journal of Quantitative Criminology, 18*(2), 159–187.

47. Javanbakht, A., King, A. P., Evans, G. W., Swain, J. E., Angstadt, M., Phan, K. L., & Liberzon, I., (2015). Childhood poverty predicts adult amygdala and frontal activity and connectivity in response to emotional faces. *Frontiers in Behavioral Neuroscience, 9*, 154.
48. Jones, N., Vargas, R., & Villar, E., (2007). *Conditional Cash Transfers in Peru: Tackling the Multi-Dimensionality of Childhood Poverty and Vulnerability.* New York: New School and UNICEF.
49. Jones, N., Vargas, R., & Villar, E., (2008). Cash transfers to tackle childhood poverty and vulnerability: An analysis of Peru's Juntos Program. *Environment and Urbanization, 20*(1), 255–273.
50. Kalil, A., Duncan, G. J., & Ziol-Guest, K. M., (2016). Early childhood poverty: Short and long-run consequences over the lifespan. In: *Handbook of the Life Course* (pp. 341–354). Springer, Cham.
51. Kaplinsky, R., (2005). *Globalization, Poverty, and Inequality*. Cambridge: Polity Press.
52. Kapoor, K., (1993). *Uganda: Growing out of Poverty*. Washington (DC): World Bank.
53. Kendig, S. M., Mattingly, M. J., & Bianchi, S. M., (2014). Childhood poverty and the transition to adulthood. *Family Relations, 63*(2), 271–286.
54. Kim, P., Evans, G. W., Angstadt, M., Ho, S. S., Sripada, C. S., Swain, J. E., & Phan, K. L., (2013). Effects of childhood poverty and chronic stress on emotion regulatory brain function in adulthood. *Proceedings of the National Academy of Sciences, 110*(46), 18442–18447.
55. Kim, P., Ho, S. S., Evans, G. W., Liberzon, I., & Swain, J. E., (2015). Childhood social inequalities influence neural processes in young adult caregiving. *Developmental Psychobiology, 57*(8), 948–960.
56. Kim, P., Neuendorf, C., Bianco, H., & Evans, G. W., (2016). Exposure to childhood poverty and mental health symptomatology in adolescence: A role of coping strategies. *Stress and Health, 32*(5), 494–502.
57. Krason, S. M., (2015). What Seems to Be a Morally Mandated Public Policy Position Really May Note Be. *Catholic Social Science Review, 20,* 143-146.
58. Lesner, R. V., (2018). The long-term effect of childhood poverty. *Journal of Population Economics, 31*(3), 969–1004.

59. Lichter, D. T., Shanahan, M. J., & Gardner, E. L., (2002). Helping others? The effects of childhood poverty and family instability on prosocial behavior. *Youth and Society, 34*(1), 89–119.
60. Lipina, S. J., (2016). The biological side of social determinants: Neural costs of childhood poverty. *Prospects, 46*(2), 265–280.
61. Lipina, S., Segretin, S., Hermida, J., Prats, L., Fracchia, C., Camelo, J. L., & Colombo, J., (2013). Linking childhood poverty and cognition: Environmental mediators of non-verbal executive control in an Argentinian sample. *Developmental Science, 16*(5), 697–707.
62. Lopez, M. H., & Velasco, G., (2011). *Childhood Poverty Among Hispanics Sets Record, Leads Nation*. Washington, DC: Pew Hispanic Center.
63. Lyytikäinen, M., Jones, N., Sharon, H., & Abramsky, T., (2006). *Childhood Poverty, Basic Services and Cumulative Disadvantage.* Oxford: Oxford University Research Archive.
64. Magnuson, K. A., & Votruba-Drzal, E., (2008). *Enduring Influences of Childhood Poverty*. Madison: University of Wisconsin-Madison, Institute for Research on Poverty.
65. Mazza, J. R. S., Lambert, J., Zunzunegui, M. V., Tremblay, R. E., Boivin, M., & Côté, S. M., (2017). Early adolescence behavior problems and timing of poverty during childhood: A comparison of life course models. *Social Science and Medicine, 177*, 35–42.
66. Mbabazi, G., & Pyeong, J. Y., (2014). Patronage-driven corruption undermining the fight against poverty in Uganda. *African Social Science Review, 7*(1), 1–17.
67. McLaughlin, M., & Rank, M. R., (2018). Estimating the economic cost of childhood poverty in the United States. *Social Work Research, 42*(2), 73–83.
68. McLoyd, V. C., Aikens, N. L., & Burton, L. M., (2007). Childhood poverty, policy, and practice. *Handbook of Child Psychology,* 4.
69. Mickelson, R. A., (2002). Globalization, childhood poverty, and education in the Americas. In: *Children on the Streets of the Americas* (pp. 15–44). Routledge.
70. Miller, G. E., & Chen, E., (2013). The biological residue of childhood poverty. *Child Development Perspectives, 7*(2), 67–73.
71. Miller, G. E., Lachman, M. E., Chen, E., Gruenewald, T. L., Karlamangla, A. S., & Seeman, T. E., (2011). Pathways to resilience:

Maternal nurturance as a buffer against the effects of childhood poverty on metabolic syndrome at midlife. *Psychological Science, 22*(12), 1591–1599.

72. Ministry of Finance, (2014). *The Poverty Status Report 2014 (Uganda).* Kampala: Economic Development Policy and Research Department.
73. Morrow, V., (2013). Practical ethics in social research with children and families in young lives: A longitudinal study of childhood poverty in Ethiopia, Andhra Pradesh (India), Peru and Vietnam. *Methodological Innovations Online, 8*(2), 21–35.
74. Muñoz, J. F., Álvarez-Verdejo, E., & García-Fernández, R. M., (2016). *On Estimating the Poverty Gap and the Poverty Severity Indices with Auxiliary Information.* Sociological Methods Research.
75. Nikulina, V., & Widom, C. S., (2014). Do race, neglect, and childhood poverty predict physical health in adulthood? A multilevel prospective analysis. *Child Abuse and Neglect, 38*(3), 414–424.
76. Nikulina, V., Widom, C. S., & Czaja, S., (2011). The role of childhood neglect and childhood poverty in predicting mental health, academic achievement, and crime in adulthood. *American Journal of Community Psychology, 48*(3, 4), 309–321.
77. Okiror, S., (2015). *Tackling Poverty and Drought in Uganda.* Kampala: United Nations Office for Disaster Risk Reduction (UNISDR).
78. Penn, H., (2004). *Childcare and Early Childhood Development Programs and Policies: Their Relationship to Eradicating Child Poverty.* London: Childhood Poverty Research and Policy Center.
79. Ratcliffe, C., & McKernan, S. M., (2010). *Childhood Poverty Persistence: Facts and Consequences* (p. 1). Washington, DC: Urban Institute.
80. Ridge, T., (2002). *Childhood Poverty and Social Exclusion: From a Child's Perspective.* Policy Press.
81. Ridge, T., (2006). Childhood poverty: A barrier to social participation and inclusion. *Children, Young People, and Social Inclusion: Participation for What,* 23–38.
82. Rowntree, S. B., (1901). *Poverty: A Study of Town Life* (1st ed.) London: MacMillan & Co.
83. Ryan, R. M., Fauth, R. C., & Brooks-Gunn, J., (2006). *Childhood Poverty: Implications for School Readiness and Early Childhood*

Education. In B. Spodek & O. N. Saracho (Eds.), Handbook of research on the education of young children (p. 323–346). Lawrence Erlbaum Associates Publishers.

84. Sánchez, A., (2008). *Childhood Poverty in Peru: An Annotated Literature Review*. Peru: Young Lives. http://repositorio.minedu.gob.pe/bitstream/handle/20.500.12799/4133/Childhood%20Poverty%20in%20Peru%20An%20Annotated%20Literature%20Review.pdf?sequence=3&isAllowed=y (accessed 13 April 2021)
85. Schickedanz, A., Dreyer, B. P., & Halfon, N., (2015). Childhood poverty: understanding and preventing the adverse impacts of a most-prevalent risk to pediatric health and well-being. *Pediatric Clinics, 62*(5), 1111–1135.
86. Schmitz, C. L., Wagner, J. D., & Menke, E. M., (2001). The interconnection of childhood poverty and homelessness: Negative impact/points of access. *Families in Society, 82*(1), 69–77.
87. Segretin, M. S., Hermida, M. J., Prats, L. M., Fracchia, C. S., Ruetti, E., & Lipina, S. J., (2016). Childhood poverty and cognitive development in Latin America in the 21st century. *New Directions for Child and Adolescent Development, 2016*(152), 9–29.
88. Serbin, L. A., Stack, D. M., Kingdon, D., Mantis, I., & Enns, L. N., (2011). Unpacking the effects of childhood poverty: A psychosocial approach to intergenerational risk. *Social Exclusion, Poverty and Social Statistics: Perspectives from Quebec, Canada and Abroad*, 113–122.
89. Sinervo, A., & Hill, M. D., (2011). The visual economy of Andean childhood poverty: Interpreting postcards in Cusco, Peru. *The Journal of Latin American and Caribbean Anthropology, 16*(1), 114–142.
90. Song, Y., & Lu, H. H., (2002). *Early Childhood Poverty: A Statistical Profile*. New York: The National Center for Children in Poverty.
91. Sripada, R. K., Swain, J. E., Evans, G. W., Welsh, R. C., & Liberzon, I., (2014). Childhood poverty and stress reactivity are associated with aberrant functional connectivity in the default mode network. *Neuropsychopharmacology, 39*(9), 2244–2251.
92. State House Uganda, (2017). *Get Rid of Poverty Through Modern Agriculture*. [Online]. https://www.statehouse.go.ug/media/news/2017/03/21/get-rid-poverty-through-modern-agriculture"---president-Museveni (accessed 13 April 2021).

93. Stewart, K., (2005). Towards an equal start? Addressing childhood poverty and deprivation. *A More Equal Society*, 143–166.

94. Torres, J. M., & Wong, R., (2013). Childhood poverty and depressive symptoms for older adults in Mexico: a life-course analysis. *Journal of Cross-Cultural Gerontology, 28*(3), 317–337.

95. Townsend, P., (1979). *Poverty in the United Kingdom: A Survey of Household Resources and Standards of Living* (1st in.) London: Penguin Books.

96. Twikirize, J. M., et al., (2014). Professional social work in East Africa: Empirical evidence. In: Spitzer, H., & Twikirize, J. M., (eds.), *Professional Social Work in East Africa: Towards Social Development, Poverty Reduction and Gender Equality* (pp. 189–216). Kampala: Fountain Publishers.

97. Vallas, R., Fremstad, S., & Ekman, L., (2015). *A Fair Shot for Workers with Disabilities*. Center for American Progress, 28.

98. Van, D. W. S., & Hens, L., (2008). Crossing the bridge to poverty, with low-cost cars. *Journal of Consumer Marketing, 25*(7), 439–445.

99. Waddington, H., (2004). *Linking Economic Policy to Childhood Poverty: A Review of the Evidence on Growth, Trade Reform and Macroeconomic Policy* (Vol. 7). Childhood Poverty Research and Policy Center.

100. Wells, N. M., Evans, G. W., Beavis, A., & Ong, A. D., (2010). Early childhood poverty, cumulative risk exposure, and body mass index trajectories through young adulthood. *American Journal of Public Health, 100*(12), 2507–2512.

101. Zembe-Mkabile, W., Surender, R., Sanders, D., Jackson, D., & Doherty, T., (2015). The experience of cash transfers in alleviating childhood poverty in South Africa: mothers' experiences of the child support grant. *Global Public Health, 10*(7), 834–851.

102. Ziol-Guest, K. M., Duncan, G. J., & Kalil, A., (2009). Early childhood poverty and adult body mass index. *American Journal of Public Health, 99*(3), 527–532.

103. Ziol-Guest, K. M., Duncan, G. J., Kalil, A., & Boyce, W. T., (2012). Early childhood poverty, immune-mediated disease processes, and adult productivity. *Proceedings of the National Academy of Sciences, 109*(2), 17289–17293.

INDEX